IMAGINING THE FED

IMAGINING THE FED

The Struggle for the Heart of the Federal Reserve
1913–1970

NICOLAS THOMPSON

Cover image: Eccles Board building under construction: 10/01/1936.
Photo Credit: Harris & Ewing/Wikimedia.

Published by State University of New York Press, Albany

© 2021 State University of New York

All rights reserved

Printed in the United States of America

No part of this book may be used or reproduced in any manner whatsoever without written permission. No part of this book may be stored in a retrieval system or transmitted in any form or by any means including electronic, electrostatic, magnetic tape, mechanical, photocopying, recording, or otherwise without the prior permission in writing of the publisher.

For information, contact State University of New York Press, Albany, NY
www.sunypress.edu

Library of Congress Cataloging-in-Publication Data

Name: Thompson, Nicolas, author. | State University of New York Press.
Title: Imagining the Fed : the struggle for the heart of the Federal
   Reserve, 1913–1970 / Nicolas Thompson.
Description: Albany : State University of New York Press, 2021. | Includes
   bibliographical references and index.
Identifiers: LCCN 2020024804 | ISBN 9781438482590 (hardcover : alk. paper) |
   ISBN 9781438482583 (pbk. : alk. paper) | ISBN 9781438482606 (ebook)
Subjects: LCSH: Board of Governors of the Federal Reserve System
   (U.S.)—History. | United States—Economic policy—20th century.
Classification: LCC HG2563 .T46 2021 | DDC 332.1/109730904—dc23
LC record available at https://lccn.loc.gov/2020024804

10 9 8 7 6 5 4 3 2 1

As a central bank, the Federal Reserve System inevitably functions as an institution which itself has its most immediate contact with other institutions. But institutions are composed of human beings and are, over time, shaped by human beings . . . this realization alone suffices to caution us toward great humility.

—William McChesney Martin Jr., 1970

*Dedicated to the generations
who struggled to shape the Fed*

Contents

List of Illustrations	xi
Acknowledgments	xiii
Introduction: Imagining a Fed in the Making	1
1 Escape from Jekyll Island: The Federal Reserve's Birth in Political Time	29
2 Making and Breaking a Hamiltonian Fed	53
3 An Engine of Inflation? The Populist Fed Interlude	81
4 Economists at the Gates: The Rise and Fall of an Egalitarian Fed	111
Conclusion: E Pluribus Unum: The Political Development of the Fed	145
Notes	163
Bibliography	203
Index	217

Illustrations

Figures

I.1	Map of the Twelve Federal Reserve Banks and Districts	14
4.1.	U.S. Monetary Gold Stock and Domestic Currency Collateral	125
C.1.	Federal Reserve Payments to the U.S. Treasury	157

Tables

I.1.	Political Time Impacts on the Federal Reserve	17
1.1.	The Federal Reserve System and Its Competitors	41
3.1.	Depression-Era Federal Reserve Legal Powers	91

Acknowledgments

This project grew out through extended conversations with several mentors. I owe a debt of gratitude to Gerald Berk, who encouraged me to think creatively and adopt a heterodox approach. David Steinberg also deserves special thanks for supporting my scholarly and professional growth. Others who stimulated my thinking while at the University of Oregon include Lars Skalnes, Mark Thoma, Karrie Koesel, Burke Hendrix, Tuong Vu, Yongwoo Jeung, and Jeremy Strickler. I also benefited from the support of my University of South Florida colleagues, especially M. Scott Solomon and Cheryl Hall. This book's arguments benefited from critical feedback at several academic conferences, and in response to the thoughtful comments of two anonymous SUNY Press reviewers. Closer to home, I would like to thank Reid Lesperance for her steadfast support, and Dita, Ophelia, and Penny, for their patient supervision.

Financial support for this project was provided by the LBJ Foundation and the University of South Florida Humanities Institute. My research was also aided by archivists at the Federal Reserve Bank of New York, the Federal Reserve Bank of St. Louis, the LBJ Presidential Library, the John F. Kennedy Presidential Library, and the United States National Archives and Administration at College Park, Maryland. The Federal Reserve Bank of St. Louis's FRASER digital library stands out as an invaluable resource for Fed researchers. It contains primary documents cited by eminent Fed historians, whose work this book problematizes and contributes to.

Introduction

Imagining a Fed in the Making

> When I was a professor of money and banking I used to wonder how Federal Reserve officials could be so stupid. Now that I've had some years as a central banker with responsibility, I often wonder how professors of money and banking can be so naïve.
>
> —Karl Bopp, President of the Federal Reserve Bank of Philadelphia

Karl Bopp, the longtime president of the Federal Reserve Bank of Philadelphia, addressed the Federal Open Market Committee (FOMC) for the final time on February 10, 1970.[1] The FOMC is the venue where representatives of all the Federal Reserve System's elements, twelve regional Federal Reserve Banks and the Washington, D.C.–based Board of Governors, come together to forge monetary policy. Bopp welcomed the new chair of the Board of Governors, Arthur Burns, and bid him farewell. After twenty-nine years at the Philadelphia Fed, Bopp was retiring. He used his parting remarks to weigh in on pressures which were forging the Fed into its modern form: an insular, board-centered technocracy. Bopp criticized a three-year-old mandate to "bring about the reduction of interest rates," which he considered futile. Unfunded wars in Vietnam and against domestic poverty fostered an inflationary environment that pushed interest rates ever higher. Bopp then turned to internal Fed politics, urging recent board appointees to "concentrate on policy" and not micromanage the Federal Reserve Bank of New York employees who implemented FOMC policy directives. Over the past decade, an influx of economists into appointed positions had transformed the Board of Governors from an occupationally diverse body into an economist stronghold.

Bopp's last remark impugned economists' ambition of consolidating Fed power. He cautioned that economists still lacked "comprehension of the linkages among financial and real economic variables . . . ignorance of the connections was colossal." Until Fed policymakers better understood monetary policy's impacts, they should "hesitate . . . to follow recommendations as to policy that might be provided by a computer."

Bopp's criticisms were not new. Five years earlier, he wrote, "The simple truth is that no one comprehends enough to be an expert in central banking. . . . Central banking is an infant, as human institutions go."[2] Economists found Bopp's critiques puzzling. Central banks had existed for centuries. Milton Friedman and Anna Schwartz had recently published *A Monetary History of the United States: 1860–1867*, which pioneered a new technique for analyzing central bank behavior by measuring monetary aggregates.[3] The Board of Governors' technical staff was expanding, forging new models and forecasts, and integrating those tools into the monetary policy process.[4] Economists believed central banking was evolving from an art to a science.

Bopp and other members of the Fed's old guard were skeptical of this notion, and believed human cognition and judgment remained crucial central banking elements. Bopp could relate to the board's new upstarts. An economics professor as a young man, Bopp had navigated the transition from academia to Federal Reserve service in the 1940s. Unlike his new colleagues, however, Bopp worked his way up through the Philadelphia Fed ranks through decades of hard work, often in deference to inherited practices and ideals he found questionable. Bopp's views carried weight among a retiring generation of Fed officials. Chief among these was William McChesney Martin Jr., the Fed chair often credited with establishing the modern Fed.[5] Martin became chairman of the Board of Governors in 1951, when the system regained independence after decades of treasury dominance. Martin had championed a "historic democratization" of the FOMC, growing its ranks to include the presidents of all twelve reserve banks in addition to the seven appointed board governors. This vacated a board advantage established in 1935, when the FOMC was constituted as a twelve-member body with seven votes reserved for the board.

Martin's diffuse Fed order was sustained through deference to the New York Fed's expertise. From the time the open market committee first formed in 1922, New York had acted as the system's agent for buying and selling government securities, the main mechanism through which monetary policy is implemented. New York's position at the commanding heights of finance and America's global trade nexus endowed its officers with a cosmopolitan outlook. They believed America had a national interest in fostering a liberal world order based on free trade and the gold standard and called for directing Fed power externally to promote dollar stability. This book identifies this ideology as Hamiltonian, reflecting an updated application of Alexander Hamilton's financial principles to a world shaped by American primacy.

The economists who invaded the board in the 1960s rejected this philosophy, and the inclusive Fed Martin fostered. The new technocrats believed monetary policy should be directed toward domestic goals, such as accelerating growth or stabilizing prices. They saw New York's aim of directing monetary policy toward sustaining international monetary stability as outdated, harmful even. Various economists had called for the system to turn its attention inward since its 1913 origin, but they were denied positions of Fed authority before the 1960s. This reflected a resilient Federal Reserve Act (FRA) clause requiring the board's ranks to reflect the "different commercial, industrial and geographical divisions of the country."[6] In practice, this meant appointed governors traditionally hailed from different regions and occupations. The law's denial of any form of central banking expertise was intended to prevent capture by Wall Street. It instead staved off an economist takeover for over half a century, when the modern Fed emerged.

Imagining the Fed traces a struggle for power that began at Jekyll Island in 1910 and ended six decades later with the establishment of a durable Fed technocracy. It shows that before 1970, the Federal Reserve was a site of institutional diversity, contestation, and change. Institutional instability grew from legal ambiguity rooted in compromises among clashing ideals, interest-based conflicts inherent in federalism, the institution-building efforts of Fed visionaries to overcome these faults, and agent-led initiatives to dismantle inherited systems. This book traces the rise and fall of three extralegal Fed regimes which predated Fed technocracy. The modern Fed was built on the legacies of these earlier Feds, which came before.

The Argument: Mapping the Fed's Struggle for Power

Imagining the Fed explains an intergenerational struggle to shape the Fed's policy regime. The title is meant to shine light on an anachronism problem common in Fed studies, and to highlight the creative element in institution building. Scholars routinely project presumed Fed identities and powers deep into the past, before such elements emerged historically. Fed analytic frames are often ideologically charged, portraying the Fed alternatively as: (1) an independent central bank, (2) a state agency charged with regulating monetary growth, or (3) the vehicle of a banker conspiracy. This book classifies these views, respectively, as progressive, populist, and Jeffersonian. It also identifies a fourth Fed genre articulated in the writings of generations New York Fed officers and researchers.[7] This latter perspective sees Fed power and responsibilities through a global lens. Hamiltonians view New York as "first among equals" within the system, owing to its unique vantage and expertise gleaned from working at the pinnacles of finance.[8]

Imagining the Fed shows that all four of these Fed images were woven into the FRA, yielding an ambiguous blueprint. The system's federalism tied representation to territory, both among the reserve banks, which governed discrete territories, and on the national board. This dispersion of power was intended to prevent New York from establishing Fed hegemony.[9] This plan would fail within a few years, however, with the first hierarchical Fed emerging in the 1920s with New York at its center. This order would be toppled by the end of the decade, however, amid internal critiques that the system was behaving like a central bank and undermining the letter and spirit of the law. A similar sequence would unfold two decades later, when William McChesney Martin Jr. tore down an inherited order to democratize the Fed.

This book argues that this developmental sequence was no coincidence. It reflected the interplay of agency and political time, set against a backdrop of institutional memory. By agency, this book means purposeful actions by individuals to change policies or institutions. This book focuses on the agency of two types of actors: Fed officials and U.S. presidents. Fed insiders are the main protagonists in the system's struggle. They build and dismantle the extralegal regimes analyzed throughout the book. Presidential agency shapes Fed institutions through its impact on political time. Stephen Skowronek developed the concept of political time to explain a recurring pattern of hegemonic parties dominating U.S. national politics, capturing the state, and directing policy for an era.[10] This book broadens the political time clock to incorporate a second developmental pattern wrought by transitions between war and peace. It identifies four political moments, partisan ascent and decay, and war and peace, and argues that each empowers an ideological reform script, which reshapes the Fed and lays the seeds of future struggles.

The rest of this chapter develops this argument. It first reviews the Fed governance literature, before theorizing the roles of ideology, agency, and political time in shaping the Fed's developmental path. The book's core claim is that "the Fed" we know today congealed in 1970, marking the culmination of the system's political development, understood as "a durable shift in governing authority," with "shift" meaning "a change in the locus or direction of control."[11] It was only at this late juncture that the board consolidated FOMC agenda control. *Imagining the Fed* makes three contributions to the American Political Development (APD) literature. The first is its theorization of the role of international factors, including wars, regimes, and interests, as driving recurring patterns of Fed conflict. The second is an agentic notion of political time, which sees the discretionary choices of presidents and central bankers as impactful. Finally, the book also contributes to an emerging literature that stresses the durable impacts of ideas and agents that lose out in reform battles at critical junctures.[12] It shows that the contemporary Fed landscape contains vestiges of all four of its founding ideologies, even though changing times have rendered some Fed value systems incomprehensible within the modern world.

Fed Governance Studies and the System's Vanishing Struggle for Power

This section introduces the Federal Reserve's struggle for power as a contest to shape its policy regime. The FRA imagined two policy instruments, the discount rate and open market investments, and splintered control of each among the reserve banks and board. The law left unclear where institutional control resided, implying alternatively that it lay with the board, the treasury, or the reserve banks.[13] Founding board member Paul Warburg reflected later that the law established a "system of checks and counter-checks—a paralyzing system which gives powers with one hand and takes them away with the other."[14] It was an invitation to struggle.

The law did not imagine a central committee where system stakeholders would come together to forge policy. The first such committee, the FOMC's forebear, was established in 1922 through a reserve bank agreement. The first committee was exclusionary, controlled by the five governors of the wealthiest reserve banks. This structure was contested immediately, and intermittently for decades thereafter. Milton Friedman and Anna Schwartz argue one proximate outcome of this struggle, a 1930 "diffusion of power" which grew the committee to twelve, foreclosed an expansionary bond-buying policy that would have steered the economy away from the Great Depression.[15] This institutional story was debunked, but the argument that Fed policy mistakes worsened the Depression remains influential.[16] Since Friedman and Schwartz wrote, the Fed's power struggle has been progressively scrubbed from the literature. Today, economists see the system's original twelve bank structure as a static source of "coordination problems," which contributed to Depression-era mistakes.[17] Most see primitive ideas as playing a more important role in leading Fed policymakers astray, however.[18] The conventional Fed history sees Congress as ending its struggle in 1935 by elevating the Board of Governors to a position of Fed primacy, reflected in an FOMC voting majority. While the new Fed would be dominated by the treasury for another decade and a half, the 1951 Treasury-Fed Accord durably restored its operational independence.[19] Afterward, new Board of Governors chair William McChesney Martin Jr. enacted procedural reforms which some argue heralded the modern Fed.[20]

An emerging Fed governance literature downplays the Fed's early power struggle, however, as well as the impact of Martin's reforms. Peter Conti-Brown's *The Power and Independence of the Federal Reserve* dismisses early Fed skirmishes as "institutional chaos" wrought by a flawed federal design, and explains Martin's legacy as mainly rhetorical, a language of independence.[21] In *The Myth of Independence*, Sarah Binder and Mark Spindel argue that Congress shapes Fed governance through the law.[22] In their view, the system's decentralized coordination problem-prone design grew from compromises among central bank champions and opponents, representatives of the nation's core and periphery, Republicans and Democrats. When later economic shocks revealed these fragilities, lawmakers responded by rationalizing the Fed. In this view, the system's structure flows entirely from the law, and agent-led reform efforts are insignificant. Lawrence Jacobs and Desmond King's *Fed Power* similarly omits any discussion of the system's internal divisions and power struggle, and portrays Martin as working to grow the Fed's power and autonomy, bureaucratic motives they claim guide all Fed officials.[23]

None of these works discuss the 1960s Fed transformation this book identifies as the culmination of its political development. Conti-Brown acknowledges that Fed power today is concentrated in an alliance between the board chair and staff, but doesn't explain the origin of this extralegal regime.[24] Jacobs and King argue that the modern Fed emerged in 1980, when it was allegedly freed from democratic oversight and embraced finance over other sectors.[25] Binder and Spindel argue that Congress changes the FRA whenever the economy tanks, and thus see the Fed as forever in the making. Yet, emerging research suggests that the 1960s reforms identified in this book are significant. Fed insiders have long recognized that decade as a time of rising board sophistication, but as two scholars recently observed, how "this transformation was engineered, by whom, and how it unfolded . . . remain a blind spot of the flourishing literature on central banking."[26] Another scholar observes that in the 1960s "the Federal Reserve System took on a new name—'The Fed.'"[27] This book shows that these developments were intertwined, and that a unified Fed identity was unthinkable just a few years before. The diffuse Fed order Bill Martin fostered emphasized inclusion, consensus, and deference to New York's expertise. The modern Fed shattered each of these pillars. While Martin's egalitarian norms were dismantled, his beliefs that the Fed should be inclusive and nonpartisan endured. The modern Fed is a composite of the institutional legacies and vestiges of the Fed regimes that came before.

The Struggle to Build a Durable Fed Regime

Imagining the Fed explains the evolution of the Fed policy regime, understood as the institutional process and values that shape its policy decisions. It analyzes the development of its two main policymaking bodies, the Board of Governors and the FOMC, from the perspective of the individuals who occupied them and remade them through time. This departs from how central banks are analyzed by economists and builds on a growing literature which interrogates how internal attributes of central banks interact with their ideational and global settings.

Many economists see central bank independence, the degree of legal separation from political authorities, as the main variable that shapes monetary policy outcomes.[28] In this view, the key to central banking success, understood as delivering low rates of inflation, is to build high legal walls separating central banks from politicians. Another literature focuses on the state of economic knowledge as the key lever that shapes monetary policy outcomes.[29] A third line of thought sees central banks' structural-institutional environments as shaping their behavior. A critical vein of this literature, which this book identifies as embodying Jeffersonian thought, sees central banks are structurally flawed due to their reliance upon elected politicians for survival.[30] A sunnier version of this theory sees the Fed as a democratically accountable central bank, which lawmakers rationalize and empower in response to economic crises.[31]

These latter approaches offer a broader view of the political forces that shape central banks and sometimes lead them astray, but they remain underdeveloped and prone to anachronism; imagining central banks as closed systems, populated by homogenous technocrats, governing strictly domestic realms. Friedman and Schwartz problematize the first assumption by arguing that the structure of policy committees shapes their policy outputs.[32] In *Bankers, Bureaucrats, and Central Bank Politics*, Christopher Adolph challenges the view that banks are populated by benevolent planners, showing that individuals' monetary policy beliefs and preferences are shaped by their experiences and career trajectories.[33] In this view, the policies and natures of central banks are shaped by the agents who populate them. Finally, a growing literature emphasizes global regimes as determinants of, and constraints on, central bank power.[34]

Imagining the Fed integrates these insights into its analysis. It differentiates among Fed regimes by their degrees of fragmentation, centers of expertise, power resources, and embeddedness. Fragmentation is a measure of the diversity of interests represented and number of veto points in collective decisions. As fragmentation grows, policy becomes harder to change.[35] When fragmentation falls, change becomes easier. This book shows that in the Federal Reserve, fragmentation entails a tradeoff between regime legitimacy and policy flexibility, as institutions that reduce fragmentation (such as committees) necessarily exclude claimants to policy authority. Expertise is a measure of where ideational authority lies within the system. It can be centralized on the board, in the treasury, or in New York, or it can be deemphasized altogether. The next section explains that these constellations of authority correspond with different ideological Fed images. Power resources refer to globally valuable goods that central banks stockpile and deploy to enact policies which shape their environment. At the system's origin, this was gold and British sterling, today it is flexible dollars. Embeddedness refers to the system's environment, including a domestic political system and a global economic regime.

This book distinguishes between secular and political time to explain the Federal Reserve's evolution. Secular time refers to periods of normal politics, when actors have time to interpret legal texts, build reform coalitions, and conceptualize their interests. These processes occur in relation to inherited institutions and agent experiences. In secular time, America's checks and balances hold, and political cleavages organize around parochial interests.[36] Political time, by contrast, refers to national traumas which change the parameters of American politics. The rise of a party to ascendancy in Washington. An economic crisis that implicates the ruling establishment. Marches to war. Returns to peace. These moments enable bursts of state building, which shatter regimes in and out of the Fed. As crises fade and secular time returns, Fed agents are forced to reconcile inherited institutions, which veer from the law, with a changed world.

Ideology, Interests, and the Battle over the Gold Standard

Congress established the Federal Reserve System in 1913, after a long dialogue over America's normative financial institutions which dated to the nation's founding. On the eve of the system's establishment, four visions vied to shape the nation's monetary authority and its purposes. Jeffersonians saw central banks as incompatible with America's constitutional order. Hamiltonians wanted a central bank modeled on the private Bank of England. Progressives looked to the German Reichsbank as a model, a joint public-private enterprise that blended public authority with private expertise.[37] Populists wanted a monetary authority constituted as an arm of the state to emit "legal tender," paper currency whose value derived from sovereign authority, to grow the money supply to create a more equitable capitalism.[38]

Support for these visions varied across America's regional divides. The industrializing Northeast was rising on the world stage, emerging as one of the world's most economically advanced regions.[39] America's abundant hinterland regions, by contrast, remained capital poor and occupied lower rungs in the international division of labor. Hamiltonian and progressive central bank champions were clustered in elite New York financial circles.[40] Most Americans were unaware of the nuances of their arguments, and many interpreted their calls to build a central bank as a plot to entrench Wall Street's power. In the South and West, populist and Jeffersonian ideologies were common. Citizens either wanted a public currency-emitting monetary authority to remedy historical grievances, or they preferred the central bank–less status quo and a gold standard regime they considered natural.

Congress's territorial makeup ensured that an elite plan to build a central bank would be defeated.[41] This book shows that changing partisan dynamics further repudiated the central bank idea, however. The Republican Party had dominated U.S. national politics since the Civil War. Its governing orthodoxy emphasized a Hamiltonian partnership between political authorities and industrialists, reflected in a mercantilist economic program, which united the gold standard, protectionist tariffs, and domestic laissez-faire.[42] This Gilded Age order was contested by a series of populist movements, culminating in William Jennings Bryan's ill-fated 1896 presidential bid on a platform to monetize silver. Bryan was defeated decisively in that contest. Republicans retained national power and legalized the gold commitment with the Gold Standard Act in 1900.

At the dawn of the twentieth century, however, the ruling party soon developed a fissure as progressivism emerged as a counterweight to mercantilism. Progressives called for lowering tariffs to improve consumer welfare and called for regulating the industrial economy. Intraparty tensions boiled over at the 1912 Republican National Convention in Chicago, where party elites nominated incumbent William Howard Taft as the party's presidential candidate over Theodore Roosevelt, the leader of the progressive wing. Roosevelt ordered his followers to leave the convention and form a Progressive Party behind his presidential candidacy. The Republican vote fractured in the fall national elections, delivering Democrats an unlikely landslide victory.

The Democratic Party was split into populist and Jeffersonian wings and anchored to a southern base. William Jennings Bryan led a populist bloc which remained committed to using state authority to regulate currency expansion. The party's Jeffersonian wing hoped to restore a more virtuous classical liberal order by breaking up trusts, lowering tariffs, staying on gold, and devolving federal power. At the Democratic convention in Baltimore, Bryan played kingmaker by endorsing New Jersey governor Woodrow Wilson as the party's nominee after several inconclusive ballots. Wilson won the presidency alongside broad Democratic majorities in both houses of Congress, but Wilson knew Democrats' grasp on national power would be ephemeral if it didn't expand its geographic base. Wilson sought to establish a new era of Democratic partisan rule by claiming the mantle of progressivism and attracting Western progressives into a broadened coalition.[43] The next chapter explains how these changing partisan dynamics resulted in a series of design compromises that layered all four central bank ideologies into the FRA.

The ideologies differ in how they imagine monetary authorities should be constituted and the ends they should pursue. Populists want a state-controlled monetary authority to emit paper currency. To do so, political authorities need to jettison the gold standard and prioritize domestic economic goals over international monetary stability. After William Jennings Bryan's 1896 presidential defeat, these ideas were taken up and refined by economist Irving Fisher and his students Milton Friedman and Anna Schwartz, who posited a stable causal relationship between the quantity of money in circulation and the domestic price level.[44] Since monetarism endorses regulating monetary growth for domestic purposes, this book identifies it as a right-leaning strain of populism. This distinction matters because it stands in stark contrast with the other three central bank ideologies, which at the time of the Federal Reserve's origin were united in support of sustaining the gold standard. Progressives wanted a public-private central bank with authority lodged in an independent board to modernize America's financial practices and integrate it within the international gold standard.[45] Hamiltonians shared these same ends, but believed a central bank structured as a private oligarchy was necessary to achieve it. Jeffersonians opposed a central bank but embraced a vision of the gold standard as an automatic institution.

These four visions vied to order the Federal Reserve's components into a system. Populists and progressives envisioned the board in Washington as the Fed's head, but populists saw it as an arm of the treasury, while progressives wanted the board constituted as an autonomous bastion of expertise. The law supported each of these views. The populist Fed vision rested on provisions that limited banker representation on the board and installed the treasury secretary as its *ex officio* chairman. It was also supported by a passage that read, "[W]herever any power vested by this Act in the Federal Reserve Board . . . appears to conflict with the powers of the Secretary of the Treasury, such powers shall be exercised subject to the supervision and control of the Secretary."[46] These design features reflected concessions made to populists.[47] They were countered, however, by progressive structures which insulated the board from politics, including lengthy, staggered terms for board members (originally five of seven members); private reserve bank ownership; and budgetary autonomy.[48] The next chapter shows that as it was being constituted, the board immediately divided into populist and progressive factions.

The law also contained passages that implied that the reserve banks were intended to be the system's leading authorities. Jeffersonian ideals infused the law's decentralization of power and deemphasis of expertise. Reserve banks were spread widely across the country and tasked with governing discrete territories. The gold standard's alleged automaticity lent plausibility to an imagined system of devolved power where reserve banks functioned as "self-regulating adjunct[s] to a self-regulating gold standard."[49] Jeffersonian thought also shaped the board requirement that its members reflect the "different commercial, industrial and geographical divisions of the country."[50] This built the nation's sectional and sectoral divisions into the board.

The FRA lent weakest support to the Hamiltonian central bank ideal. Hamilton endorsed private governance, with the bank wholly controlled by shareholders with common "experience guided by interest."[51] This design was engineered to advance Hamilton's purposes for the bank, which included lending out a stable currency to unlock commercial growth and acting as a source of government energy by helping elected officials navigate "certain emergencies." Hamilton warned that if lawmakers kept the currency-issuing power to themselves, they would be tempted to respond to crises by expanding the currency and debasing its value through inflation. He wrote, "The stamping of paper [is] so much easier than the laying of taxes, that a government in the practice of paper emissions would rarely fail in any such emergency to indulge itself too far . . . [resulting in an] inflated and artificial state of things incompatible with the regular and prosperous course of the political economy."[52] In Hamilton's view, the bank's credibility would spring from the diverging interests of its owners and elected officials.

Hamilton believed that to be effective in safeguarding the currency and spurring lawmakers to tackle looming problems, the central bank needed to be structured in the opposite way of the American government. Rather than dividing authority vertically among national and subnational units, or apportioning representation inside the bank by territory or in response to national elections, the bank's corporate structure would empower shareholders with shared, long-term material interests. "To attach full confidence to an institution of this nature," Hamilton wrote, "it appears to be an essential ingredient in its structure, that it shall be under a *private* not a *public* Direction, under the guidance of *individual interest,* not of *public policy.*"[53] The FRA decisively rejected this Hamiltonian vision. The law's architect, Rep. Carter Glass (D-VA), explained that the Federal Reserve was "modeled upon our Federal political system. . . . The regional banks are the states and the . . . Board is the Congress."[54]

The system's Hamiltonian tradition would be pioneered by Benjamin Strong, the New York Fed's founding governor. As the FRA neared final passage, Strong complained that Democrats had thrown "the central bank idea . . . upon the brush-heap."[55] Their "mongrel institution" was "nothing but a central bank with some of the most vital advantages of such an institution so bound up with red tape . . . that it would fall down in its practical working and bring disaster upon the country." Strong would spend the rest of his life forging cooperative linkages among the reserve banks, enabling them to act more like a central bank, and with central banks overseas. The law's two concessions to Hamiltonian ideals included the location of a Federal Reserve Bank in the nation's financial capital, as well as its endorsement of the gold standard. The Hamiltonian theory of the Fed shares with its Jeffersonian counterpart an emphasis on reserve bank autonomy. Instead of imagining each reserve bank as sovereign and independent, however, reserve banks are understood as united by a national interest in preserving the gold standard, understood as a working international regime. In this vision, New York is imagined as "first among equals," owing to its position atop America's financial capital and global trade nexus.[56]

Federalism structured uneven support for the law's embedded ideologies across its envisioned units (see Fig. I.1 on page 14). Because the United States had been without a central bank for nearly eight decades when the Federal Reserve was established, early officials had "little understanding of central banking theory and . . . no experience of central bank administration except that gained on the spot."[57] Because the system was composed of thirteen separate entities, however, each tied to a separate location, central banking lessons were learned unevenly. Barry Eichengreen observes "officials of the Federal Reserve Bank of New York, the seat of international finance, were better attuned to the advantages of international cooperation than . . . the Board of Governors" and reserve banks in the "interior of the country."[58] Eichengreen sees these differences as "doctrinal," but Jeffry Frieden maps them onto diverse sectoral interests regarding national currency policy.[59] To maintain currency stability in an

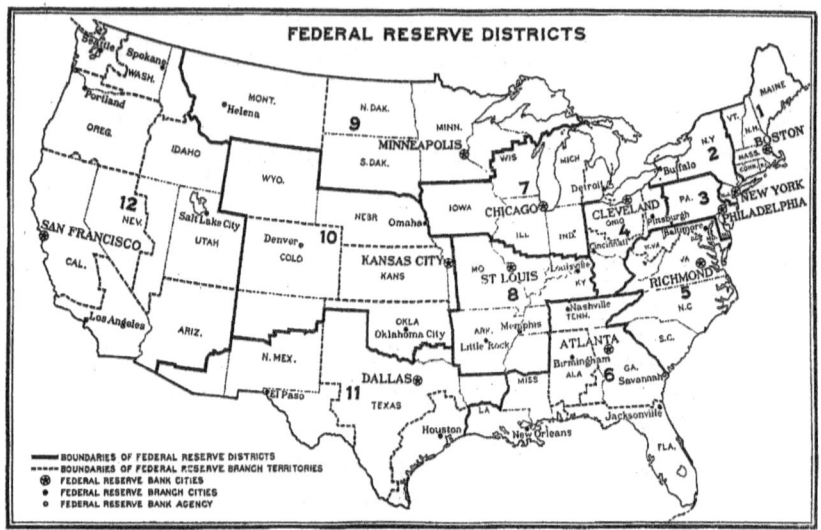

Figure I.1. Map of the Twelve Federal Reserve Banks and Districts. Map by Federal Reserve Board, Federal Reserve Bulletin, January 1925, Washington, DC.

open economy, monetary policy must be directed entirely toward replicating foreign monetary conditions.[60] In hard times, however, individuals whose fortunes are tied to the state of the domestic macroeconomy prefer expansionary monetary policies to maintain their incomes.[61] These discretionary policies cause domestic inflation rates to surpass those prevailing abroad, however, causing the currency to become overvalued. To stabilize an overvalued currency, states can enact austerity to push down domestic prices, devalue the currency, or float it on foreign exchange markets.[62] Internationally oriented sectors, including exporters and international traders and investors, prefer to forego monetary stimulus in downturns to maintain currency stability. When the Federal Reserve was established, these interests were clustered in New York and along the eastern seaboard.[63] Territorial representation thus hard-wired currency conflict into the system.

This problem would be compounded by Americans' gold standard naiveté. Many imagined the gold standard as an automatic, self-enforcing institution. Jeffersonians believed the gold standard was natural, following David Hume's price-specie-flow mechanism. In this view, when gold enters a country, the money supply automatically expands, causing local prices to rise relative to foreign prices, making imports cheaper. Rising imports are paid for with an outflow of specie, which contracts the money supply, pushing down prices and restoring international equilibrium. These simple beliefs jarred against the way classical gold standard operated in practice, however. Scholars sometimes argue that central banks administered the gold standard by applying "rules of the gold standard game." Arthur Bloomfield has shown, however, that no such rules existed when the classical gold standard operated.[64] Central banks prioritized maintaining gold convertibility above other goals, but their policies routinely flouted supposed "rules of the game." This layer of discretion was essential for sustaining ongoing patterns of international central bank cooperation, where central banks could call on their foreign counterparts for support in emergencies.[65] This cooperative regime was crucial for the sustaining the gold standard by preventing financial contagion and promoting global financial stability.

The central bank–less United States was a pariah within this cooperative system. Instead of presenting the world with a unified face, the Federal Reserve had thirteen separate heads. To beneficially engage central bank networks and promote international monetary stability, the system would need to select a diplomatic interlocutor, which would lead the system to adopt unified policies that bent in response to monetary developments overseas. Whether monetary policy would be aimed externally to promote dollar stability or inward toward domestic goals would hinge crucially on the constitution of the Fed policy regime. The median citizen in any democratic country is employed in domestic sectors, which favor monetary policy flexibility over currency stability.[66] Consequently, the more the Fed regime approximated the political order, fragmented by veto points and parochial interests and ideas, the less likely it would be to make the timely policy adjustments needed to sustain dollar stability. To contribute to world monetary order, the system would need to devise institutions to reduce its fragmentation and empower New York to shape the system's policy agenda.

When the Federal Reserve was born, these contradictions were not yet apparent. Since America had not had a central bank under the classical gold standard, Americans were blissfully ignorant as to its operations. As the system was first being established in 1914, World War I broke out, collapsing the international gold standard. It would only be after that crisis passed and the fixed currency regime remained broken that Fed agents would begin grappling with contradictions among its federal structure and international monetary order.

Agency, Political Time, and Fed Reform Catalysts

Stephen Skowronek developed the concept of political time to describe a recurring American pattern where ascendant parties dominate national politics for an extended era before being supplanted by a new hegemonic party.[67] Wesley Widmaier has extended the concept to explain the rise and fall of international economic regimes.[68] Both theories are structural, envisioning regimes as born with built-in half-lives. Partisan regimes unravel as factions diverge, governing orthodoxies grow stale, and minority parties regain strength. International regimes devolve as their embedded ideas are converted from pragmatic principles into rigid policy scripts. In each theory, regimes collapse when their policies and ideals are implicated in crises and repudiated, and the political time cycle begins anew as new regimes are formed.

Conspicuously missing from these theories are factors that bridge domestic and international realms, such as wars and societal interests. Consequently, political time theories miss crucial contingent relationships between actors and their environments. For example, the outbreak of war overseas presents U.S. presidents with strategic choices of whether to engage or abstain from conflicts, which impact their domestic political survival.[69] Similarly, individuals form economic policy preferences in response to assessments of whether the world economy is opening or closing.[70] These relationships impact the health and vitality of both global and domestic regimes. Presidents who lead the nation into unpopular wars see their parties punished by voters, potentially cutting short a partisan regime. Waning foreign participation in global regimes can similarly weaken domestic support. These relationships are crucial in the monetary realm, where fixed currency regimes rely on ongoing patterns of mutual international adjustment.

An agent-centered theory of political time looks to the rhetoric and actions of regime leaders to explain how they navigate a changing structural landscape.[71] In this view, regimes are not born with built-in half-lives, but survive or fail based on their capacity to maintain authority and popular support amid changing circumstances. Leaders make choices that shape regime longevity, including questions of war and peace and how to respond to crises. Once these choices are made, however, they set in motion patterns of state building and demolition which move beyond a leader's control. These political moments penetrate the Federal Reserve and reshape its environment, setting the stage for its next round of

Table I.1. Political Time Impacts on the Federal Reserve

	Partisan Ascent	Partisan Decay	War	Peace
Reform Script	Populist	Progressive	Hamiltonian	Jeffersonian
Autonomy	↓	↓	↓	↑
Capacity	↓	↑	↑	↑
Locus of Authority	Party	Board	New York	System Agents

struggle. This book conceives of political time as four moments: partisan ascents and implosions, war and peace. Each event shifts the parameters of U.S. politics and empowers an ideological state-building script. Table I.1 (above) theorizes how each moment reshapes the Federal Reserve's attributes and environment.

Partisan Regime Origin and Collapse: Wellsprings of Populism and Progressivism

The rise of a newly ascendant party unleashes populist forces throughout the polity. Partisan regimes are founded by presidential candidates who successfully link the old regime's ideas and policies to emergent crises. The transition to unified government reduces the political system's veto points, opening reform opportunities.[72] Legislative reforms are shaped by factional compromises, but are often pushed past the finish line by invoking the "democratic wish," a populist reform script that promises to strip power from corrupt elites and restore it to "the people."[73] This invites the construction of sprawling federal agencies, which splinter authority across regions and institutional borders, sowing the seeds of interest-based conflicts and power struggles. The populist impulse also reshapes the bureaucracy and courts. Party activists are tapped to fill vacancies in state agencies and the judiciary.[74] Partisans first clash with holdovers from the old regime, but as partisan appointments accumulate the bureaucracy and legal system bends to the ruling party's priorities.[75]

This book shows these same dynamics reshape the Federal Reserve Board of Governors. Board appointees serve lengthy, staggered terms, which expire biennially, to ensure that individual presidents cannot load the board with loyalists. Presidents nevertheless see these appointment opportunities like all others, as opportunities for patronage and shifting policy priorities.[76] Partisan implants first grow the board's fragmentation, as newcomers clash with holdovers beholden to older visions of the board's mission. If partisan rule is sustained across multiple electoral cycles, however, the board grows more unified as old members cycle off and are replaced with like-minded partisans, remaking the board's value system.

In America's competitive electoral environment, ruling parties inevitably lose their grip on national power. As partisan regimes mature, agencies of state are increasingly seen by the party faithful and opponents alike as an extension of the ruling party.[77] In the face of emergent crises, however, America's inherited state is often revealed as parochial and lacking capacity.[78] When confronted with such a crisis, declining partisan regimes grapple toward progressive reform. Presidents look to delegate authority to public and private actors to contain the crisis. New agencies are also forged, but the shadow of future elections hangs over bipartisan legislative negotiations, so new agencies are constituted as independent and located outside the executive branch, to prevent them from becoming instruments of the ruling party.[79]

Partisan regime collapses remake the Federal Reserve and its environment. Scholars have identified a recurring pattern whereby lawmakers respond to a faltering economy by changing the FRA to reshape its powers, governance, and mandate.[80] This book shows that Fed empowerment processes begin earlier in the political time cycle, before crises spiral to slay partisan regimes. Presidents commanding declining regimes push their thumb on the system's internal power struggle to elevate the board's status. Likewise, crisis-induced progressive state building is an open-ended process. New financial agencies are layered onto an unwieldy state, shrinking the Fed's autonomy, muddling its responsibilities, and often taxing its resources.

War and Peace: Founts of Hamiltonian State Building and Jeffersonian Repudiation

War empowers Hamiltonian state-building scripts.[81] Only in the face of grave national emergencies do Americans set aside their antistatism and consent in the construction of coercive institutions imported from

Europe, including armies, taxes, and central banks.[82] War reshapes the Federal Reserve in three ways. Wars are costly and financed through a combination of taxes, loans, and monetary expansion. The Fed assists with each of these tasks. As banker to the state, it mobilizes and deploys revenues, helps the treasury gain access to capital markets, and creates reserves to provide subsidized credit. The process of drafting the Fed into providing war finance is enabled by constitutional provisions that grant the U.S. president greater wartime authority. A Hamiltonian alliance between the New York Fed and the treasury is forged, centralizing Fed authority along a New York–Washington axis. Congress rewards the Fed for wartime service by removing legal restrictions on its actions. By strengthening the system and concentrating its power, war makes the Fed "more like a central bank."[83] War also transforms the Fed's global setting. Wars destroy fixed currency regimes and catalyze shifts in economic power. These shifts occur across national borders but also within them. War increases the power of New York compared to other Fed outposts, setting the stage for future institutional skirmishes.

Returns to peace empower Jeffersonian critiques that war-swollen institutions depart from foundational ideals.[84] Claims of presidential authority lose force as the wartime emergency fades. Fragmentation re-emerges as other actors reassert their governing prerogatives. Fed actors seize onto these fragmenting currents to demand restoration of the system's autonomy. Once independence is restored, however, Fed agents inherit a central bank that concentrates power in New York. Antistatist sentiments flare throughout the country, and Americans demand dismantlement of a war-swollen state.[85] These forces are also projected inside the Fed, especially when demobilization is accompanied by economic problems. The system's struggle reemerges as actors in and out of the Fed invoke Jeffersonian scripts to attack Fed hierarchies and policies.

Wars leave behind several legacies that shape the Federal Reserve's problems moving forward. One is debt. Congress readily approves wartime deficits, but its fragmented structure makes it hard to develop fiscal plans to pay debts in war's aftermath.[86] If taxes are not raised or spending cut, the Fed can find itself pressured into monetizing debts and fueling inflationary forces. The second legacy concerns world order. Throughout this book, the United States emerges from wars in a hegemonic position, giving it opportunities to shape the peace and rebuild fixed currency orders. After World War I, the United States spurned overtures to rebuild a liberal international order, setting the world on a path toward crisis.[87] It took the opposite approach after World War II, spearheading international order building. These choices crucially shape the Fed's environment.[88] If political authorities endorse projects of rebuilding fixed currency regimes, the Fed must direct its powers externally. Even then, its capacity to stabilize the dollar is shaped by fiscal and trade policies.[89] If politicians enact policies that generate inflationary or deflationary pressures, the Fed must counter them to keep the dollar stable. This book shows that policy changes in the name of dollar stability (or other goals) are not always feasible, however, and the system's uneven integration into the world economy was a recurring source of policy gridlock and institutional conflict.

A final impactful war legacy is voters' verdict on the ruling party's decision to lead the nation to war. If, looking back, voters decide that war was too costly or corrosive of American ideals, they punish the leaders who led them there at the voting booth. Minority party leaders can foster their own party's ascendancy by successfully painting the war as a failure. When this happens, the polity-shaking impacts of partisan regime formation are layered atop the traumas of demobilization. This book shows that this sequence occurred three times during the Fed's maturation, each time recasting its developmental path. Democratic presidents led the nation to wars in World War I, Korea, and Vietnam, which resulted in Democrats losing power. Each time, budding partisan regimes were cut short, and the Fed's problems and possibilities shifted.

Ideas and Agents: The Struggle to Shape Fed Institutions in Secular Time

The FRA imagined an amorphous, fragmented landscape. In underinstitutionalized, complex environments, agents have incentives to devise rules and procedures to advance shared goals.[90] Some such goals are universal, such as institutional survival and prestige. Others are more particular, like institutions that enfranchise certain actors while excluding others. Reform-minded agents can package ideas into "common carrier" reforms to unite coalitions with diverse goals.[91] Enacting or changing extralegal rules requires building internal majorities. Ideas play important roles in constructing, stabilizing, and contesting such regimes.[92] The FRA's embedded ideologies are resources agents can invoke to attack or defend the institutional status quo, or which can be fused creatively to imagine a Fed with different processes and purposes.[93]

Populist, progressive, and Hamiltonian ideologies imagine different Fed hierarchies, while Jeffersonian ideas are weapons for attacking institutional hierarchies. Ideas operate at multiple levels of generality, however, ranging from broad ideologies to microlevel scripts for how to interpret and respond to given situations. Ideas can be usefully understood as "discrete diagnoses of problems, priorities and solutions in a realm of policy."[94] Agents use ideas to interpret their structural positions and define their interests.[95] One crucial way ideas shape institutions lies in their rejection after guiding policy through a period of crisis.[96] Ideas are repudiated through their association with crises regardless of whether they are the mechanism at fault, reducing their salience as ordering principles or institutional weapons moving forward.

This book traces the construction, decay, and collapse of three Fed regimes that predated modern Fed technocracy. Each was forged in response to a set of national and global circumstances and linked a set of Fed values to an institutional process. Each provisional order was forged in response to changing political times. The first regime analyzed in chapter 3 is the open market committee forged in the 1920s. It was built in an uncertain global context, where U.S. authorities rejected calls to spearhead the reconstruction of a liberal world order and the gold standard remained broken. New York Fed governor Benjamin Strong cited a mix of global and domestic threats to call for uniting the system's investment powers in a committee controlled by five reserve banks. Strong then peddled a "great idea" that the system was united by a national interest in helping restore the gold standard overseas to boost exports and to shield the United States from destabilizing gold imports.[97] Strong developed this idea in collaboration with his foreign counterparts. In 1924 and 1927, Strong's great idea united the system behind coordinated expansionary policies, which Strong deemed experimental, to lower U.S. interest rates and push capital across the Atlantic to create conditions that would enable other states to return to gold.

Strong's idea succeeded because it appealed to multiple ideologies. Most Fed officials agreed with Strong that the system's mission was to sustain the gold standard, and a world with only the U.S. dollar linked to gold was dangerous. Strong pitched his project as *restorative*, appealing to Jeffersonian ideals by promising that the restored system would function automatically. Foreign gold restoration was completed by 1927, but New York's requests for unified policies to promote international monetary stability persisted. In this changed environment, agents throughout the system reassessed their interests through parochial lenses. Officials from the nation's interior and West did not experience lasting material benefits from Strong's collaborations. Board member Adolph Miller fanned these regional divisions by tying bond purchases to surging stock market speculation. After the 1929 stock market collapse, Miller would deploy Jeffersonian and progressive ideas to topple Strong's hierarchical Fed through board regulations and repudiate his internationalism. In 1930, Miller would lead an obstructive coalition to block New York's repeated calls to use Fed stimulus to fend off a global crisis.

Fed regimes constructed in the 1930s and 1950s would follow a similar pattern. Each would be founded on a set of values and forged in relation to national and global settings and memories of the past. The international gold standard again collapsed in 1931, tarnishing both Hamiltonian and Jeffersonian Fed ideologies. A few years later, Marriner Eccles would invoke populist ideals to reimagine the Fed as an engine of the New Deal. Chapter 4 shows that Eccles was both the architect and repudiator of a populist Fed. In the 1930s, Eccles steered the Fed's powers toward fighting deflation and supporting the treasury. By the late 1940s, however, after an intervening world war, Eccles became a vocal opponent of treasury dominance. He denounced his Fed creation as an "engine of inflation," paving the way for its reconstitution.[98]

Chapter 5 traces the 1950s construction of William McChesney Martin Jr.'s egalitarian Fed regime and its eclipse by the modern Fed in the 1960s. Martin became Fed chair after the 1951 Treasury-Fed Accord ended an era of Treasury dominance. After World War II, U.S. political authorities spearheaded the construction of the Bretton Woods fixed currency regime with a gold-linked dollar at its core. Bretton Woods was founded on an "embedded liberal" compromise informed by a Keynesian view of the Depression, that states should maintain autonomy to shield their societies from international adjustment costs while working toward trade liberalization.[99] In this environment, Martin appealed to each of the system's ideologies and invoked idealized images of the system's pre-1935 past to dismantle inherited hierarchies that lodged open market power in New York and to foster an inclusive Fed order.

This system collapsed amid severe domestic and international cross-pressures in the 1960s. By 1960, Bretton Woods's future was being called into question because America's once impregnable gold reserves were being depleted. The world's central banks sprang to Bretton Woods's defense, forging new cooperative linkages to combat currency speculation.

Foreigners called on the Fed to raise U.S. interest rates to stem the capital outflow, but a rising chorus of American economists on both ends of the political spectrum called on U.S. political authorities to abandon the gold standard and turn the Fed's powers inward. An emergent era of Democratic partisan dominance provided a pathway to power inside the Fed to a left-leaning set of economists who called for severing the system's board occupational diversity norm. Democrats then cut taxes before launching wars in Vietnam and against domestic poverty, unleashing a Great Inflation, which rendered attempts to save Bretton Woods futile. The modern Fed, which crystalized in 1970, was founded on a mix of progressive and populist principles. Moving forward, monetary policy would be understood as a domestic tool for regulating monetary *growth*. As a new age of floating currencies dawned, the system's long debates about whether to stabilize the dollar and how to make policy was gradually forgotten.

Impacts of Fed Development: Global Power, Political Time, and Legacies of Loss

Milton Friedman and Anna Schwartz made the Federal Reserve's struggle for power famous by arguing that a 1930 open market committee "diffusion of power" led to a "policy of drift and inaction," which they claim caused the Great Depression.[100] Scholars reject this institutional claim, but embrace their broader argument that Fed inaction worsened the depression. At Friedman's ninetieth birthday in 2002, future Fed chair Ben Bernanke proclaimed, "You're right. We did it. We're very sorry. But thanks to you, we won't do it again."[101] Bernanke meant that most economists now agreed that the Fed had the responsibility to grow the money supply in recessions and financial panics to stabilize the macroeconomy.

Unbeknownst to most observers, this endorsed an anachronistic understanding of Fed power and purpose. Responding to rising political attacks amid the Depression, an internal Federal Reserve memorandum struck a defensive tone, observing that before the 1930s central banks were not commonly understood as responsible for using credit levers to end stock market booms or fight depressions. The Depression's severity grew from declining "soundness of bank assets" and "international maladjustments that developed in the decade after the war."[102] A New York Fed memorandum agreed that fixing "disorganization caused by the war and the peace . . . was beyond the powers of any central banking mechanism."[103] Before the 1930s, Fed insiders did not use the term *monetary policy*. They spoke of "credit policy," which was understood as a limited tool to be used within gold standard constraints. Lester Chandler observes, "The difference was not merely semantic; it both reflected and affected ways of thinking."[104]

Friedman and Schwartz imagine the Depression-era Fed as unencumbered by structural constraints. But before 1933 the system was bound by the gold standard, and reserve banks needed gold to buy bonds and to back the currency they issued. Friedman and Schwartz dismissed reserve bankers' claims that they lacked gold to support bond buying programs in 1931 because the system *as a whole* had sufficient reserves to buy bonds until 1933, "the free gold problem . . . played no role in the outcome."[105] This ignores the collective action problem inherent in forging an expansionary system policy which relies upon voluntary contributions of gold by self-regarding units. Further, it crucially ignores the context Fed officials operated within, one where currency hoarding by Americans required reserve banks to expand their stockpiles of gold.

Charles Kindleberger, who worked as a New York Fed researcher in the 1930s, blasted Friedman and Schwartz's "uni-causal" Depression explanation, arguing that the Depression was global in scope and grew from a broader U.S. failure to rebuild and stabilize the world economy.[106] Retired New York Fed president Allan Sproul was even blunter. In a peer review of the manuscript, Sproul claimed Friedman and Schwartz arrived "at a conclusion, determined in advance, that 'business dances to the tune of money,'" and demonstrated "disregard for the realities of the market place in a dynamic, complex economy." Sproul saw the book as a ploy to strip the Fed of autonomy by forcing it follow their favored rigid policy rule. "To proceed from such a study . . . to suggest explicitly with regard to the past and implicitly with regard to the future, that here is a touchstone—a steady rate of increase in the stock of money . . . that if this arithmetic guide is followed, fiscal policy, debt management, the cost-price push, the balance of payments . . . will fall nicely into line. . . . Such an arithmetic guide . . . would be more wispy, if not more willowy, than the general guide of economic stability now followed."[107] The analysis missed crucial contextual factors that changed the Fed's powers and responsibilities, including "changes in the monetary system and our banking structure, during and after two World Wars . . . the purging of the commercial banking system in 1929–1933, the organization of the Federal Deposit

Insurance Corporation, the progress of the Federal Reserve System in learning its job."

These New York Fed practitioners hearkened back to an earlier conception of central banking pioneered by Alexander Hamilton. In Hamilton's view, the purpose of a central bank lay in promoting financial and currency stability by providing a counterweight to elected officials who would prefer to evade tackling emerging problems by mindlessly printing money. Hamilton's logic informs modern arguments in favor of central bank independence.[108] It diverges markedly from modern Fed practice, however, where the Fed draws upon a well of global power to stabilize the domestic American economy. Friedman and Schwartz imagine that the Federal Reserve was born with these powers and purposes. Others see Fed power as springing from the law.[109] Both of these views reflect populist understandings of currency's value and, by extension, central bank power, as springing from sovereign authority, rather than flowing from control over valuable resources. They imagine the Fed and America as exceptional, uniquely unconstrained by the global structures and contexts they are embedded within.

There is some truth in this sentiment, but it ignores the crucial ways America's national choices shape the world.[110] The six decades surveyed throughout this book are an era of U.S. primacy, where its policies shaped and foreclosed opportunities for global order. The world was repeatedly faced with problems of halting American leadership, which grew from its fragmented political order and shifting partisan dynamics. Federalism makes enacting policies in service of strategic goals difficult, especially when they entail distributing domestic costs.[111] The essence of monetary power lies in a nation's ability to exploit its currency's global position to avoid international adjustment costs, or shift adjustment costs onto others.[112] The wars of the twentieth century expanded America's monetary power through successive waves of dollarization. When the Federal Reserve was conceived in 1913, the dollar was a mere measure of gold embodied in a variety of currencies, which circulated domestically. By 1970, the Fed would hold a monopoly on production of globally valuable dollars, which were already effectively de-linked from gold.

In this changed world, it no longer made sense to look to Hamiltonian or Jeffersonian ideologies to understand the Fed's structure or purpose. As the board's capacity expanded, it was natural to look its chair and staff to shape the FOMC agenda. The modern Fed's emergence completed a historic migration of ideational authority from New York to Washington which began four decades earlier. The modern Fed crystalized as an insular technocracy, founded on a melding of progressive and populist ideals. Moving forward, monetary policy would be forged through a battle of ideas about how best to regulate monetary *growth*. No longer would Fed authorities allow falling gold stockpiles or international imbalances to dictate credit contraction.

The modern Fed vacates the oppositional stance to government, which Hamilton saw as among a central bank's primary virtues. Hamilton wanted the central bank to act as a spur to government energy; to alert election-minded politicians to looming problems and force them to tackle them expeditiously. Hamilton saw the institutional features of his envisioned bank, including private ownership, limited capital, and corporate governance, as endowing it with the capacity to force lawmakers to reconcile means with ends, and balance guns with butter. In Hamilton's view, a central bank that refracts the political order's instincts to respond to crises by mindlessly printing money is worse than no central bank at all. Yet, this is the impact of the collective embrace of Friedman and Schwartz's understanding of the Depression. The modern Fed is America's frontline economic stabilizer and defender. Lawmakers rely on Fed power to fill the void left by decades of attacks on national fiscal capacity and regulatory authority.

Through its actions, which ease the government's financing burden and prevent crises from spiraling, the Fed steers the nation away from critical junctures.[113] This book argues the modern Fed's narrow focus on sustaining economic growth has contributed to the "waning of political time."[114] Stephen Skowronek argues that the transformative impact of political time has fallen in recent decades due to "institutional thickening," the development of an enduring welfare and regulatory state, which limits all presidents' abilities to dismantle inherited programs and structures. From this book's perspective, the modern Fed's macroeconomic stabilization efforts have relaxed the nation's budgetary constraint and emboldened lawmakers to enact short-sighted policies. This dynamic also extends to the international realm. Fed largesse and privileged access to global dollar reserves allows U.S. politicians to fight wars entirely on credit, prolonging conflicts by masking their costs from the public, and blurring lines between war and peace.[115]

The story of Fed development told throughout this book differs from historical institutionalist accounts of critical juncture–induced reform.[116]

In the common telling, the Federal Reserve was born with flaws owing to its origin in a legislative compromise. These fragilities were allegedly revealed through economic crises in which the Fed was deemed complicit, resulting in its legislative reconstruction in 1935 and a durable grant of autonomy in 1951. These three moments: 1913, 1935, and 1951, together form the progressive Fed synthesis, a view of Fed history that sees its modern form as both desirable and inevitable.[117] Populist and Jeffersonian Fed histories similarly see the system's developmental path as prelaid. Populists sees the Fed as a once-virtuous monetary authority that devolved through capture either by Wall Street, claim populists on the Left, or by discretion-wielding bureaucrats, according to Right populists. Jeffersonians see the Fed as the institutional vehicle of a bankers' conspiracy to entrench their power, a fount of corruption by design.

This book finds greater contingency and variation in the Fed's developmental path. In each of the Fed regimes surveyed, all four of its ideologies were reflected to greater or lesser degrees. The system's cumulative layered development reflects patterns identified by Jeffrey Tulis and Nicole Mellow in *Legacies of Losing in American Politics*.[118] In this view, agents and ideas that lose out in critical junctures can still leave marks on the institutional fabric, and often become empowered later on to shape longer-term outcomes. This book shows that all Fed regime builders, a pantheon of heroes ranging from Paul Warburg to William McChesney Martin Jr., left behind a mix of durable and passing legacies, forged both in victory and in defeat. The concluding chapter shows how these different elements come together to form the contemporary FOMC process. When you finish this book, you will understand why the Fed's essence cannot be neatly captured by any timeless ideological frame. Rather, Fed culture is best understood as a braid of four ideological strands, whose positions of hierarchy and subordination vary with each Fed regime, and the contexts they are forged in relation to.

1

Escape from Jekyll Island

The Federal Reserve's Birth in Political Time

> The position of the Reserve Board, as designed by the Act, was bound to prove exasperatingly difficult and trying. The office was burdened with the handicap, commonly imposed upon so many branches of administration in a democracy, of a system of checks and counter-checks—a paralyzing system which gives powers with one hand and takes them away with the other.
>
> —Retired Board member Paul Warburg, 1930

Conspiracy theorists and Fed sympathizers alike trace the Fed's origin to Jekyll Island, a remote private club off the Georgia coast. In 1910, Senator Nelson Aldrich (R-RI) summoned a handful of elite financiers there for a conference where they hatched a plot to build an American central bank. Jeffersonians see the cabal as evidence that the Fed was born of a conspiracy to entrench bankers' power.[1] Progressives celebrate the meeting for yielding an enlightened central bank design based on Paul Warburg's ideas.[2] While the FRA departed from the Aldrich Plan by creating twelve central banks instead of one, each was tasked with purposes imagined at Jekyll. Progressives trace the Fed's essence as an independent central bank to these *functions*. They see the system's evolution into the modern Fed as vindicating Warburg's progressive ideas.

Each of these views contains a kernel of truth but overstates Jekyll Islanders' influence. Both misinterpret the Aldrich Plan's envisioned central bank, which wasn't exclusively progressive, but also contained Hamiltonian design principles. They likewise underestimate the lasting impacts of Jeffersonian and populist beliefs held by Democratic partisans who forged the Federal Reserve Act. This chapter traces the Federal Reserve Act's construction and enactment through political time. Nelson Aldrich's 1910 endorsement of a central bank was an act typical of a leader of a dying partisan regime. Aldrich was the face of the Republican old guard in the Senate, where he flexed institutional muscle to defend mercantilist policies that benefited Eastern capitalists and infuriated Western progressives. Aldrich's heavy-handed tactics drove a wedge through his party, contributing to a split with progressives on the eve of the 1912 elections, which handed control of government and financial reform to Democrats. This political time sequence, partisan collapse followed by reformation, activated progressive and populist reform scripts, which combined to render the FRA an ambiguous blueprint.

This chapter proceeds through three sections to illustrate how partisan forces shaped the FRA's design, propelled it into law, and structured its early power struggle. It begins by locating the Jekyll Island meeting in the context of political time, arguing that Aldrich's behavior reflects this book's expectations for a leader of a declining regime. It then traces a series of bargains brokered by President Wilson that shaped the law. Rather than endorsing a single ordering principle, philosophical compromises were scattered throughout the legal text, imagining a federal sprawl amendable to multiple constructions. The final section explains how the system's struggle unfolded while Democrats remained ascendant in Wilson's first term. In this setting, populists, progressives, and Hamiltonians worked at cross-purposes to institutionalize their Fed visions, but Democrats obstructed reforms to successfully defend a weak and fragmented partisan design.

The Aldrich Plan as a Republican Hail Mary

Declining partisan regimes make last-ditch efforts to restore order and sustain partisan rule by delegating authority to experts. This progressive reform strategy is fraught with danger, however, because weakened parties have limited control over the national agenda and factions have differing goals. This section applies this logic to explain the Aldrich Plan's emergence and repudiation. It first explains the weaknesses of America's early-twentieth-century banking system and Paul Warburg's solution. It then explains how the Aldrich Plan favored Hamiltonian over progressive principles, infuriating the party's progressive wing and fanning partisan divisions.

STUCK IN THE PAST: AMERICA'S PREMODERN FINANCIAL REGIME

Three Civil War legacies—greenbacks, Republican rule, and the National Banking System—animated U.S. monetary politics through the 1890s. The treasury issued paper currency, "greenbacks," to prosecute the Civil War, demonstrating the feasibility of Edward Kellogg's call for state-issued money. Afterward, creditors persuaded lawmakers to make greenbacks convertible into gold.[3] This dovetailed with movements overseas, as states followed Great Britain's lead by making their currencies convertible into gold at stable rates. The world then entered an era of deflationary pressures.[4] Falling commodity prices increased U.S. farmers' real debt burdens, fueling waves of populist agitation. William Jennings Bryan's ill-fated 1896 presidential bid on a bimetallic currency platform marked the peak of these movements. The same year, the application of new mining techniques caused the world's monetary gold stocks to begin rising.[5] Suddenly, decades of falling prices gave way to a new era of inflation.

This fortuitous turn benefited the long-ruling Republican Party, which used control of the presidency in the decades after the Civil War to defend a mercantilist policy mix of high tariffs, the gold standard, and domestic laissez-faire.[6] Republicans passed the Gold Reserve Act in 1900, legalizing the gold standard. Waves of industrial and financial consolidation remade the American corporate sector, giving rise to massive trusts. Burgeoning wealth grew America's power on the world stage, but fragmented institutions rendered its development chaotic.

The National Banking System was established during the Civil War as a new class of federally chartered banks empowered to issue currency, national bank notes, collateralized by federal bonds instead of gold. This system was layered atop a diffuse state-chartered banking system regulatory regime. Competition to issue bank charters among state and federal regulators inspired a "competition in laxity."[7] At both the state and national levels, banks were prohibited from establishing branches, rendering each a freestanding unit tied to a discrete territory. Banks in the countryside and small cities could deposit some of their required reserves in banks in larger cities, however, where they could earn interest. America's bank reserves pyramided in big New York City banks, where they were loaned to stockbrokers on the call loan market.[8]

This system supported New York's primacy in the nation's financial system. Wall Street's power derived from elite financiers' ties to European banking houses, however. America remained an agricultural, debtor nation. Much of its capital was locked up in fixed, long-term investments. The United States depended on seasonal inflows of European capital to bring its produce to world markets. While a common condition, America's lack of a central bank and crude financial practices rendered it a global pariah.[9] Other countries accessed capital markets by selling bills-of-exchange, loans tied to specific transactions, on secondary markets. This practice was once common in the United States, but fell by the wayside after the second Bank of the United States was dissolved in 1836.[10] In its wake arose a system of localized finance based on promissory notes, where banks loaned funds directly to individuals, against stocks of goods and promises of future sales, rather than through trade-linked bills guaranteed by multiple signatories.

In America, elite financiers, partisan treasury secretaries, and city-level clearinghouse associations all performed central bank functions. As the fall harvest approached, country banks would withdraw deposits from correspondent banks and seek to borrow funds to help local farmers bring their produce to market. To handle a surge of withdrawals, New York banks would call in call loans, sometimes triggering security liquidations and sharp stock market falls. Elites such as J. P. Morgan would borrow from European banks on their own lines of credit to access funds to loan to farmers. This process was clunky in the best of times. Funds were physically dispatched and moved slowly across the country. Farmers paid steep rates to borrow money. These problems were reinforced by the nation's limited currency stock. Quantities of greenbacks, national bank notes, and gold- and silver-certificates, were all fixed in the short run. Farmers needed cash to pay laborers, but national bank notes were concentrated in the Northeast.[11]

This system came under strain at the dawn of the twentieth century, when New York banks began seeking emergency government deposits to avoid liquidity crises. Treasury Secretary Leslie Shaw authorized this practice in 1902, agreeing to deposit funds in New York banks on the condition that funds be loaned to the interior.[12] Rural borrowers saw this practice as corrupt because New York banks paid little interest on treasury deposits, but loaned them out at emergency rates. This system was prone to contagious banking panics. Rural banks waiting for funds to arrive from New York would sometimes be overwhelmed by withdrawals.[13] As word of bank closures spread, bank runs would ensue in adjoining regions. City-level clearinghouse associations formed islands of stability amid financial chaos. In crises, these local bank clubs would suspend gold payments and issue clearinghouse loan certificates as scrip currency.[14] These actions protected local banks, but pushed adjustment costs into the countryside. U.S. financial crises would become internationalized when the New York City Clearinghouse Association suspended gold payments, facing foreign creditors with prospects of U.S. defaults.

Paul Warburg's Progressive Central Bank Idea

When Paul Warburg migrated to New York in 1901, he began a crusade to persuade Americans to build a progressive central bank modeled on his native German Reichsbank. Warburg argued that America's proclivity to financial crisis grew from its archaic practice of loaning funds through promissory notes rather than trade-linked bills of exchange. A central bank was needed to modernize U.S. financial practices by remaking it in the European image. It would do so by discounting (loaning funds against) bills of exchange endorsed by two or more parties. This would cultivate the growth of secondary bill markets, allowing banks to raise cash by selling bills. America would also gain easier access to European capital if "we could offer American paper drawn in dollars, showing its commercial origin and indorsed by . . . banks . . . we should vastly multiply the avenues leading into the portfolios of the European banks . . . millions of even Russian bills are constantly held by French, English, and German banks . . . there is no reason . . . to doubt that these same avenues could be readily opened to American paper."[15] Reaping these global benefits would require fostering vibrant domestic bill markets. "To make our paper part and parcel of the means of the world's international exchange. . . . It must always have a ready home market. . . . This is insured in nearly every country of the world . . . [by] some kind of a central bank, ready at all times to rediscount the legitimate paper of the general banks."

Warburg had a specific central bank in mind. He noted that the German Reichsbank is "the most perfect organization of its kind. The capital stock . . . is owned partly by the government and partly by the public. The Reichsbank has a central board in Berlin, consisting of the foremost men in financial and commercial circles. The president of the bank is a salaried officer, a trained banker (no politician) who retains his position irrespective of the party in power, like the president of any private bank who remains in office as long as he does his work well."

Warburg's new Wall Street colleagues at first rejected his central bank idea.[16] The Panic of 1907 changed Wall Street's calculus, however. J. P. Morgan personally intervened to defuse the crisis, but only after several bank closures, a stock market crash, and gold suspension.[17] After the crisis, elites warmed to the central bank idea, but only one they could control.

Nelson Aldrich: The Face of a Dying Republican Regime

Congress responded to the crisis by establishing the National Monetary Commission, a bipartisan panel of eighteen senators and representatives, tasked with recommending "to Congress at the earliest date practicable what changes are necessary or desirable in the monetary system."[18] Sen. Nelson Aldrich (R–RI), known as the "general manager of the nation" due to his influence over economic policy, chaired the commission. He was known for authoritarian tactics in the Senate, which he brought to bear on the National Monetary Commission's proceedings. Aldrich made a European fact-finding tour in Summer 1908, where he warmed to the central bank idea.

He returned to face a looming tariff battle, however.[19] For years, he had partnered with House Speaker Joseph Cannon (R–IL) to suppress calls from Republican progressives for freer trade, exploiting his position as chairman of the Senate Finance Committee to shape the agenda. In 1909, Cannon allowed a progressive tariff to pass through the House, knowing that Aldrich would restore protectionism in the Senate. Aldrich intervened to raise duties, setting the stage for a conference committee showdown. President William Howard Taft sided with Aldrich, securing a high tariff rate schedule.

Aldrich's hubris drove a wedge through the Republican Party. In March 1910, progressives allied with house Democrats to strip Speaker Cannon of control of the House Rules Committee. Aldrich responded to his ally's enfeeblement by announcing he would not seek reelection that fall.[20] The November elections yielded the first Democratic house majority in sixteen years. Afterward, Aldrich invited a clique of financiers to Jekyll

Island to develop a central bank plan. They were struck by his obliviousness to his own collapsing power.

Aldrich renamed Paul Warburg's proposed central bank from a United Reserve Bank to a National Reserve Association to avoid public opposition.[21] He submitted his "suggested plan" to the National Monetary Commission in January 1911, nearly three years after it was charged with delivering legislation "at the earliest date practicable." When the new Congress assembled in March, it cut off the commission's funding and demanded a final report. The Aldrich Plan was submitted to both houses of Congress in January 1912. The design was progressive insofar as it was structured as a bankers' club. The National Reserve Association would only provide services to banks, not compete with them for loans and deposits. It would issue currency against a mix of gold and commercial assets and provide liquidity to the banking system by rediscounting bills of exchange. To quell fears of Wall Street control, Warburg designed voting rules that limited big banks' power within the association and ensured broad regional representation.[22] The corporate board's governance shaded the bank Hamiltonian, however. It would be dominated by bankers, with few state representatives. This departed from Warburg's beloved Reichsbank model, where bankers staffed and managed the bank, but state authorities retained ultimate authority.[23]

When the Aldrich Plan arrived in congress, progressive Sen. Charles Lindbergh (R–MN) called it a "wonderfully clever" bill which would invite "capture by Wall Street as soon as it should get into operation."[24] He called on House Democrats to investigate the "combinations of financiers and financial institutions . . . who control the money and credit and . . . operate in restraint of trade and in violation of the law." Rep. Arsene Pujo (D–LA) began "money trust" hearings in May, which became a public spectacle. Prominent financiers were forced to testify and disclose the extent of their empires. Louis Brandeis reported that the hearings confirmed a growing fear among the public that financial power had grown dangerously concentrated.[25]

When Theodore Roosevelt, while in Africa on safari, heard of President Taft's capitulation to Aldrich on the tariff issue, he saw it as a betrayal of the progressive cause. Roosevelt challenged Taft for the Republican nomination in 1912 and campaigned vigorously in states with primaries. Taft retained the support of the Republican establishment, however, who nominated him for a second term. The Republican National Convention ended in chaos when Roosevelt instructed his followers to leave and form a Progressive Party behind his presidential bid.

The Federal Reserve Act's Construction by an Ascendant Democratic Coalition

Democrats exploited the Republican implosion to win unified control of government. President-elect Woodrow Wilson understood that Democrats' grasp on national power would be short-lived unless they expanded their base beyond the South. He believed the key to cementing a partisan realignment lay in tailoring reforms promised in the party's platform to appeal to Western progressives, whom he hoped to convert into Democrats.[26] This section shows how Wilson took advantage of his political moment to broker compromises that shaped the FRA.

The Democratic Party platform included a plank endorsing financial reform, while rejecting a central bank.[27] "We oppose the so-called Aldrich bill or the establishment of a central bank; and we believe our country will be largely freed from panics . . . by such a systematic revision of our banking laws as will render temporary relief in localities where such relief is needed, with protection from control or dominion by what is known as the money trust." Democrats were divided into two factions, which saw this mandate differently. Jeffersonians remained ideologically opposed to central banks in general, while populists only opposed a private central bank. They wanted a public monetary authority to right historical wrongs by printing and distributing currency. President Wilson wanted financial reform to appeal to progressives. His advisor Colonel House quietly reached out to Paul Warburg for advice.[28]

Brokering a Partisan Reform Compromise

President Wilson navigated this partisan thicket by brokering sequential compromises on the Federal Reserve's structure. In December 1912, Rep. Carter Glass (D-VA), the new chairman of the House Currency and Banking Committee, approached Wilson with a plan to build a system of twenty central banks spread across the country. Glass was a Jeffersonian who saw the Aldrich Plan's fault as lying in its "monopolistic tendencies," not its private control.[29] He hoped to end Wall Street's hegemony by cultivating "rival aggregations of financial power."[30]

Wilson agreed to endorse Glass's plan under the condition that an "altruistic" board be included to serve as a "capstone . . . atop the structure."[31] This demand reflected Wilson's desire to appeal to progressives. Faced with little choice, Glass accepted Wilson's demand, while worrying that Wilson had been influenced "by those who are seeking to mask the Aldrich plan and give us dangerous centralization."[32] Indeed, Wilson was impressed with Paul Warburg's diagnosis of the nation's financial problems, but his institutional solution, a central bank, was incompatible with the Democrats' party platform and Wilson's own campaign trail rhetoric.[33]

The Wilson-Glass compromise envisioned a diffuse federal system of privately owned and controlled central banks overseen by a public board. This creditor-friendly design was unacceptable to populists. William Jennings Bryan had acted as kingmaker at the Baltimore convention, throwing his support behind Wilson after the New York delegation endorsed frontrunner James "Champ" Clark of Missouri. Wilson rewarded Bryan by naming him secretary of state. When details of Wilson and Glass's plan were circulated inside the administration in May, Bryan lectured Wilson that Democrats were "committed by Jefferson and Jackson and by recent platforms to the doctrine that the issue of money is a function of government and should not be surrendered to banks."[34] Bryan made two demands to secure his support, a public guarantee of reserve bank currency and exclusion of bankers from the board.

Wilson gathered warring factions at the White House in June to broker a compromise. Populists pushed for state control. Senator Robert Owen (D-OK) wanted the board constituted as "exclusively a political agency." Treasury Secretary William McAdoo agreed that "the right measure is the one which puts the Government in the saddle."[35] Glass warned that caving to populist demands would make the reform unacceptable to business. At an impasse, Wilson sought advice from progressive Louis Brandeis. He counseled the president, "The power to issue currency should be vested exclusively in Government officials, even when the currency is issued against commercial paper. . . . The conflict between the policies of the Administration and the desires of the financiers . . . is an irreconcilable one."[36] Wilson then conceded to Bryan's demands, drawing Glass's criticism that the currency guarantee would be harmful. Wilson explained that the guarantee was symbolic, since currency would still be backed by gold. Wilson asked rhetorically, "If we can hold to the substance of the thing and give the other fellow the shadow, why not do it, if thereby we may save our bill?"[37] Historian Arthur Link observes that the Wilson administration then "united in a solid phalanx that never broke during all the ensuing controversies."[38]

Democrats and Progressives Unite to Advance the Glass-Owen Bill

To move the reform through Congress, Wilson intervened personally, enlisted William Jennings Bryan to do so, and took advantage of a resilient party caucus. When radicals complained in the house Democratic caucus that the bill was "written wholly in the interests of the creditor classes," Carter Glass read a letter from William Jennings Bryan urging his supporters to "stand by the President and assist in securing the passage of this measure at the earliest possible moment."[39] This triggered a caucus vote where Democrats labeled the bill a party measure, binding all Democrats to support it on the House floor.[40] The caucus endorsement put Glass in "undisputed control of the Democratic steamroller."[41] Later, on the House floor, Republicans proposed an amendment reaffirming the gold standard. Bryan again intervened and urged his followers to support the amendment, which passed with wide Democratic support. The House passed the Glass-Owen bill the same day with only three Democrats, out of 257, voting nay.

The bill faced a more difficult path through the Senate, where populists wielded power on the Senate Finance Committee. Three of seven Democrats joined Republicans to obstruct the bill's advancement out of committee.[42] Hearings ground on for months. In October, Frank Vanderlip, a Jekyll Islander and the president of National City Bank, proposed a treasury-housed central bank. A majority on the committee united behind Vanderlip's plan. Wilson responded by inviting committee Democrats to the White House for a scolding, telling them he would not support a Wall Street–backed plan.[43] Two withdrew their opposition to the Glass-Owen bill, but deadlock continued. The impasse was resolved when the committee agreed to advance both bills for Senate consideration. On November 30, the Senate Democratic Caucus passed a resolution making the Glass-Owen bill a party bill. Progressives then joined Democrats to pass a resolution requiring continuous Senate debate of the bills for thirteen hours per day until they were voted on. On December 19, the Senate narrowly rejected Vanderlip's plan. The Glass-Owen bill then passed fifty-four to thirty-four, with all forty-eight Democrats voting yes.[44]

Partisan Enactment of the Federal Reserve Act

The FRA pushed crucial governance decisions into the future. This section shows how Democrats continued working to shape the system after the bill was signed into law. The House version of the bill called for at least twelve reserve banks, while the Senate bill required "not less than 8 nor more than 12." The Senate language was adopted by the conference committee. A Reserve Bank Organization Committee, composed of the secretaries of the treasury and agriculture and the comptroller of the currency, was constituted to decide the number of reserve banks within this range and their locations. The law gave the president an important role in shaping the Federal Reserve Board, which was constituted as a seven-member body with five presidential appointees, appointed with the Senate's advice and consent, and two *ex officio* members of the administration, the treasury secretary and the comptroller.

The task of drawing the Federal Reserve's map was delegated to the Reserve Bank Organization Committee. Congress appropriated the committee one hundred thousand dollars to survey the country's seven thousand nationally chartered banks regarding their reserve bank location preferences and to undertake a ten thousand mile "listening tour" to hear the cases of eighteen cities vying to land one. On April 2, the committee announced reserve banks would be incorporated in Boston, New York, Philadelphia, Cleveland, Richmond, Atlanta, Chicago, Dallas, St. Louis, Kansas City, Minneapolis, and San Francisco. This maximally decentralized system located three reserve banks in the capital-poor, but solidly Democratic, South.[45] Five were placed in capital-abundant regions, while seven others were spread across the rural periphery. This decentralized design appealed to each Democratic faction. Glass believed that decentralization would cultivate the rise of new financial centers. Treasury Secretary William McAdoo hoped to use his board perch to steer resources to cash-starved Democratic constituencies.[46]

To bring his populist vision to life, McAdoo sought to establish command over the board. When Wilson considered his board appointments, McAdoo demanded "at least four members of known sympathy with the spirit and purposes of the Federal Reserve Act and of undoubted loyalty to the Administration."[47] The law named the treasury secretary the board's chairman and the comptroller of the currency, his subordinate, an *ex officio* member. This administration faction shared power, however, with five appointees from "different commercial, industrial and geographical divisions of the country."[48] McAdoo warned Wilson that if he wasn't provided a pliant board, he might "be forced to act independently." The law authorized but did not compel the treasury to designate reserve banks as fiscal agents. If McAdoo preferred, he could bypass the reserve banks and run the existing Independent Treasury System as a *de facto* central bank.[49]

Despite McAdoo's veiled threat, Wilson heeded Colonel House's advice to make conservative appointments, which would win the confidence of business.[50] Wilson announced his initial nominees on May 4, 1914. He chose Richard Olney, a former attorney general, to serve as the board's governor, or "active executive officer." He also nominated Paul Warburg, Henry A. Wheeler, vice president of Union Trust Co., W. P. G. Harding, president of Alabama's largest bank, and Thomas D. Jones, a director of International Harvester Company. One senator observed, "A more reactionary crowd could not have been found with a fine-tooth comb."[51]

Wilson's nominees drew cries of betrayal from populists, setting up a confirmation battle on the Senate Finance Committee. Olney and Wheeler announced they would not accept their nominations. In their place, Wilson nominated Adolph Miller, an academic economist, and Charles Hamlin, an assistant treasury secretary. Senators Reed (D-MO) and Hitchcock (D-NB) demanded that Jones and Warburg testify before the committee. Jones appeared and faced hostile questioning. International Harvester was under federal investigation at the time for operating as an illegal combination. Jones admitted that he had approved of all the company's policies since he joined it in 1909, prompting Reed and Hitchcock to demand the withdrawal of his nomination. At Wilson's urging, William Jennings Bryan spoke with the senators to try to persuade them but failed to change their minds.[52] Wilson angrily withdrew the nomination.

Paul Warburg was not interested in subjecting himself to similar humiliation.[53] He declined to appear before the committee and asked Wilson to withdraw his nomination. Wilson refused. Sen. Hitchcock (D-NB) then reached out to Warburg and promised that his appearance would be a conference rather than an interrogation. Warburg agreed, and the Senate promptly approved his nomination. The first Federal Reserve Board was sworn in on August 10, 1914.

The Federal Reserve Act: An Invitation to Struggle

The compromises among opposed principles littered throughout the FRA formed a plan to build a sprawling structure. The law invited a struggle for primacy both among and within the reserve banks and the board. Wilson's partial accommodation of populist demands left the board's nature uncertain. If McAdoo prevailed in his quest for power, the resulting Fed would lean populist. If the board instead established autonomy from the treasury and gained supremacy, the Fed would be structured as a progressive agency. A second struggle was imminent, however, between the reserve banks and board to determine who were the system's most powerful actors. If power remained devolved among the reserve banks, and new financial centers emerged, the system would lean Jeffersonian. If the reserve banks' inherent power imbalances were instead allowed to shine through, the Fed would approximate the Hamiltonian-leaning Aldrich Plan.

The FRA was an impenetrable blueprint which left open each of these possibilities.[54] Table 1.1 compares its envisioned institutions with Alexander Hamilton's Bank of the United States and the Aldrich Plan's envisioned National Reserve Association. These latter central banks were envisioned as powerful, nationally branched corporations. Each lodged authority in a banker-controlled board that would formulate policy,

Table 1.1. The Federal Reserve System and its Competitors

	Bank of the United States	National Reserve Association	Federal Reserve System
Structure	Corporate	Corporate	Federal
Governance	Private	Private	Public-Private Hybrid
Capital	$10 million (1791)	$300 million (1912)	$48 million* (1913)
Duration	20 years	50 years	20 years
Membership	Voluntary	Voluntary	Compulsory for National Banks
Currency Restrictions	None	Moderate	High

Sources: Alexander Hamilton, "Report on a National Bank, December 13, 1790," in *Writings*, ed. Joanne B. Freeman, 613–646 (New York: Library of America, 2001); J. L. Broz, *The International Origins of the Federal Reserve System* (Ithaca: Cornell University Press, 1997), 178–185; Federal Reserve Act, Public Law 63-43, 63d Cong., 2d sess. (December 23, 1913).

*Reserve Banks each required to have a minimum $4 million capital.

supervise the bank's executive officer, and oversee subordinate branches. The Federal Reserve was more complex and less coherent. The board was a constituted as a public entity, but the nature and extent of its authority was unclear. Some hoped it would be limited to light-handed oversight, while others envisioned it as exercising command over the reserve banks. The choice to locate reserve banks in capital-poor regions required low minimum-capitalization levels. If each reserve bank were capitalized at the law's $4 million minimum, the system's capital would be one-sixth of the proposed National Reserve Association's. If reserve banks in more developed regions had larger capitals, by contrast, power disparities would be baked into its structure.

Beyond light capitalization standards, the law contained several other checks on the system's power. These included limited-duration reserve bank charters, complicated membership requirements, and draconian currency restrictions. Hamilton's original Bank of the United States blueprint contained twenty-year sunset provisions. Time-limited charters proved to be the plan's Achilles' heel, as both the First and Second Bank of the United States died at the expiration of its twenty-year charter. The Aldrich Plan sought to avoid this outcome with a fifty-year charter, which would provide the central bank plenty of time to demonstrate its usefulness.[55] The FRA culled this innovation, however, issuing separate twenty-year charters to each reserve bank.

Reserve banks were to be owned and organized by local commercial banks. Nationally chartered banks were required to join the system by buying stock in their local reserve bank at a cost of 6 percent of their paid-in capital and surplus.[56] By joining, banks gained access to their reserve bank's discount facilities, voting rights to select six of its nine directors, lower reserve requirements, and annual dividends on the stock of up to 6 percent.[57] National banks also were authorized to manage estates, making them more competitive with state-chartered banks.[58] State-chartered banks and trust companies lacked incentives to join the system, however, as they benefited from weaker regulations. Further, while a national bank could exit the system by re-chartering as a state bank, no such mechanism was imagined for state banks to exit the system.

Two final legal hurdles prevented the efficient concentration of bank reserves: clauses requiring members to deposit only five-twelfths of their required reserves in reserve banks, and sharp restrictions on reserve bank currency emissions.[59] Banks could keep seven-twelfths of their legally required reserves in their own vaults. This made them unavailable for reserve banks to loan out to quell nascent panics. While many Americans understood the law as primarily establishing a new currency which would expand and contract with the needs of the economy, the FRA's currency provisions were quite stringent. Reserve banks were required to back currency 100 percent with short-dated commercial paper and 40 percent in gold. When member banks repaid discount loans, Federal Reserve notes would return and be removed from circulation. Unlike other central banks, reserve banks were not allowed to issue currency directly against gold. Nor were Federal Reserve notes constituted as lawful money. These restraints would make it hard for reserve banks to issue notes to soak up gold and replace other circulating currencies.

ORGANIZING FOR COMBAT: THE FEDERAL RESERVE ACT'S CRITICS AS FED AGENTS

The Jekyll Island conspirators blasted the FRA as it wound through Congress. Nelson Aldrich, now retired from the Senate, predicted the "radical and revolutionary" bill would yield "unbounded inflation" and be the "most important step toward changing our form of government from a democracy to an autocracy."[60] Benjamin Strong complained that Democrats, acting on "party prejudices," had thrown "the central bank idea . . . upon the brush-heap."[61] Paul Warburg later explained that elite opposition stemmed from "excessive decentralization by the creation of too large a number of Federal reserve banks . . . complete political control of the Board . . . [and the currency] obligation of the United States—a concession made to the extreme Bryan wing."[62]

Compared to other central bank champions, Warburg was the most amenable to working with Democrats on financial reform. He published a friendly critique of the Glass-Owen bill while it was in the House, warning that "division of the country into twelve Federal Reserve Banks . . . would be the destruction of a reliable and strong discount market, the weakening of the reserve power of the country, the undoing of the hope of developing . . . the American bank acceptance, and the sacrificing of a strong and efficient . . . gold policy . . . while all these advantages of a frank centralization have been lost, the Owen-Glass plan cannot avoid the same degree of centralization . . . by conferring autocratic powers upon a small group of men."[63] Warburg endorsed the government currency guarantee, however, explaining, "It is not the United States upon whom rests the primary obligation, but the Federal Reserve Banks . . . the Treasury would be called upon to pay only after the Federal Reserve Banks are in default."[64]

Warburg's endorsement drew a rebuke from his friend Benjamin Strong. Warburg wrote back that he considered it "almost a joke to receive a letter from you, emphasizing your position of loyalty to your Government and its institutions, and upbraiding me as favoring the issue of 'fiat' money."[65] He was "as heartily opposed as you are to the issuance of elastic currency by the Government . . . there is a great difference, however, between a guaranty and a direct issue. Nobody would call the notes of the German Reichsbank 'fiat' money, if the German Government would decide to-morrow, that it wanted to guarantee those notes." He suggested the two get together to solve "the question of 'fluidity' and very liquid assets, by taking a cocktail together."

Warburg thus began lobbying Strong to join his effort to make the Federal Reserve a success. This effort intensified over the summer of 1914, when Warburg agreed to serve on the board. He believed a federal system would only succeed if its reserve banks were well managed and commanded respect in their communities. He made it his mission to recruit talented financiers to work in the reserve banks' officer corps.[66] While Strong was reluctant, Warburg prevailed on him to accept the post of the New York Fed's founding governor. They agreed to work together as insiders to build a more coherent Fed from within, but their collaboration would be undermined by Democratic obstruction and their own diverging philosophies.

Independent or Instrument? McAdoo's Populist Bid for Fed Dominance

Processes of constituting the board and reserve banks over the summer of 1914 brought diverging Fed visions into conflict. Treasury Secretary McAdoo sought to subordinate the board but was opposed by Warburg, who fought for its autonomy. As board members first gathered in Washington, McAdoo worked to establish his dominance.[67] He apportioned the board space in the Treasury building and insisted that it meet there. When board members inquired about the formal rank of their positions, McAdoo lampooned their efforts to President Wilson, "They must swim in the luminous ether close to the sun!" Getting in on the joke, Wilson quipped back that they should rank "right after the fire department."[68] McAdoo told board members that Wilson decided their rank would be equal to assistant secretaries, two full ranks below himself. When Charles Hamlin, the board's first governor, proposed one rank higher, McAdoo replied doing so would "make the Board more obstructive than ever and it will swell their heads."[69] Hamlin observed that McAdoo "degraded and humiliated" board members, and told Colonel House that McAdoo's imperious behavior would make it hard to attract first-rate men in the future.[70]

McAdoo's power grab imperiled Warburg's progressive project. Warburg saw the board as charged with leading a long-term transformation of America's banking laws and institutions. To succeed, it would need to attract and sustain top talent, a task made difficult by paltry salaries, forced divestiture of bank interests, and board occupational and regional diversity requirements. Warburg himself gave up a lucrative partnership to accept his appointment. Other elites would not make similar sacrifices to serve as the treasury secretary's lackey.

The board divided into two factions. The comptroller and Hamlin answered to McAdoo. Warburg led a group that strived to build autonomy. W. P. G. Harding straddled these factions, casting the decisive vote in early decisions. The board's first crucial choice involved constituting reserve bank hierarchies. The law called for each reserve bank to be controlled by a nine-member board of directors, six of whom would be selected by member banks from the region's bankers and businessmen, and three appointed by the Federal Reserve Board.[71] One of the latter appointees was to be designated Federal Reserve Agent and "chairman of the board." The law imagined no other reserve bank officers. This created awkwardness, because reserve banks were widely understood as intended to be locally controlled. At Warburg's suggestion, the board tasked each bank's board of directors with appointing its own "governor," the title held by European central bank executives.[72] Seeking to exert command, McAdoo pushed to make the Federal Reserve Agent each bank's top officer, because he saw the agent as his subordinate.[73] As the reserve banks prepared to open, locally elected governors and Federal Reserve Agents found themselves in strange standoffs. In St. Louis, the Federal Reserve Agent initially took charge.[74] In New York, Benjamin Strong took command from day one. Warburg's faction scored an institutional victory by endorsing this latter hierarchy in the Board's 1914 *Annual Report*, granting the governor "general charge of the bank."[75] Defeated, McAdoo suggested a legal amendment to empower the board to appoint five of nine reserve bank directors.[76]

McAdoo then asked the attorney general to issue an opinion clarifying the extent of his authority. The law required the board to impose biannual levies on the reserve banks to fund its operations.[77] McAdoo asked the attorney general to classify these levies as "public moneys," making them subject to treasury audits. The resulting opinion agreed they were public moneys, but auditing authority hinged on "whether the Federal Reserve Board is an independent board . . . or a bureau . . . of the Treasury . . . the history of the Federal reserve bank act . . . leads me to the clear opinion that the board is an independent board."[78] McAdoo complained to Wilson that "the provision that the Federal Reserve banks shall pay the expenses of the Federal Reserve Board" was "unfortunate."[79] Budgetary independence "influences members . . . to feel that they are less of a Government institution than a part . . . of the reserve banks themselves." The law "should be changed . . . [so] the expenses of the . . . Board should be approved by the Congress and paid out by the Treasury." McAdoo then gave up, finding little use for a diffuse system beyond his control.

Warburg's Ill-Fated Quest to Redraw the Federal Reserve's Map

One of Paul Warburg's main motivations in accepting a board appointment was his belief that the system could be improved by eliminating marginal reserve banks. While he had first championed a corporate bank, as the FRA would through Congress, Warburg argued that a regional system might be equally effective if it were composed of a small number of self-sufficient banks.[80] America's uneven regional development ensured that a twelve-bank structure would be divided among a handful of strong, capital-abundant reserve banks and a larger mass of weaker banks in poor rural economies. During fall harvests, rural reserve banks would inevitably exhaust their resources and turn to larger banks for assistance. Weak banks could call in the board to adjudicate the terms of intrasystem loans, potentially granting it "autocratic powers."[81] A federal system of fewer reserve banks with larger districts which linked urban creditors and rural debtors would work more effectively. When exceptional circumstances demanded policy coordination, voluntary cooperation would arise spontaneously in a system of fewer, more equal, reserve banks. An internal balance of power would reduce the threat of board politicization.

Warburg thought his advice to centralize the system had been heeded the night the FRA was signed into law. He wrote Rep. Carter Glass (D-VA) congratulating him on "steering [the bill] through the many cliffs," while wondering whether "concentration has gone far enough with eight Federal reserve banks."[82] Warburg promised to submit the law "to fairest and fullest test. If, after a few years of actual experience, it should be shown that the business community was . . . right . . . representatives at Washington will then be perfectly willing to amend the law." The Reserve Bank Organization Committee's decision to create twelve districts drew Warburg back into the fight. The law stated that districts "may be readjusted and new districts may from time to time be created by the Federal Reserve Board, not to exceed twelve in all."[83]

Warburg headed a board subcommittee on redistricting. Its final report reflected his thinking: "Of the twelve Federal reserve banks one half may be said to be strong and the other half weak. The remedy for this situation . . . is such a readjustment of the districts as will leave us with perhaps eight or nine districts, all of adequate extent and banking power and each able to support a strong and active regional center."[84] To reach this figure, Warburg proposed merging weak Southern reserve banks with their stronger Northern neighbors.[85] He warned against delay: "[T]he longer the friends of the System wait in applying a remedy, the stronger the reaction will be when the defects are cured by its enemies." Democratic partisans saw the plan as a threat to their hard-fought gains, however.[86] McAdoo secretly sought a legal opinion on redistricting authority and avoided board meetings until it was issued.[87] The attorney general ruled that the board couldn't dissolve reserve banks which had already been established.[88] Warburg was thwarted.

Benjamin Strong's Quest for Reserve Bank Autonomy

In October 1914, the board invited reserve bank governors to Washington, D.C., for an organizational conference. Benjamin Strong used this opportunity to organize the governors' conference, an ongoing forum where the twelve governors would gather to establish shared practices, discuss policy, and confront shared problems. At the top of the agenda was imperious board actions regarding discount rates.[89] Discount rates are the fee charged member banks to borrow from reserve banks against commercial assets. Higher rates disincentivize borrowing from the reserve banks, while lower rates make borrowing cheaper. The law tasked reserve banks with setting "rates of discount . . . subject to . . . review and determination" by the board.[90] Governors expected this policy lever to be wielded locally, but the board sent out a letter as reserve banks prepared to open instructing them not to announce rates before receiving board approval.[91]

It would soon pressure some banks to lower their rates. The conference responded by issuing a unanimous statement that "the function of initiating discount rates . . . should be exercised by the Federal Reserve Banks without pressure from the . . . Board."[92]

Board members saw the governors' conference as an extralegal rival. The conference inflamed these fears by hiring a permanent secretary and establishing an executive committee. The board sought to destroy the executive committee by denying funds for its secretary's salary and for travel expenses.[93] After three years, the conferences were suspended, according to Warburg, due to opposition "from members of the Board, as well as from certain individuals 'on the hill' who believed that the conferences were an illegal . . . attempt to create a central bank."[94]

Progressive and Hamiltonian Fed Reform Collaboration

Strong and Warburg's collaboration got off to a rocky start. Strong wanted to fix the FRA's flaws on day one, but Warburg warned him, "Do not forget that I am not acting alone either and we two, acting as buffer states, will have to do the best to cooperate as well as we can. With the best of intentions on both sides I have no doubt we shall succeed."[95] Strong and Warburg soon found themselves on opposing sides of institutional conflicts, however, starting with the discount rate controversy. Strong argued that the law intended for reserve banks to control discount rates. "Voicing the opinion of all the members of the Board," Warburg replied, "To concede that the Board should . . . only . . . review rates when Federal Reserve Banks shall indicate their willingness to make a change, would . . . be abdicating a power. . . . The law clearly contemplated a central authority as a means of coordinating the twelve banks under a comprehensive policy, and the Board has determined to act upon these lines."[96] This skirmish revealed a tension between Warburg's and Strong's Fed visions. Warburg imagined the board as the system's supreme authority, while Strong saw the reserve banks as the system's key actors.

Warburg and Strong nevertheless agreed on the law's basic problems. They agreed the eligibility criteria for which assets could be discounted needed to be clarified; that state banks needed incentives to join the system; that reserve banks should be empowered to issue currency against gold; that national banks should be granted authority to open branches within city limits; and that member banks should be required to deposit all their legal reserves in reserve banks. They advanced these goals by shaping board regulations and recommending legal amendments.

Warburg hoped to modernize U.S. financial practice by encouraging banks to issue bills of exchange, also known as trade acceptances, instead of promissory notes. The law legalized acceptances for international exchange but not for domestic commerce. Discount-eligible commercial paper was required to be self-liquidating with a maturity of less than ninety days. Member banks were confused whether they could discount promissory notes. In a speech to Atlantic City bankers, Strong explained that promissory notes were eligible for discount if they were tied to commercial transactions. Such notes "constituted the vast majority in volume of the paper which our bank has thus far discounted."[97] Congress resolved this puzzle in 1916 through liberalization. Domestic acceptances were legalized, and promissory notes were endorsed.[98] This was a pyrrhic victory for Warburg. By codifying existing practice, discount liberalization undermined Warburg's dream of remaking the U.S. financial system in the European image.[99]

A second rupture between Warburg and Strong occurred over trade acceptance policy. Like the discount rate, the law empowered reserve banks to set administered rates at which they would freely buy acceptances from member banks. Both viewed cultivating markets in dollar-denominated bills as essential for regulating gold flows and helping New York compete in the lucrative international trade finance market.[100] Strong wanted to subsidize this market by "establish[ing] the preferential rate for the dollar acceptance wherever rates are being quoted in other parts of the world."[101] Onerous acceptance regulations discouraged state banks from joining the system, however.[102] Warburg shrugged off this complaint, writing that the board "must not upset our banks needlessly by subjecting them again to brand new regulations."[103]

The acceptance clash between Strong and Warburg soon exploded over the Fed's role in financing World War I. War broke out in July 1914, before the board or reserve banks were organized. The war caused Europeans to cancel import orders and repatriate gold, threatening to push the United States into a currency crisis. Treasury Secretary McAdoo shut down the New York Stock Exchange and issued emergency currency to quell the crisis.[104] Warburg and Strong organized a gold settlement fund, which tempered demands for gold shipments. While threatening crisis in the short run, as the war lingered the United States benefited from an export boom.[105] Belligerents liquidated their citizens' U.S. securities at fire sale prices, effecting a de facto capital transfer from Europeans to Americans. After exhausting their means of paying for imports, European powers turned to their banks for credit, which was borrowed from New

York banks using long-dated finance bills. This was the same mechanism U.S. financiers had used to access European capital for agricultural purposes before the advent of the Federal Reserve, so Strong believed these finance bills were eligible for discount.[106] Warburg disagreed: "In the past, in the United States, there have been no commercial bills of exchange which could flow from one country to another, and, owing to the fact that large crop movements had to be anticipated, the finance bills have played a legitimate role."[107] This did not apply to war finance bills, however, which Warburg deemed unscientific.[108] Strong dismissed Warburg's objection as impractical: "This is not the time when nice theories of the way commerce should be financed can be strictly applied."[109]

Warburg and Strong achieved greater harmony in forming a legislative agenda. They agreed the reserve banks needed to be strengthened by enabling them to capture imported gold. Since the war started, the United States had imported $600,000 in gold, but little had made its way into reserve bank vaults.[110] Instead, the treasury impounded gold imports and issued gold certificates against them, which circulated as currency. Warburg and Strong feared that this would make it hard for the reserve banks to regulate a surge of gold outflows after the war. In 1916, the board proposed a slate of amendments to "strengthen the gold holdings of the Federal Reserve Banks."[111] It proposed raising the proportion of reserves held by banks in the reserve banks and "issuance of Federal Reserve notes not only against commercial paper, but also against gold."

Rep. Carter Glass (D-VA) used his power as chairman of the House Currency and Banking committee to block currency reform. Warburg "found Glass very shakey as to the power of the Federal Reserve Banks to issue notes against gold."[112] When a reform passed without the gold clause, Warburg called it a "disheartening blow. . . . Maybe if we get a Republican House in the fall . . . we can do more."[113] Strong was also "terribly disappointed about the . . . note issue."[114] Reserve banks were empowered to establish relationships with foreign central banks, however. Strong wrote Warburg, "When this miserable war is concluded . . . I have hope that you and I will journey to Europe together and perfect these arrangements all around. Possibly, that can be the finishing stroke of the job before we both take to the woods."

Strong and Warburg were optimistic that Republicans would be returned to power in the 1916 elections, paving the path for currency reform. Strong, once an ardent FRA critic, now claimed it was time to "take up energetically the completion of the reform. The Federal Reserve

System is a good basis on which to develop it . . . if Mr. Hughes is elected [president] it can be made a part of the Republican legislation program."[115] Warburg saw a return of Republican rule as essential to bypass Carter Glass. He lamented, "Glass's power appears to be absolute."[116]

These hopes were dashed in November when Wilson narrowly won reelection on his record of keeping the nation out of war. Progressive House members caucused with Democrats, forming a majority coalition, which left Glass in power. On November 27, 1916, the board issued a notice drafted by President Wilson that discouraged member banks from increasing their loans to European banks.[117] Wilson would soon change course, however, and ask Congress to declare war against Germany to make the world safe for democracy. While Strong and Warburg saw the return of Republican rule as the key to Fed reform, the next chapter shows that this other change in political time, the transition to a wartime footing, would end Democratic obstruction.

Conclusion: The Federal Reserve Act as a Partisan Creation

Progressives and Jeffersonians trace the Fed's origin to Jekyll Island, where a deal was struck to build a central bank founded on progressive and Hamiltonian principles. Jeffersonians see that envisioned institution as a bankers' conspiracy. Progressives see it as a prudent plan to build an independent central bank, not much different from the Fed of today. While progressives admit that the Aldrich Plan was rejected by Congress, they see its essence as permeating the Federal Reserve System, which they paradoxically imagine as a decentralized, central bank.

This chapter has shown that these interpretations are flawed, each projecting an anachronistic Fed image deep into the past. The Aldrich Plan further divided an already splintering Republican Party, giving Democrats a chance to repudiate it and take national power. Democrats were united rhetorically against a central bank but divided into opposing populist and Jeffersonian camps. President Wilson brokered compromises among them while shaping the reform to appeal to progressives to support his bid for a partisan realignment. The FRA was forged by layering conflicting ideals, imagining a diffuse and incoherent federal structure.

Hamiltonians were the clearest losers from the FRA's passage. New York received a private central bank its bankers could control, but it was forced to share status and rank with eleven other central banks in lesser financial capitals and a public board in Washington. Carter Glass explained the design as "modeled upon our Federal political system. . . . The regional banks are the states and the . . . Board is the Congress."[118] President Wilson described the law as a "constitution of peace" and pitched the public-private collaboration necessary to bring the system to life as an example of "democracy in action."[119] As observers of U.S. politics past and present are aware, however, America's fragmented institutions are often not up to the task of solving problems. Alexander Hamilton believed that a central bank needed to vary structurally from other U.S. political institutions through unified control by shareholders with common "experience guided by interest." Benjamin Strong channeled this sentiment.

Democrats remained ascendant throughout Wilson's first term. Sustained control of the levers of national power enabled Democrats to defend key aspects of their partisan design. Legal questions of the Federal Reserve Act's meaning were adjudicated by a partisan attorney general. Democrats who served on the Reserve Bank Organization Committee worked to scuttle Paul Warburg's attempt to redraw their partisan map. Partisan control of Congress enabled Carter Glass to obstruct reforms he disagreed with. Sustained Democratic rule ensured elements of their foundational bargain would hold. To this day, the Federal Reserve is made up of twelve separate reserve banks and a distinct board. Peter Conti-Brown notes, "the Fed is a 'they,' not an 'it.'"[120]

Other aspects of this foundational bargain would unravel through changing times. The next chapter shows how World War I shattered the international order the Federal Reserve was intended to inhabit and invited a return of Republican rule. Advancing political time would enable Benjamin Strong to forge a New York–centered Fed order, which used the reserve banks' combined resources to manage financial markets and rebuild the international gold standard.

2

Making and Breaking a Hamiltonian Fed

> Whenever the Federal Reserve System operates through the open-market committee, it operates . . . as a central bank. . . . You strip your regional banks of their separate control of credit . . . when you operate with their resources in the central money market.
>
> —Board Member Adolph Miller, Congressional Testimony, 1931

Could the Federal Reserve have steered the economy away from the Great Depression? This question has loomed large over the system since the depths of that crisis. In 1935, economist Irving Fisher told lawmakers, "This depression . . . would have been prevented if Governor Strong had lived. . . . He discovered . . . that open-market operations would stabilize—he discovered for himself what was necessary to cure the deflation that started in May 1920 and to prevent an inflation . . . only a few of us knew what he was doing. His colleagues did not understand it."[1] Monetarists claim that the advent of open market operations in the 1920s vested the Fed with a powerful tool capable of stabilizing the macroeconomy and domestic prices. The FRA empowers reserve banks to "purchase and sell in the open market . . . bonds and notes of the United States" within a framework of "rules and regulations prescribed by the Federal Reserve Board."[2] In 1922, Benjamin Strong persuaded the reserve banks to delegate their investment powers to a committee controlled by the governors of the five wealthiest reserve banks. The New York Fed would act as the committee's agent, using its facilities to buy and sell securities for the system.

Scholars debate how this policy instrument was envisioned and the purposes toward which it was first deployed. Monetarists claim open market policy was geared domestically, representing "a conscious attempt, for perhaps the first time in monetary history, to use central-bank powers to promote internal economic stability."[3] Strong's New York Fed colleagues also saw open market operations as useful for countering business cycles, but understood Strong's 1920s discretionary policies as aimed toward rebuilding the international gold standard, a World War I casualty.[4] These Hamiltonians understood American and global prosperity as interwoven. Unless the United States spearheaded the reconstruction of a liberal world economy, they feared, a looming crisis would shatter global capitalism and empower radical reform impulses.

The four ideologically inflected developmental portraits presented in the introductory chapter offer diverging views of the Federal Reserve's evolution in the 1920s. Left-leaning populists see the Fed as corrupted by the advent of an exclusionary open market committee, which "provided the arrangement of power [financiers] had originally wanted in the new central bank."[5] Jeffersonians tell a similar story, arguing that the committee fostered a speculative stock market boom that ended in calamity. Right-leaning populists flip this story on its head, arguing that the first open market committee was the system's rightful order. Friedman and Schwartz lament a 1930 "diffusion of power" on the committee as the fountainhead of Depression. Progressives reject this claim, arguing that crude ideas and static decentralization bred "coordination problems," which prevented policymakers from forming a coherent response to shocks in the early 1930s.[6] Hamiltonians also reject the monetarist claim, instead seeing the depression as springing from global dislocation wrought by World War I and myopic U.S. foreign economic policies.[7]

This chapter uses the lens of political time to arbitrate these competing arguments. It first shows that World War I established a more powerful and hierarchical Fed, as America's abrupt rise to global creditor status, cumulation of gold, and dollar internationalization, endowed the Federal Reserve with global power. The war and its aftermath also remade the system's global and domestic environments. It shattered the classical gold standard and the broader liberal world order it supported. Domestically, it fractured Wilson's partisan coalition. In 1920, voters restored Republicans to national power on promises of a "return to normalcy," understood as a rejection of Wilson's liberal internationalism. Republicans would ratchet up protectionism and demand repayment of European war debts, pushing the world to the brink of renewed crisis.

This chapter shows that Benjamin Strong's Fed fended off a global crisis for years. Congress would reward the system in 1927 by extending reserve bank charters indefinitely, granting them permanence. After Benjamin Strong died in 1928, however, and a new Republican president was elected on promises of more tariffs, the Fed regime Strong forged came under attack. Herbert Hoover urged the board to take a confrontational approach to the New York Fed.[8] Through a series of skirmishes, the board emerged as a powerful veto player on the eve of the Depression. In the pivotal year 1930, when an expansionary policy might have steered the economy away from depression, the board blocked New York's attempts to lower its discount and bill rates to maintain its portfolio. As New York's investments collapsed and the open market committee rejected its calls for new bond purchases, Fed policy turned contractionary. As the Depression deepened, a bitterly divided Federal Reserve stood idly by, unable to respond.

War as Developmental Catalyst: The Fed's Rebirth in World War I

Benjamin Strong recognized war's developmental possibilities. After Woodrow Wilson won reelection, he wrote "the Federal Reserve System and particularly the New York Bank will not establish itself with its members and with the country generally until it has met the test of a real crisis."[9] When Congress declared war in April 1917, Strong wrote, "We must . . . persuade [treasury secretary McAdoo] to permit the Reserve Banks to become the real, active and effective fiscal agents for the Government. If he does that, our place in the country's banking system will be established for all time."[10] McAdoo made the reserve banks fiscal agents in exchange for a wartime finance subsidy. They distributed war bonds and discounted them at below market rates. After the war, Congress would reward the system by abolishing the Independent Treasury System, the reserve banks' competitor for fiscal agency duties.[11]

After war was declared, President Wilson intervened to end Carter Glass's FRA reform obstruction. Warburg recalled that Glass agreed "to remove himself from the Congressional field of battle . . . if, during his absence, we should be able to secure the coveted legislation, he would not obstruct it."[12] Wilson signed a bill making Federal Reserve notes lawful money and issuable against gold, adding incentives for state banks to join the system, and requiring members to deposit all their reserves in reserve banks.[13] The reform enabled the reserve banks to absorb a $1 billion wartime inflow of gold.[14] Wilson urged state banks to join, writing system "membership . . . is a distinct and significant evidence of patriotism."[15] State bank and trust company membership grew from thirty-four units in 1916 to 1,042 in 1919.[16] All of the largest state banks joined the system, concentrating the nation's bank reserves in reserve bank vaults.

Europeans financed wartime imports by liquidating U.S. securities, shipping gold, and borrowing dollars. The world economy dollarized along two tracks. European governments borrowed more than $10 billion directly from the U.S., creating future streams of public dollar payments. Benjamin Strong also set the New York bill rate below global market rates to encourage Europeans to finance trade by using dollar-denominated acceptances. In the 1920s, the dollar would gain equal footing with British sterling in financing world trade.[17]

While a crucial developmental catalyst, the war also caused an important Fed casualty. Paul Warburg's initial four-year term was set to expire in 1918. Responding to public criticisms "that a naturalized citizen of German birth, having near relatives prominent in German public life, should not be permitted to hold a position of great trust in the service of the United States," Warburg asked President Wilson not to be reappointed.[18] Warburg's departure contributed to the board's subsequent marginalization by removing its most capable leader and chief interlocutor with Strong and the New York and European financial communities.[19]

Fumbling the Return to Peace: Democratic Decline and Global Crisis

Wilson led America to war to make the world "safe for democracy." He called for a "peace without victory" and envisioned a collective security organization called a League of Nations. Wilson wielded less power than expected at the negotiating table in Versailles, however, and conceded to demands for assigning war blame and a large indemnity against Germany to secure European support for the League.[20] British economist John Maynard Keynes left the negotiations early to write *The Economic Consequences of the Peace*, which predicted that a crushing German reparations burden would prevent lasting peace and prosperity.[21]

The Treaty of Versailles's harsh terms caused Wilson's domestic progressive support to collapse.[22] Many Americans were wary of joining a

League of Nations, which would require the United States to intervene in future European conflicts. Senate Democrats supported joining the League by ratifying the Treaty of Versailles, but 1918 elections had relegated them to the minority. Republicans divided on the issue, with former president William Howard Taft leading a pro-League faction, and Sen. Henry Cabot Lodge (R-MA) opposing the security commitment.[23] Rather than seeking a compromise, Wilson embarked on an ill-fated national tour where he sought to rally support for the League. Senate Treaty ratification votes failed in 1919 and 1920.

Months after the armistice was signed, Benjamin Strong complained that the Federal Reserve remained in "government debt bondage" and its cheap credit policies were fueling postwar inflation.[24] In early 1919, Strong wrote the assistant treasury secretary, "WE MUST DEFLATE."[25] Doing so was necessary to remain on the gold standard, even though "the process of deflation is a painful one, involving loss, unemployment, bankruptcy, and social and political disorders." The treasury faced the daunting task of financing a national debt that had ballooned from $1 billion to more than $25 billion during the war, however. Carter Glass, now treasury secretary, demanded that the Fed subsidy remain in place. Inflation surged. In November, Strong told the governors' conference "We are emancipated now or we are not."[26] The New York and Boston Feds voted to raise their discount rates, which the board vetoed.

Strong then traveled to Washington to confront Glass, threatening to raise New York's rate unilaterally if the board didn't consent. Glass replied that he would have President Wilson remove Strong for subordination.[27] After the showdown, Glass asked the attorney general for an opinion interpreting the FRA clause that made discount rates "subject to review and determination of the Federal Reserve Board" to mean that the board held ultimate discount authority. The attorney general obliged, writing that the "Board has the right, under the powers conferred by the Federal Reserve Act, to determine what rates of discount should be charged . . . [and] to require such rates to be put into effect."[28] Afterward, Glass left the treasury to fill a Senate seat in Virginia, and Strong left for a year's sabbatical to recover from tuberculosis.

The board wasted little time in wielding its new discount power. In January, the New York Fed's directors voted to raise the discount rate and eliminate the treasury subsidy. The board governor replied that the board had "determined" its commercial rate would be 6 percent, half a percent *higher* than the directors requested, while keeping the subsidy in place.²⁹ When New York's ratio of gold to currency issues fell below the law's required 40 percent threshold, the board agreed with the New York directors to raise its discount rate to 7 percent and treasury certificate rate to 5.5 percent.³⁰ This dose of restraint came a half-year after the budget moved into surplus, creating a contractionary policy mix, which worsened an emerging global recession.

The onset of hard times exacerbated growing domestic social disorder. In 1919, waves of influenza, industrial strikes, race riots, and lynching broke out across the country.³¹ Republican presidential candidate Warren G. Harding repudiated Wilson's internationalism by calling for a "return to normalcy," declaring that "tranquility at home is more precious than peace abroad."³² Harding called for fiscal restraint and detachment from Europe's problems, arguing, "If we put an end to false economics which lure humanity to utter chaos, ours will be the commanding example of world leadership today." Harding's calls resonated in a speculative atmosphere in which the price level had doubled over the past five years.³³ Americans punished Democrats at the voting booth in November 1920, restoring united Republican rule on promises of an inward turn.

Republican Ascendance, Global Imbalance, and Strong's Great Idea

The return of Republican rule would have a devastating global impact. Republicans called for raising tariffs, collecting $10 billion in allied war debts, retiring the national debt, and lowering income taxes. The U.S. embrace of austerity unleashed a global deflationary shock.³⁴ European currencies slumped on foreign exchange markets and the gold-linked dollar began surging. These pressures would grow as Republicans enacted their neo-mercantilist agenda.

Eastern industrialists and financiers called on the United States to rebuild a liberal international order by entering the League of Nations, providing war debt relief to Europe, supporting gold standard restoration, and institutionalizing a low tariff regime through reciprocal treaties. These elites wielded little power, however, in the Republican Party and Congress.³⁵ Western corn and wheat growers benefited from surging exports during the war and took out loans to expand their production, but the return of European farmers after the war fueled an overproduction crisis. Fearing foreign competition, Western farmers had "little incentive to support government efforts to liberalize and stabilize the international system."[36] By the time Republicans took office in March 1921, the wholesale price level had already fallen 39 percent.[37] Republicans passed an "emergency" tariff bill raising agricultural duties. Industrial tariffs would be restored the next year. Protectionism clashed with another partisan goal, however, of collecting allied war debts.

Benjamin Strong was critical of these policies. He spent 1920 surveying European damage and meeting foreign central bankers. Strong decided "a positive helpful policy by the United States was essential, and that an American policy of withdrawal and aloofness would be tragic."[38] He initially pushed the lame duck Wilson administration for greater European support to little avail. When Republicans passed the "emergency" tariff bill in 1921, Strong wrote the Republican Party chairman attacking the incoherence of the party's economic agenda. "These gentlemen at the Capitol seem to think that we can continue to export, without importing. . . . This is an age and era of people of inconsistency. We say to the nations of Europe—pay us the eleven billions that you owe us—and then we make it impossible for them to pay it by the prohibitive tariff . . . this tariff bill . . . strikes me as being economically unsound, politically unwise, and likely to be suicidal in its effect."[39] Strong's warning went unheeded. Moving forward, Republican administrations would avoid international conferences out of fear that the United States would be overwhelmed by demands for debt relief. Indeed, most financiers agreed that global recovery hinged on a deal to reduce German reparations in exchange for U.S. debt relief. Most Americans wanted war debts repaid in full, however, so Republicans pressed forward with debt collection.[40]

A final pillar of the Republican program, debt retirement, would further imperil global stability. Republican treasury secretary Andrew Mellon, a millionaire industrialist, wanted to lower income taxes and pay down the national debt. Fiscal surpluses would be extracted through war debt collection and higher tariffs, shifting the taxation burden onto Europeans and U.S. consumers. High tariff walls made it hard for Europeans to export to the United States to earn dollars, so debt payments pushed gold across the Atlantic. From 1920–24, U.S. gold stocks would grow by 70 percent to $4.2 billion, approaching nearly half the world's supply. In coming years, America would become "a great sinkhole for gold."[41]

Political Attacks and the Federal Board's Populist Makeover

The postwar recession hit farmers hard. In April 1920, the Atlanta, Dallas, Kansas City, and St. Louis Feds enacted progressive discount rate schemes which penalized heavy borrowers.[42] Farmers blamed high discount rates for their falling fortunes. Rural congressmen proposed radical FRA amendments, such as requiring congressional approval before discount rates could be raised above 5 percent.[43] The board was "besieged by farmers" demanding lower rates.[44] Treasury secretary Andrew Mellon also demanded discount rate reductions.[45]

The formation of a Republican administration booted Wilson-era Democrats from the board. As his tenure ended, comptroller John Skelton Williams accused the New York Fed of instigating the postwar deflation and illegally concentrating power. He told the congressional Joint Commission of Agricultural Inquiry, "The theory, conception, and purpose of the Federal reserve . . . are as near perfection as the human mind can produce . . . but from the very outset Secretary McAdoo and the more liberal elements of the board had to combat . . . the reactionary faction which fought for the centralization rather than the democratization of banking power."[46]

Benjamin Strong defended the Fed's policy record in three days of congressional testimony. Citing centuries of historical examples, Strong argued that inflation inevitably grew from war but financial orthodoxy was subsequently restored through periods of falling prices. The system "would have been inviting disaster" if it rejected treasury demands for subsidies, Strong claimed, noting there was "no limit to the level to which [interest rates] would have gone." Strong agreed that sustained cheap credit policies after the war fueled inflation but defended the system by citing his letter to the treasury demanding restraint. Strong's testimony impressed colleagues and lawmakers. The New York Fed's counsel wrote that he had never "heard anyone who was so obviously a master of himself and his subject as the Governor was before this commission."[47] The resulting *Report of the Joint Commission of Agricultural Inquiry* absolved the Federal Reserve of Williams's charges by pinning blame on the previous administration for blocking Strong's moves to raise discount rates earlier in 1919.[48]

Congress did make a concession to farmers, however, by growing the Federal Reserve Board. An agricultural representative was added to effect "a fair representation of the financial, agricultural, industrial, and commercial interests, and geographical divisions of the country."[49] An FRA requirement that two board members have banking experience was removed, pushing the board in a populist direction. Board governor W. P. G. Harding warned that an eight-member board would be prone to tied votes, gridlock, and parochialism. The structure would "localize each member, and each man would say to himself, 'I do not represent the country at large; I represent my particular district."[50] Harding proposed instead waiting until his term expired a few months later and replacing him with a farmer. The *New York Times* demanded that Harding be reappointed, however, warning against an "intrusion of politics" and "sectional influences" onto the board.[51] President Harding appointed his boyhood friend, Ohio lawyer Daniel Crissinger, as board governor.[52] Supporting this book's theoretical expectations, the rise of an ascendant party remade the board along populist lines. These institutional changes would eventually provide a path to power for a revisionist, agrarian board faction.

The Federal Reserve's Search for New Policy Ideas

In October 1921, Benjamin Strong told the governors' conference that the practice of maintaining a penalty discount rate, set one or two points above market rates, was having harmful consequences. Surging gold imports had pushed the New York Fed's gold reserve ratio to 82 percent, up from below 40 percent in early 1920. The previous summer, the reserve banks had lowered their discount rates in response to treasury pressure, but Strong was convinced that market interest rates were falling because of gold imports, not discount rate cuts. "The reduction in our rate had no influence in the market. It was the competition to lend money that did it."[53] Strong argued that the system needed to abandon the British practice of maintaining a penalty rate and instead forge a new policy guide tailored to American circumstances.

Strong saw surging gold inflows as an existential threat. He feared a repeat of the postwar boom and bust cycle, which saw inflation spike before giving way to collapsing prices. Deflation invited political attacks. In this context, Strong began pitching a program of collaborating with foreign central banks to help restore the gold standard abroad. During the war, Strong had developed a friendship with Bank of England governor Montagu Norman, with whom he remained in close contact. Strong believed restoring fixed exchange rates would tame gold imports and increase European demand for U.S. produce. He told the governors' conference, "we are going to have to take some part in this situation abroad. We probably won't do it politically, but we have to do it financially and economically."[54] Philadelphia Fed governor George Norris endorsed Strong's plan as a second-best option: "The three great opportunities that we have had to accomplish the stabilization of foreign exchange were, first, to go into the League of Nations; second, to make a readjustment of our tariff . . . and the third was to empower the Secretary of the Treasury to deal in an intelligent way with refunding of foreign obligations. . . . But because we have lost those three it does not follow . . . that we ought to throw aside and discard all others . . . the proposition [Strong] has suggested is one that undoubtedly has merit and may be reasonably be expected to accomplish some results." Chicago Fed governor James McDougal agreed, stating "the entire System will be sympathetic" to Strong's international collaboration if it "can be worked out on a safe and workable basis."

Strong initially proposed that the Federal Reserve use its surplus gold to establish an international stabilization fund other countries could borrow from when restoring gold convertibility, but Norman told Strong that such "artificial means" wouldn't be "practicable until the [war] debts have been settled, the Reparations adjusted, and free Gold Markets" restored, when the gold standard could operate the "old-fashioned way."[55] The Bank of England governor's response struck an orthodox tone, but he actually had a grander scheme in mind. He wanted Strong to host a central bank conference to negotiate an international return to gold. Strong resisted out of fear that he would be overwhelmed by extraordinary demands for support.[56] In 1922, the United States boycotted an international economic conference in Genoa, Italy. The Genoa Conference passed a British resolution to establish a gold exchange standard whereby central banks, moving forward, would supplement their gold reserves with foreign currencies. Central banks were instructed to shape credit policies "with a view to preventing undue fluctuations in the purchasing power of gold."[57]

Afterward, Strong wrote Norman that he worried the declaration implied that "the United States, with its currency at a premium the world over, should . . . regulate credit policies as to expand credit and currency to a point where the value of our currency would decline and consequently other currencies would approach the value of ours."[58] Strong's letter revealed a central obstacle to restoring fixed exchange rates. America's relatively low wartime inflation experience resulted in a strong (undervalued) dollar. To restore a fixed exchange rate regime, other states would have to deflate their prices, or the United States would have to allow its prices to rise. Strong was unwilling to countenance inflation, writing Norman, "You may be sure that inflation has no charms which have not been analyzed by Reserve Bank men and rejected as spurious."[59] Changing circumstances would soon lead Strong to reconsider these beliefs, however.

The Advent and Struggle over Open Market Operations

In late 1921, the reserve banks began independently buying government bonds on the open market for the first time. By June 1922, these purchases would exceed $350 million.[60] Treasury secretary Mellon complained the purchases were disrupting treasury financing operations. He instructed the reserve banks to begin selling their bonds. Strong warned the reserve bank governors that "if we do not do something they will. The . . . Board has power to regulate this matter."[61] Strong asked them to delegate authority to execute investments to a committee of the New York, Chicago, Philadelphia, and Boston governors. Thus, the Committee on the Centralized Execution of Purchases and Sales of Government Securities was born.

Over the summer, the New York Fed began selling bonds from its own account to counter the expansionary influence of gold inflows to prevent inflation. In October, Strong asked the governors' conference to endorse this gold sterilization practice as a system-wide policy. The governors rejected the gold sterilization plan, but empowered the committee to chart a discretionary policy and added the Cleveland governor to its ranks.[62] The Chicago and Richmond governors expressed reluctance toward this new arrangement, warning that a central investment policy would undermine the autonomy of reserve banks over their portfolios.

After establishing the committee, Strong was forced to take another leave of absence to fight tuberculosis. In his absence, board member Adolph Miller, its lone economist, sought to assert board control over open market operations. Miller wrote a regulation reconstituting the governors committee as the Open Market Investment Committee. Its membership would remain the same, but the board would "limit and otherwise determine" its purchases, restricting them "primarily [to] commercial investments."[63] Miller presented his regulation at a joint meeting of the board and governors. The Boston governor protested, "It is very doubtful . . . whether the Federal Reserve Board has specific power to fix a definite limit as to the amount of the legitimate open-market operations that a Federal Reserve Bank may engage in. . . . [N]owhere is the Federal Reserve Board given specific power to limit the amount of bonds and notes of the United States that the Board of Directors of the Federal Reserve Bank may wish to buy." The Philadelphia governor agreed, accusing Miller of trying to establish a central bank in Washington. Miller admitted that "there has even been some question in the Board itself as to whether it had the power. . . . I think we have got the power; to me it is almost as clear as though it were there." The governors accepted the committee's reconstitution and board supervisory authority but rejected its power to limit investments. Board member Charles Hamlin agreed to amend the regulation. When Strong learned of Miller's power grab in Colorado, he wrote, the "Board had no right to discharge the committee and wouldn't have done so had I had a crack at them. . . . Every time the Board assumes some power like this, we approach nearer to actual management (instead of supervision) by a political body."[64]

International Liberalization and Strong's Great Idea to Restore Sterling

Many Republican elites recognized that restoring a more liberal world order was in America's interest. They embraced the "diplomacy of the dollar" by encouraging Americans to invest in European reconstruction.[65] In 1923, Bureau of the Budget director Charles Dawes led a multilateral effort to renegotiate German reparations payments, yielding the Dawes Plan, which stabilized the German currency and arranged for floating German bonds in New York.[66] These negotiations were ongoing when Strong returned to the New York Fed in November 1923.

At the time, an emerging New York Fed orthodoxy held that open market operations could be deployed countercyclically to stabilize the economy. Officer W. R. Burgess wrote, "There would be very general agreement to the principle that the Reserve Banks should purchase securities at periods when liquidation in business seems to be going faster than fundamental conditions warrant, and that . . . we should sell securities when business is moving forward so rapidly that the tendency has become unduly speculative in nature."[67] When Strong returned, New York's deputy governor warned that a recession was on the horizon but argued gold inflows and a proposed income tax cut would combat it.[68]

Aligning global and domestic conditions led Strong to reimagine Fed power and purpose. Burgess recalled, "The skies were a bit dark in this country, and the world over there was a good deal of disturbance because England was not yet back on a gold basis, and most of the other countries of the world were in great uncertainty. The Dawes Plan had not yet been concluded, although the experts were working on it. Agricultural prices were on the toboggan."[69] In this context, Strong "had a great idea . . . that the Federal Reserve System had a responsibility that went far beyond our domestic situation at that time alone . . . that this country could never hope for a permanent groundwork of prosperity until the world was back on a gold basis. . . . One way we had to help was by making conditions here favorable to the return of the world."

Strong hoped to lower interest rates in New York below those in London to push capital back across the Atlantic and entice Americans to invest abroad. Moving funds into London would increase demand for sterling, whose foreign exchange value was "constantly depressed." The logic of Strong's idea was that an expansionary Federal Reserve policy would nudge up U.S. prices and boost the sterling exchange. To put his plan in motion, Strong would need to build a broad coalition spanning the reserve banks, the board, and elements of the administration.

Strong's plan received a warm welcome on the open market committee. The five banks it represented governed America's capital-abundant, industrialized core. This region occupied a hegemonic position in the world economy, and experienced steady trade surpluses with Europe on manufactured goods throughout the 1920s.[70] It was these reserve banks that had surplus gold which could be invested. New York had the largest surplus, with Chicago and Philadelphia occupying a second tier. It was these reserve banks' constituents, bankers and investors, who were to be enticed to invest abroad on a massive scale. The open market committee embraced Strong's "great idea," authorizing progressively larger bond purchases in December, February, and May. By the end of the summer, the system's bond portfolio would grow by $500 million.

Strong believed bond purchases needed to be complemented with more visible discount rate reductions. He explained his logic to Norman: "The effect of changes in the discount rate is more like a sledgehammer blow to sentiment, while the effect of our transactions in the open market is much gentler."[71] The New York directors began seeking discount reductions when Strong visited Norman in April. The Boston Fed governor told board member Charles Hamlin "the movement for lower rates at New

York was inspired by Governor Strong, now sick in Governor Norman's house in London; that Norman wanted inflation in United States to put us more nearly on a parity with Great Britain."[72]

After returning home, Strong wrote Treasury Secretary Mellon, "Our own interests demand that no effort be spared to secure a return to the gold standard, and so arrest the flood of gold which threatens in time to plunge us into inflation. We now hold one-half of the world's monetary gold, and our holdings increase steadily."[73] Gold restoration would help our "own trade advantage" because, "Stable exchange rates will facilitate foreign trade just as greatly as stable credit facilitates domestic trade." Strong calculated a 10 percent gap in British and U.S. price levels needed to close to facilitate restoration. It would "be difficult politically and socially for the British government and the Bank of England to force a price liquidation in England beyond what they have already experienced," so the adjustment burden "must fall more largely on us than upon them." Strong's appeal won over Mellon, who would become a New York ally on the board and in successive administrations. The board approved three half-point discount rate reductions, pushing New York's discount rate below the Bank of England's.

Burgess later described the policy as a stunning success: "Sterling began to climb upward . . . balances moved from New York to London . . . in the spring of 1925 England was able to go back on the gold standard."[74] By April, sterling was trading on exchange markets at its prewar parity and British prices had fallen 3 percent below the United States'.[75] Winston Churchill announced sterling's return to gold at the prewar parity. Americans also began buying large quantities of Dawes Plan bonds, helping Germany return to gold.[76]

Testifying before Congress the following year, Strong defended his international project as a boon for farmers: "The interest of the United States in the restoration of . . . stable exchanges lies largely in the fact that we have the largest foreign trade of any country, and . . . the one industry . . . which . . . has not yet fully recovered, is the farming industry [which] largely depends upon foreign markets. Roughly one-half of all that we export is produced by farmers and one-half of that produce is cotton."[77] Strong explained that America had a national interest in restoring European prosperity: "This country, with its vast resources, is interested in maintaining its markets and consequently in the general restoration and elevation of living standards, which have been so greatly impaired because of the war." Strong bragged to lawmakers that sterling restoration had spurred "resumption of gold payment in Holland, Switzerland, the Dutch

Indies, Australia, and New Zealand; South Africa and Sweden . . . exportation of American cotton to Germany since the adoption of the Dawes plan [had expanded] tenfold."

Not everyone was pleased with the fruits of Strong's project, however. The choice to restore sterling's prewar parity was a windfall for London financiers but a loss for British industrialists. John Maynard Keynes had called for restoring instead at a lower parity that accounted for wartime inflation, to avoid what he foresaw would be period of painful austerity to push down domestic wages and force industrial restructuring.[78] W. R. Burgess, Strong's lieutenant, admitted a lingering "gold problem" remained.[79] When interest rates in New York rose above those in Europe, capital moved to the United States, depriving European central banks of gold. As the U.S. fall harvest approached, global credit markets tightened, and the open market committee was confronted with a choice between buying bonds to expand liquidity or fostering a global credit crunch. This dynamic combined with uneven regional benefits from international collaborations and Adolph Miller's claims that bond purchases supported stock market speculation to soon cause support for Strong's great idea to wane outside New York and the cotton-exporting South.

International Collaboration and the Chicago Discount Rate Controversy

In 1926, France stabilized the franc on a de facto basis while lowering its exchange rate to account for wartime inflation. The depreciated franc made French exports cheaper on world markets, revealing sterling's overvaluation.[80] Currency misalignment weakened global headwinds toward liberalization. In 1927, the Banque de France and German Reichsbank began buying gold in London to fight domestic inflation, which threatened to push the Bank of England off gold.[81] Fearing a global crisis, Strong agreed to host a secret conference attended by British, French, and German central bankers, at the undersecretary of the treasury's Long Island estate.[82] The system was represented by the open market committee and the board governor. Montagu Norman explained that the Bank of England was in desperate straits. Once again, Strong agreed to shoulder the adjustment burden by persuading his colleagues to ease their credit policies.

The open market committee and board endorsed a program of $50 million in bond purchases and coordinated discount reductions at all twelve banks. Two governors from interior reserve banks said conditions in their districts didn't warrant discount reductions but thought their directors would go along to support the national program. Chicago governor James McDougal stated that his directors saw no need for a discount reduction and would not seek one.[83] In following weeks, eight reserve banks would seek and receive board permission to lower their discount rates. Chicago, Philadelphia, Minneapolis, and San Francisco did not. In early August, the *Wall Street Journal* published an anonymous article saying Chicago would resist the change.

Strong complained to the board governors that Chicago's behavior was disruptive, but warned the rate was "for them to decide."[84] Strong wrote to the Chicago and Philadelphia governors pleading with them to lower their rates. McDougal replied Chicago would "if and when it seemed expedient to do so."[85] Strong wrote back, "I have read that austere letter of yours . . . and after finishing it feel as though I were sitting in an unheated church in midwinter somewhere in Alaska. The fact is, my dear Mac . . . that the objects which we sought to accomplish by our rate reduction are mainly for the benefit of the producers of exportable crops in your district and the other districts . . . it is neither a New York question nor a Chicago question . . . but a national question bearing upon our markets in Europe, consequently an international question."[86] Board governor Daniel Crissinger reported that he heard Chicago's directors would consider lowering their rate three days. This did not satisfy board members who were "already sore," however, that they were excluded from the July central bank conference.[87] The agricultural representative called a motion to force Chicago and San Francisco to lower their rates, which passed by four votes to three.[88]

The board's show of force sent shockwaves across the country. Sen. Carter Glass accused members of seeking to aggrandize the board. He was shocked when Hamlin reminded him that he had sought the opinion establishing board discount primacy in 1919.[89] Strong blamed the controversy on "inept language in the statute," worrying, "If Congress inquires into this matter . . . it will involve the appearance of various members of our own institution who hold contrary opinions on this subject, and the country will be concerned less internal war lead to a situation in which the whole country might suffer."[90] Strong wrote Glass, "Whether the law intends that the Reserve Board should initiate changes or not . . . an attempt to exercise that power by the board will . . . be fatal to the regional character of the System. . . . [A]ll of our directors and all of my associate officers . . . feel as I do that this tendency to centralize the . . . authority to execute policies taken by the Board in Washington is a mistake and will be detrimental to the System."[91]

The board governor resigned in the wake of the controversy. Secretary Mellon tapped Minneapolis Fed governor Roy Young to replace him. Many viewed Young's appointment as an endorsement of greater reserve bank autonomy, because Minneapolis was the last reserve bank to lower its discount rate. The *St. Louis Star* wrote that Young would make a fine governor so long as he kept "his Western atmosphere enough to realize that all of the banks and all of the money are not in New York, nor all of the nation's industries in Wall Street."[92]

Hamlin later learned that Adolph Miller had fomented the crisis. Before leaving for a two-month trip to his California home in July, Miller warned Hamlin that if system policies were directed "to help the gold standard in Great Britain we should get into an awful mess."[93] On his trip, Miller stopped in Chicago and Minneapolis to encourage bankers to resist the discount rate change and also allegedly provided the inflammatory *Wall Street Journal* statement.

Board Rising: Republican Weakening and Growing Board Veto Authority

In Friedman and Schwartz's telling, Benjamin Strong's 1928 death triggered the "crucial engagement in the struggle for power within the system," resulting in a harmful 1930 "diffusion of power" on the open market committee.[94] They blame Depression-era Fed mistakes on the "shift of power from New York to the other Federal Reserve Banks and the weakness of the Reserve Board." From Strong's October 1928 death to the committee's 1930 expansion, however, they trace repeated skirmishes between the board and New York Fed. They and progressive Fed scholars consider the board–New York feud as inconsequential, however, because the same policy beliefs allegedly held in both outposts. A Fed historian describes the fight as "about procedure, not substance."[95] In this view, shared policy ideas ensured that "conflict between Washington and New York was not that great" in the opening years of depression.[96]

This section uses this book's theory to reassess the causes and consequences of the board's bid for power. Strong's international project yielded uneven regional benefits. Other than New York, only the cotton-exporting South saw its fortunes durably lifted by sterling's restoration. From 1925–29, cotton exports surged 41.7 percent compared to 1921–24.[97] Western and interior farmers did not experience similar recoveries.[98] This made Western Fed officials doubt Strong's claim that international monetary stabilization efforts boosted produce exports.

Experience had taught the new board governor, Roy Young, to be skeptical of Strong's great idea. When Young led the Minneapolis Fed from 1921–27, its district experienced 1,282 bank suspensions, nearly 30 percent of the national total.[99] While respectful of Strong, Young was skeptical of New York's leadership, and would soon join an aggrieved faction of Westerners Adolph Miller (San Francisco), George James (St. Louis), and Edward Cunningham (Chicago). This board faction's growth to four members put it on par with a pro–New York faction led by Secretary Mellon.[100] The Westerners could now block discount rate changes with a tie vote. Further, when the treasury secretary or comptroller missed meetings to fulfill their other public duties, the revisionist faction would constitute a majority with power to pass regulations.

At the beginning of 1927, Congress had passed the McFadden Act, which extended reserve bank charters indefinitely.[101] The same day the system won its de facto permanence, an anonymous *Wall Street Journal* article read, "Foundations have already been laid . . . to centralize control of the system in the Federal Reserve Board, and restrict the powers for individual action gradually acquired by the twelve Federal Reserve banks."[102] Harvard economist Allyn Young published a Hamiltonian rebuttal in the *Annalist*, writing that it was better to "insist upon separate regional responsibilities of the different Reserve Banks, even if this means frankly conceding larger responsibilities and larger powers to the New York Bank . . . than to run the danger of 'unifying' the system into a cumbrous and slow-moving substitute for a single central bank, with divided authority and divided responsibilities."[103] The board's heavy-handed enforcement of Strong's international policy later that summer was the first step in a sustained bid for power.

The board's revisionist faction would be further emboldened by the election of Adolph Miller's Georgetown neighbor Herbert Hoover in 1928.[104] On the campaign trail, Hoover promised higher tariffs to protect Western farmers, who were now threatened by cheaper imports. Hoover's election deflated the sails of global liberalization and imperiled the gold standard. After years of U.S. trade and investment surpluses, the gold standard's functioning and survival now depended on vast U.S. capital exports. In 1927 and the first half of 1928, surging overseas investments pushed the U.S.'s annualized balance-of-payments deficit to $1 billion. Prospects of higher U.S. tariffs caused investors to rethink European growth prospects, however. By the time Hoover took office in 1929, the New York stock market would be enraptured in a surging bubble, which halted U.S. capital exports and threatened to drain gold from Europe.[105]

The Board's Bid for Power and New York's Stock Market Bubble

The New York Stock Exchange began surging in early 1928. The board and reserve banks agreed to fight speculation by selling bonds and raising discount rates. In May, Adolph Miller told lawmakers that stock speculation was fueled by the previous summer's bond purchase. When a lawmaker observed, "We are exporting an enormous amount of cotton," Miller replied that export gains were "largely scenery . . . you cannot affect the international-exchange situation without affecting the . . . stock exchange loan situation."[106] He complained that the open market committee was controlled by a "majority of one . . . too sensitively attuned to foreign viewpoints." To remedy this fault, Miller suggested that Congress require "purchase of securities . . . be made subject to the affirmative vote of at least five [board] members." Benjamin Strong's testimony stressed the extraordinary nature of recent collaborations; "The world is gradually emerging from a period of the most extraordinary disorder ever known in the history of monetary affairs." When the gold standard was fully restored, Strong promised it would be "more automatic."[107]

Strong then sailed for Europe. When he returned in August, he told the New York directors that his doctor had ordered him to retire due to failing health.[108] A few days later, the open market committee approved $100 million in bond purchases "to avoid undue credit stringency" during the fall harvest. Previously, the board had approved open market directives on a pro forma basis, but now its governor proposed that reserve banks instead satisfy seasonal needs by offering preferential discount rates for agricultural paper. After the committee rejected Young's proposal as impractical, the board narrowly approved the first open market directive, warning that it "would not care to agree to the purchase of Government securities, except as a last resort." Two Western board members remained "unalterably opposed," with one suggesting the board revise the system's open market procedure at a future meeting.[109]

In September, the Federal Advisory Council, a member bank consultative council established by the FRA, proposed growing the open market committee to include all twelve reserve bank governors, while keeping "an executive committee . . . of five members with full power to act."[110] The governors' conference endorsed this proposal, stating the procedure "shall be in the future as in the past, to wit: that the Committee Shall consider and act upon the recommendations of the Executive Committee." This did not satisfy the angry board members, who complained it "would result merely in an enlargement of the present Open Market Investment Committee without any practical change in . . . procedure."[111]

The revisionist faction grew bolder after Benjamin Strong died in October and Herbert Hoover was elected president in November. Miller proposed a regulation to reconstitute the Open Market Investment Committee as an Open Market Policy Conference. The new proposed committee would include representatives of all twelve reserve banks and be chaired by the board governor. Mirroring Miller's 1923 proposal, investments would be "subject to [board] review and determination" and bond purchases would be prohibited. The Boston governor challenged Miller, arguing the board lacked authority to change the procedure. Miller admitted he might be right, but he hoped to "effect a mutual agreement in the matter; that the open market power was the very heart of the System policy."[112] The governors again rejected Miller's bid for power.

By January 1929, the stock market boom was in full swing. Strong's handpicked successor, George Harrison, called the board governor to inform him that the New York directors had chosen to raise the bank's bill rate to limit bills flowing into its portfolio. Unlike the discount rate, reserve banks had heretofore set their bill rates independently. The board governor ordered Harrison to suspend the change, stating "he did not intend any longer to be a rubber stamp."[113] Young called an emergency board meeting, where the member from New York warned that a veto would be "a slap in the face of the New York directors . . . [the board] always approved the actual rate as a matter of course, after it had taken effect." The board approved the hike, while authorizing Miller to write a regulation requiring board approval before future bill rate changes.

Bank of England governor Montagu Norman came to New York that month and proposed sharp discount hikes to pop the bubble.[114] The Bank of England was hemorrhaging gold. Norman and Harrison agreed global interest rates would fall once the stock bubble burst. Harrison told the board that "we should increase discount rates and through sharp incisive action quickly control the long continued expansion in the total volume of credit so that we might then adopt a System policy of easing rates."[115] In February, the New York Fed requested a discount rate hike. The board unanimously rejected the request, citing New York's failure to provide an official justification for its request, a reporting requirement the board began demanding four months before.[116] At Miller's urging, the board instead urged reserve banks to fight speculation by applying "direct pressure" on member banks, forbidding them from loaning discount proceeds to stock brokers.[117] The New York directors renewed their request at their ten next meetings. The board denied each request by shrinking majorities, over unanimous reserve bank endorsement. The board governor privately complained that Harrison "lived and breathed for Norman."[118]

In August, the board and New York Fed reached an agreement to raise New York's discount rate to 6 percent while purchasing bills to provide seasonal financing. The program avoided a global liquidity crunch during the fall harvest, but the stock market began its infamous crash on October 23. The next day, the New York Fed requested authority to lower its discount rate, which the board denied unanimously.[119] Norman cabled New York, "[L]iquidation in your stock market and reduction in call money rates have been satisfactory and have helped to re-establish international position."[120] At three a.m. on October 28, after consulting with a couple of directors, Harrison phoned the open market trading desk agent and ordered him to buy $100 million in bonds before the day's trading began.[121] In coming days, the New York Fed advertised its "discount window is wide open." As investors fled, member banks absorbed more than $1 billion in call loans and extended $300 million in new loans. Friedman and Schwartz credit New York's "timely and effective" response with preventing the crash from spiraling into a broader crisis.[122]

New York's bond purchases nevertheless incensed rural board members. Miller argued banks should have been forced to borrow at the discount window. Charles Hamlin was "inclined to agree . . . but excused the New York bank on grounds that it was a critical emergency."[123] George James argued the purchases violated the system's "gentlemen's agreement" on open market procedure. Governor Young disagreed, stating that Benjamin Strong had always claimed reserve banks had a right to buy bonds in a crisis. The next week, the board passed a regulation requiring reserve banks to seek board approval before making future unilateral purchases.[124]

The open market committee authorized $200 million in additional bond purchases, declaring that recent liquidations posed "a serious threat to business stability . . . [indicating] the need of having the Federal Reserve System do all within its power toward assuring the ready availability of money for business at reasonable rates."[125] The board rejected the directive, ordering the committee to seek the board governor's approval before making any purchases. The New York directors responded by approving $50 million in purchases for its own account.

Harrison then asked the board governor to have a "frank and complete conversation."[126] Harrison complained that the "Board's idea of not being a 'rubber stamp' is to have veto over everything . . . the logical consequence [being the] Board would become a central bank operating in Washington . . . contrary to the whole principle of the Federal Reserve Act." Young replied that the "Board had been given most extraordinarily wide powers . . . Congress could determine whether they objected to having a central bank operating in Washington." Rebuffed, Harrison agreed to seek board approval before undertaking independent bond purchases in the future in exchange for Young's promise that the board would approve the recent open market directive.[127]

On January 16, 1930, the board completed its historic fragmentation of the Fed policy regime by approving Adolph Miller's regulation establishing an Open Market Policy Conference composed of all twelve reserve bank governors and the board.[128] After the vote, governor Young explained he had cast a dissenting vote because he had earlier reached an agreement with the treasury secretary and New York Fed directors to delay a committee restructuring. Acting on the new information, Charles Hamlin proposed a vote to reconsider the previous vote, which lost on a three-three tie. Miller's regulation stated that committee directives would "be submitted to each of the Federal Reserve Banks and the Federal Reserve Board for consideration and/or action." After all bodies approved, the policy would be implemented by a five-governors executive committee.

The board circulated a memorandum explaining the new procedure and soliciting feedback. Five reserve banks that were previously excluded voiced approval.[129] Six others described the plan as "manifestly unworkable" (Chicago); a "machinery . . . so cumbersome as to seriously retard action" (Cleveland); maybe "prov[ing] disastrous" (Philadelphia). The executive committee's power needed to be "materially enlarged" (Richmond). New York defended reserve banks' rights to buy bills unilaterally and to leave the conference if they so decided.

This section has shown that an aggrieved board faction, acting in a context of a faltering Republican regime, flexed uncertain regulatory authority to overthrow Strong's hierarchical Fed. While progressives paint the struggle between the board and New York as inconsequential, the next section shows board obstruction patterns continued throughout 1930 to devastating effect.

Strong's Great Idea Repudiated: Policy Gridlock after the Crash

After the crash, New York Fed officers saw favorable headwinds for the world economy. Pressure on European central banks receded, and they eased policy.[130] Multilateral negotiations yielded the Young Plan, which extended the German reparation payment schedule and established the Bank for International Settlements, a supranational central bank club to manage reparation payments. European prospects were improving. The U.S. began exporting gold. For the first six months of 1930, U.S. foreign lending surged to the vast scale achieved in 1927.[131]

New York Fed officers hoped to exploit these favorable dynamics by easing credit to fuel a global investment-led recovery. The Republican Party's isolationist drift undermined this logic, however. Congress took up Hoover's promise of higher tariffs. What was originally conceived as targeted relief for farmers, however, logrolled into the most protectionist tariff in U.S. history. Further, the Hoover administration barred the Federal Reserve from joining the Bank for International Settlements, depriving the new body of its most powerful potential member.[132]

In this context, the New York governor invoked Benjamin Strong's great idea to build support for an expansionary program. Harrison wrote to the reserve banks in January, "It cannot be stated the country has yet the full benefit of freely available credit at reasonable rates. The bond market is . . . still restricted. Mortgage money is difficult to obtain . . . evidences of business recession have become constantly clearer." Harrison noted that the expansionary effect of $255 million in bond purchases had already been wiped out by gold exports and reduced discounts. He called for an active credit ease to stimulate the bond market and thereby spur a global recovery.

Many Fed officials were swayed by Adolph Miller's argument that bond purchases fueled speculation, however. Before the 1929 crash, the San Francisco governor wrote Harrison that "the 1927 experiment, [is] now ... admitted to have been disastrous ... [T]he purpose of the Federal Reserve System is to provide and assure adequate finance for trade. ... [O]ur policies should be formulated to that end without being too much influenced ... by the gyrations of the stock market or the desire to create or promote a bond market."[133] At the first Open Market Policy Conference, on January 28, the system's divide was on full display. Harrison called for a program of bond and bill purchases to effect "affirmative ease."[134] Only the Atlanta and Richmond governors backed Harrison's call for stimulus. The Philadelphia governor summarized the majority view: "We feel that it is better that the situation should clear up further, that the extent and duration of this recession should be more ascertainable ... rather than to exhaust our ammunition now in what may be perhaps a vain attempt to stem an inevitable recession."

This same dynamic would unfold at conferences in March and May. In early March, the board statistical director delivered a "very pessimistic" report on business conditions to the board, which led governor Roy Young to propose that the board encourage the New York Fed to buy $50 million in bonds for its own account, noting that "no harm could be done and some good could be accomplished."[135] The board went along, and the New York directors readily complied. When Harrison called for more purchases at the open market policy conference later that month, however, the other governors deemed New York's purchases "unwise" and approved no more.[136]

Before the May conference, Harrison circulated a memo noting that commodity prices had fallen "to new low levels [not seen] since 1916." In Harrison's view, recovery hinged on "restoration of [European] purchasing power through the medium of foreign borrowings in the New York money market, just as the recovery of domestic trade ... depends on the new financing for domestic enterprise." Harrison called for more bond purchases, but the Philadelphia and San Francisco governors demanded sales. The divided conference agreed to leave the account unchanged, while leaving open the possibility of purchases "if the situation so develops as to require an Open Market operation by the System."[137] The next week, the New York directors voted unanimously to request bond purchases.[138] Harrison wrote the other banks that "even a slight addition to the available reserve funds might prove helpful both from the point of view of its direct influence on the bond market and in the psychological benefit." Harrison informed the board on June 3 that seven banks supported a $50 million purchase, which the board approved over dissents by three members of the rural faction.[139] Two days later, a New York director observed that recent declines in New York's bill portfolio had already wiped out the expansionary effect of the $50 million purchase.[140]

This contractionary dynamic was reinforced by persistent board obstruction of New York attempts to lower its bill and discount rates. At the first conference in January, the board governor had asked the other reserve banks if the board should approve a pending New York request to lower its bill rate. Eleven reserve bank governors said yes. Two days later, the board approved a bill reduction half the size requested by New York's directors and blocked a discount reduction request on a tie vote.[141] At the March conference, the board governor again asked if the board should approve a New York bill rate reduction request, and the governors said yes. The board then waited forty-one days to approve a bill rate reduction half the size requested. In May, Harrison complained the board was breaking the law by using the conference as a referendum on New York's bill and discount requests.[142] The conference approved resolutions declaring the discount rate "not within its proper province" and endorsing "downward flexibility" on bill rates.

Despite broad endorsement of New York bill and discount rate autonomy, two policy choices that shaped its ability to sustain its investments, the governors denied Harrison's calls for more bond purchases. These rejections were cast at a normative level, claiming New York was distorting the system's purpose. At a June open market executive committee meeting where Harrison again sought more purchases, the board governor read a letter from the San Francisco governor stating, "We . . . do not consider the promotion or creation of a bond market one of the functions of the Federal Reserve." The Philadelphia governor agreed, stating the system had no responsibility "to develop or foster the bond market."[143] No more purchases were approved.

Harrison then told the New York directors they had three options. They could wait for the governors to change their minds, persuade them to embrace purchases, or withdraw from the conference and buy bonds unilaterally. The directors agreed that delay was "tantamount to retarding business recovery."[144] Harrison circulated a letter explaining that his directors had considered leaving the conference but decided to stay because they "preferred persuasion . . . to independent action." He explained, "Our directors have believed . . . whatever steps the Reserve System may take . . . to facilitate a more active and stronger bond market through which capital funds may be made available for new enterprise or distributed to those parts of the world where purchasing power is now seriously curtailed, should be taken promptly and courageously." Only the Atlanta and Richmond reserve banks replied saying they supported further bond acquisitions.

Harrison then suspended his quest for credit expansion. At the September 25 conference, he voted with the majority to leave the bond portfolio unchanged. The Chicago and San Francisco governors cast dissenting votes from the directive because they wanted sales. When Harrison presented the directive for board approval, Adolph Miller, the arch foe of investments, asked why the governors hadn't considered "purchases of Government securities . . . [to] force banks and others to seek new investments."[145] Harrison was also criticized internally. New York deputy governor W. R. Burgess and statistician Carl Snyder led a faction calling for aggressive bond purchases to combat deflation.[146] Harrison criticized their plan for pushing "forced investments . . . the dangers of such a policy of 'inflation' were great and the advantages doubtful." Purchases might push gold abroad to France where "it would be less useful, from a world standpoint, than in this country." Most practically, the other governors would not go along.

The governors rejected Harrison's calls for stimulus, in part, because Strong's great idea no longer made sense. In June, Hoover fulfilled his campaign pledge by signing the Smoot-Hawley Tariff into law over objections by 1,028 economists and denunciation by thirty-four countries.[147] Harrison's call for a Fed-fueled global recovery hinged on a belief that low U.S. interest rates would entice Americans to make long-term foreign investments. In a context where foreigners were cut off from U.S. markets and unable to earn dollars to pay loans, this plan was untenable. Capital exports plunged in the year's second half and the banking system grew fragile.

Progressive Fed scholars argue that the board–New York conflict was procedural, with minimal impacts on policy.[148] Yet, board obstruction of New York bill and discount rate reductions in 1930 had a devastating impact. New York's unbending administered rates, amid falling market interest rates, caused its investments to collapse. System bond holdings grew by $448 million in the year after the October 1929 crash, but these purchases were surpassed by a 77.8 percent fall in New York's bill portfolio and 44.8 percent decline in its discount loans. Outstanding system credit shrank by 25.9 percent, turning the thrust of policy contractionary.[149]

The literature's underestimation of the negative impact of the board's pre-Depression rise grows from an outsized focus on open market policy in 1930. This is Friedman and Schwartz's legacy, who contend a living Strong would have willed the Fed to buy $1 billion in bonds in early 1930, double the size of any previous bond-buying program. While looking back from a modern vantage it is easy to believe that the Fed had the power to stave off depression, the humans who lived in and struggled over the system at the time were, rightfully, more skeptical.

Conclusion: A Hamiltonian Central Bank in the Breaking

This chapter has traced the rise and fall of a Hamiltonian Fed across four political moments. The first section showed that U.S. entrance into World War I ended Democratic obstruction of Paul Warburg and Benjamin Strong's reforms. Currency liberalization enabled the reserve banks to capture a $1 billion wartime gold inflow, and the reserve banks benefited from fiscal agency duties, becoming the government's banker. America's rise to global creditor status, and the attendant dollarization of sovereign debts and international trade, grew the reserve banks' global power. These war-wrought legal and structural changes durably grew the system's power.

The Democratic Party's collapse helped the system regain independence. Afterward, however, it found that the practice of maintaining penalty rates was self-defeating in a world where the dollar was the only currency linked to gold. Amid a sharp postwar recession, lawmakers from rural areas attacked the system's power and discretion. These creedal attacks were blunted and channeled by an ascendant Republican Party, which remade the board into a patronage instrument and added a "dirt farmer" to its ranks. Republican ascent unleashed populist forces through adoption of mercantilist policies, which grated against America's hegemonic global position. Steady U.S. trade and payments surpluses drained European purchasing power, reinforcing a strong (undervalued) dollar. Financiers understood the incoherence of the Republican program but wielded little political power. Benjamin Strong warned the Republican chairman in 1921 that the emergency "tariff bill . . . will come back some day and work the destruction of the political party that adopts it."[150] Strong's own creative actions and policy initiatives put off the Republican day of reckoning for more than a decade.

Strong built a broad coalition, spanning the Federal Reserve and government, behind his "great idea" that the Fed had the power and responsibility to help rebuild the gold standard. He promised that gold restoration abroad would cure a domestic agricultural crisis by reviving European purchasing power, and that the restored gold standard would be "more automatic." Instead, gold restoration increased demands on Strong and his New York colleagues to advocate for internationally geared policies to avoid a global crisis. Support for Strong's experimental easing policies grew thin in agricultural regions, which did not experience post-1925 recoveries.

Adolph Miller's repudiation of Strong's internationalism hastened this process. Amid an environment of Republican decay, Miller leveraged his connection with Hoover and argument that bond purchases fueled stock speculation to engineer the board's rise as a powerful veto player. The board created new requirements for reserve banks to officially justify discount rate change requests, used policy veto threats to negotiate procedural compromises, and forced an ill-timed restructuring of the open market committee. Miller thus toppled Strong's Hamiltonian Fed.

Congress would recognize the Open Market Policy Conference as the Federal Open Market Committee in 1933, enshrining its place in law for the first time. It was a "bicameral system" where policy changes approved by a committee of twelve governors had to then be approved by a fragmented board.[151] Harrison complained to the New York Fed directors, "Direction of system policies by a conference of twelve men who must also consult the Federal Reserve Board means . . . we run a real risk of having no policy at all."[152] Nor was Adolph Miller happy with his creation. He had always sought a positive board authority to shape policy, not just a negative veto power. Miller would spend the rest of his board career attacking Strong and calling for more board empowerment. As Congress prepared to do so in 1935, Miller linked the Depression to Strong's 1927 program, insisting it "was not . . . a policy either developed or imposed by the Board on the Reserve banks against their will. It was distinctly a Reserve bank policy."[153] Miller would not be around to wield Fed power, however. Changing political times would lead to his expulsion from the board, and its reconstitution as an arm of the New Deal.

3

An Engine of Inflation?

The Populist Fed Interlude

> To this public body Congress has entrusted broad powers which enable it to affect the volume and cost of money. . . . Much as they may contribute to the country's progress, monetary powers possess no peculiar magic. They are not omnipotent. To be effective in performing their function, they must be closely coordinated with the other major powers and policies of government which influence the country's economic life.
>
> —Franklin Roosevelt, Federal Reserve Building Opening, October 20, 1937

The Banking Act of 1935 recast the Federal Reserve Board as the Board of Governors, elevated it to a position of Fed primacy, and established the modern office of chairman. The law is widely seen as a developmental watershed, durably growing the board's power, authority, and independence. Progressive scholars celebrate the reform but struggle to explain how it became instantiated in Fed practice. The system would remain captured until 1951, when a bureaucratic agreement, the Treasury-Fed Accord, would restore its autonomy. Progressives see these two moments, 1935 and 1951, as together laying the foundations for the modern Fed. This composite view implies that a Fed not much different from today's was built in the 1930s. While the legal framework laid in these years would later justify the modern Fed, this chapter shows that the Fed built by chairman Marriner Eccles was a populist vehicle of the New Deal. Its fate was linked to the strength and resilience of an ascendant Democratic Party.

Eccles was a Fed outsider. He accepted Franklin Roosevelt's 1934 appointment as board governor contingent on Roosevelt's support for a system overhaul that empowered the board. Eccles's bid for Fed primacy encountered stiff resistance. Opposition by Sen. Carter Glass (D-VA) and Fed insiders ensured legal reform would be incremental. Despite receiving a weak legal warrant, Eccles would go on to establish a populist Fed with a hierarchy extending to the White House, with Eccles positioned as the Fed's administration interlocutor. This regime would never be fully accepted internally as legitimate nor actualized in everyday Fed practice.

This chapter relativizes the scope of Fed changes in the Depression and World War II, emphasizing the role of political time in empowering and eroding Eccles's Fed vision. The first section shows how Herbert Hoover's collapsing partisan regime began the process of board empowerment. The second section explains how Democratic ascent unleashed populist forces, which diminished the Fed and severed the dollar's link to gold. Eccles won Roosevelt's support for a Fed overhaul after it was already degraded. Despite opposition in Congress and in the Federal Reserve, Eccles leveraged his personal ties to Roosevelt to build an extralegal Fed hierarchy. The final two sections explain how Eccles's Fed unraveled in World War II and its aftermath. War weakened Eccles's standing within the system by growing New York's power. Roosevelt's death diminished Eccles's influence in the administration. While fighting stopped in 1945, America would continue occupying Germany and Japan. In this environment, Eccles began a public campaign against inflation, which cost him the Fed chairmanship. Disempowered, Eccles turned on his populist creation. His denunciations of Fed capture and a new war in Korea weakened the Democratic Party, paving the way for the 1951 Treasury-Fed Accord.

Republican Collapse: Invitation for Progressive Reform

The 1930 congressional elections dealt a devastating blow to Republicans. On election night, Republicans lost fifty House seats to cling to a one-seat advantage. A wave of subsequent Republican deaths triggered a series of special elections, however, which handed Democrats a narrow House majority. Republicans lost eight Senate seats, leaving the chamber evenly divided. Amid deepening depression and collapsing electoral support, Republicans reassessed their laissez-faire commitments and began groping toward progressive reform.

The international gold standard unraveled in Europe over the summer of 1931. The Federal Reserve and President Hoover sought to stave off its collapse. In April, the New York Fed governor told the Open Market Policy Conference, "The central position of the United States in the whole world picture makes it desirable to tax our ingenuity that the Federal Reserve System may put forth every possible effort . . . towards maintaining a measure of credit stability throughout the world and towards eventual business recovery."[1] One hundred million dollars in bond purchases were authorized. The board permitted New York to extend emergency credits to distressed central European central banks. In June, Hoover announced a one-year moratorium on war debt and reparation payments. The next day, the New York Fed governor told the open market executive committee that "there had been a threat of a . . . breakdown of capitalism in Europe. . . . He could see no risk in buying governments at this time, but considerable advantage." The Atlanta governor agreed, "The President . . . had taken a constructive step which should be backed up to the limit."[2] The committee authorized $50 million of bond purchases.

Most Europeans welcomed Hoover's moratorium, but France received it as a "bombshell."[3] Treasury Secretary Andrew Mellon went to France to negotiate. Two weeks later, the Bank of England governor cabled New York complaining, "[W]hile folks have been talking and arguing in Paris, the Reichsbank has been bleeding to death."[4] Germany imposed draconian capital controls, effectively leaving the gold standard. Speculation then turned against the Bank of England, which lost $200 million in gold two weeks. Montagu Norman wrote in his diary on July 27, "danger of suspension of gold payments."[5] Two days later, he collapsed.

In August, the New York Fed governor and board sought to persuade the Open Market Policy Conference to enact a bold bond buying program to lift the world economy. A newly installed governor said the board would approve up to $300 million in purchases. The Cleveland governor proposed a $120 million purchase instead. The New York Fed governor objected, stating only a "bold stroke" might succeed. Board member and open market foe Adolph Miller agreed, stating as "skeptical as he might be toward Open Market Policy . . . if there ever had been a justification for its bold, experimental use . . . that situation exists at present time." The conference demurred, approving the smaller package. Britain suspended gold on September 21. Speculation turned to the United States the next day, which suffered its largest daily loss of gold ever.[6]

New York's directors wanted to keep its discount rate low to avoid reinforcing perceptions that America's gold stock was vulnerable.[7] The board governor intervened, telling the directors that "foreigners would regard it as a lack of courage if the rate were not advanced." New York's rate advanced 2 percent. In September and October, 827 American banks failed. A wave of bank failures across the Mid-Atlantic in November created a "credit blockade."[8] Bank suspensions grew 86 percent from the second half of 1930 and defaults on foreign dollar-denominated bonds grew seventeenfold.[9] The six months after Britain's suspension "witnessed the most rapid contraction of bank credit and the money supply ever experienced in America."[10]

Banking collapse worsened Republicans' problems. Falling tax revenues posed an urgent problem. The conservative orthodoxy of the day held that balanced budgets were integral to restoring business confidence and economic recovery.[11] Income and estate tax reductions enacted in the late 1920s suddenly became liabilities. The Smoot-Hawley Tariff raised taxes, but its sharp restriction of trade limited revenue gains. In December, Hoover asked Congress to pass the largest peacetime tax hike in U.S. history. The Revenue Act of 1932 sharply raised taxes on the rich and corporations. The estate tax doubled. Excise taxes were reintroduced. Rather than restoring confidence, austerity compounded deflationary pressures, worsening the Depression.

Hoover sought to create new agencies to recapitalize ailing sectors of the economy. In October 1931, Hoover announced a privately organized National Credit Corporation to relieve illiquid banks. The scheme failed because healthy banks didn't want to bail out those that were insolvent.[12] In December, Hoover revived the World War I–era War Finance Corporation, rechristened as the Reconstruction Finance Corporation, to recapitalize banks and railroads. It was given $500 million in public funds and authorized to issue to $1.5 billion in federally guaranteed bonds.[13] A Home Loan Bank System was established to support saving and loan associations.[14] These agencies acted as lenders-of-last resort, muddling the Federal Reserve's responsibilities.

Republicans also goaded and empowered the Federal Reserve to fight the Depression.[15] In 1931, reserve banks requested an amendment to weaken the dollar's tie to gold by allowing government bonds to be used as collateral. Federal Reserve notes were required to be 100 percent backed by commercial paper and gold, but collapsing world trade made commercial paper scarce. As their discounts and bill holdings fell, reserve banks were forced to hold larger portions of gold reserves to back their currency. This problem was exacerbated by widespread public currency hoarding. Some reserve banks cited a lack of "free gold" to oppose aggressive bond purchases in August 1931. The 1932 Glass-Steagall Act ended this problem by granting reserve banks temporary authority to issue currency against government bonds.[16] It also added FRA sections 10(a) and 10(b), giving the board authority to authorize reserve banks to loan funds to groups of five or more banks and discount otherwise ineligible assets in "exceptional and exigent circumstances." In July 1932, Congress granted emergency authority to reserve banks, contingent on board approval, to open their discount windows to "any individual, partnership, or corporation" unable to access financing.[17] Congress thus began endowing the board with new powers as the Republican regime was unraveling, reflecting this book's theoretical predictions.

Threats of congressional action also spurred the reserve banks to belatedly engage in large-scale bond purchases. Sen. Elmer Thomas (D-OK) proposed legislation requiring reserve banks to print $2.4 billion dollars to buy bonds from the treasury.[18] To preempt this action, the New York Fed proposed that the Open Market Policy Conference aggressively buy bonds on an unprecedented scale. From April to August, the conference bought $1 billion in new bonds. This program temporarily arrested the deflationary slide and restored bank reserves destroyed by the 1931 credit crunch. When Congress adjourned in August, however, the Boston and Chicago Feds scuttled the program.[19] Boston was now headed by Roy Young, whose 1920s experiences at the Minneapolis Fed and battling New York on the board made him an ardent opponent of bond purchases. While double the size of any earlier bond purchasing campaign, the 1932 purchases were too little, too late. Prices again soon started to fall, and the economy cratered.

Voters punished Republicans in the 1932 elections. Franklin Roosevelt won the presidency with 57.4 percent of the national popular vote. Democrats picked up twelve seats in the Senate, taking control, and added ninety-seven more seats to their House majority. Roosevelt blasted Republican protectionism on the campaign trail and blamed Hoover for growing deficits. Roosevelt called for a stronger federal response to combat the crisis, which he called a New Deal, but his other proposals were orthodox, including balanced budgets and freer trade.[20] This did not add up to a coherent plan. The New Deal's content would be flushed out through the churnings of an ascendant partisan regime, which this book argues empowers populist forces.

The banking system collapsed in the months before Roosevelt took office in 1933.[21] In February, negotiations broke down between the Reconstruction Finance Corporation and the Guardian Group, a Michigan bank conglomerate. Michigan's governor declared a bank holiday, closing all banks and freezing deposits. This triggered bank runs in neighboring states, causing more bank holidays. In his last days in office, Hoover reached out to Roosevelt and the Federal Reserve Board to form a joint response but was mutually rebuffed.[22] Hoover asked Roosevelt to publicly pledge to keep the United States on gold, but Roosevelt replied that "mere statements" would not stop bank runs.[23] When Roosevelt took office on March 4, thirty-three states had declared bank holidays and the New York Fed lacked gold to export.[24] Roosevelt invoked the 1917 Trading with the Enemy Act to declare a national bank holiday and embargo gold exports.

Reform trends started under Hoover would continue in the New Deal, with a populist twist. A smattering of new financial agencies would be created to revive the economy, eroding the Federal Reserve's autonomy. The next section shows partisan ascent unleashed populist forces by taking the United States off gold, devaluing the dollar, and expropriating Fed resources. Only after this series of humiliations would Roosevelt back Eccles's partisan Fed makeover.

Eclipsed by the New Deal: The Fed's Marginalization and Rebirth

As Democrats descended on Washington in March 1933, they inherited a peacetime crisis of unprecedented scale. Every sector of the economy was distressed. Banks were closed. Crisis-changed social expectations presented Democrats with a mandate to build a more activist state. State building surged on several fronts, but few were as prolific as in the financial sphere.[25] Agencies were created to recapitalize railroads, banks, and corporations, to insure deposits, and to channel funds into residential and farm mortgages. A banking structure based on gold and commercial assets was remade into one based largely on government securities. By 1936, only 7 percent of member bank assets would satisfy the FRA's original discount requirements.[26] This section explains how these processes recast the Federal Reserve's institutions and environment.

Leaving Gold, Devaluing the Dollar, and the Creation of a Populist Fed Competitor

The process of leaving gold and devaluing the dollar was long and painful, and involved many Federal Reserve sacrifices. In July 1933, Franklin Roosevelt embarrassed the New York Fed by blasting a London Economic Conference communique it had helped craft which pledged a coordinated return to gold. When the statement was released, Roosevelt declared in the United States, "The sound internal economic situation of a nation is a greater factor in its well-being than the price of its currency. The old fetishes of so-called international bankers are being replaced by efforts to plan national currencies with . . . continuing purchasing power."[27] Roosevelt's rebuke cost the New York Fed prestige overseas while undermining its gold restoration project.[28]

When Roosevelt became president, gold suspension was inevitable because the New York Fed lacked gold to export.[29] The Emergency Banking Act, signed during Roosevelt's first week in office, authorized the president to recall domestic circulating gold.[30] In April, Roosevelt issued Executive Order 6102, requiring Americans to turn all gold holdings above $100 dollars in to reserve banks in exchange for lawful currency.[31] The Thomas Amendment to the Agricultural Adjustment Act empowered the president to devalue the dollar by up to 50 percent against gold.[32] Roosevelt signed the Legal Tender Act on June 5, constituting all government-issued currencies legal tender. The same day, Congress passed a joint resolution abrogating gold clauses in public and private contracts. These legal devices shifted losses incurred through currency devaluation onto borrowers.[33] If the dollar was now devalued, borrowers would reap a windfall. In August, Roosevelt ordered all private gold to be turned in to the reserve banks.

In October, Roosevelt announced in a fireside chat that he planned to devalue the dollar against gold as a one-time adjustment. Thereafter, the United States would stabilize the dollar's "purchasing and debt-paying power during the succeeding generation."[34] To implement this plan, Roosevelt authorized the Reconstruction Finance Corporation to buy gold above market rates to depress the dollar. The Bank of England governor "hit the ceiling" when told about the plan, explaining it would "undermine confidence in all currencies" and bring "exchange chaos in Europe." The New York Fed governor explained that Roosevelt was acting for domestic purposes only, but Norman complained his "domestic operation" would drain gold from Europe.[35]

Congress passed the Gold Reserve Act in January 1934. It authorized the president to lower the dollar's gold content by up to 60 percent and then restore gold-dollar convertibility. Reserve banks were required to exchange their gold reserves for treasury-issued gold certificates *before* the devaluation. Roosevelt then announced the dollar would be re-pegged to gold at $35 per ounce, a 59 percent devaluation from its long-standing $20.67 parity. The reserve bank gold transfer yielded a nominal devaluation profit of $2.8 billion for the treasury. This was a tax on reserve bank resources. The law set aside $2 billion of the windfall for an Exchange Stabilization Fund. It was modeled on a similar agency in Great Britain and empowered to buy and sell currencies to regulate the dollar's exchange value. For practical purposes, it was a treasury-housed central bank, which operated using reserve bank resources.[36] A board memo warned that the treasury now had "authority to assume complete control of general credit conditions and to negate any credit policies that the Federal Reserve might adopt."[37]

The Federal Reserve did receive one benefit from this traumatic process, growing domestic dollarization. As Federal Reserve notes were extended to soak up circulating gold and gold certificates, it raised the ratio of Fed currency in circulation relative to other currencies. This was a mixed blessing at best. When Congress and Roosevelt devalued the dollar, Americans saw the Federal Reserve as complicit. In 1935, the Supreme Court would uphold dollar devaluation in a five-four ruling in the *Gold Clause Cases*, which declared that Congress had constitutional authority to abrogate gold clauses in contracts.[38] The next section shows how concurrent financial state-building further weakened and humiliated the Federal Reserve.

FINANCING A RAMSHACKLE FINANCIAL STATE

Before Congress asked the reserve banks to turn over their gold to the treasury, it requisitioned half of their surplus accounts to capitalize a national deposit insurance scheme, the Federal Deposit Insurance Corporation. Many Fed officials opposed national deposit insurance because they feared it would encourage banks to make riskier loans. This concern was more general, however, and applied to a universe of new financial programs and agencies, which fostered moral hazard by weakening incentives for banks to make prudent lending decisions and for borrowers to repay their debts. This trend began with late-Republican-era agencies, including the National Credit Corporation, Reconstruction Finance Corporation, and Home Loan Bank System. It continued under the New Deal in 1933 and 1934 with the advent of the Federal Deposit Insurance Corporation, the Exchange Stabilization Fund, the Securities and Exchange Commission, the Homeowners' Loan Corporation, and the Federal Farm Mortgage Corporation.[39] This proliferation of agencies muddled Federal Reserve responsibilities. W. R. Burgess reflected in 1936, "[B]ecause every move was made in haste it grew a bit haphazard, with responsibility for supervision . . . divided among a number of different bodies."[40]

The rapid construction of a financial state reduced the system's autonomy and capacity to shape its environment. Lester Chandler observes that before the 1930s, "government itself had assumed almost no role in . . . economic recovery. The Federal Reserve had held the center of the stage, almost without competition. Now the roles were almost reversed. The Federal Reserve and its policies did not become insignificant, but they were overshadowed as the government seized the initiative and took bold and far-reaching actions in the monetary area and many others."[41] The Federal Reserve was enlisted to finance this surge of state building. Under pressure from lawmakers in 1933, the Open Market Policy Conference bought $595 million in government bonds, raising its portfolio to $2.4 billion. This action eased the treasury's financing burden. Reserve banks were also taxed to fund the Federal Deposit Insurance Corporation. In 1934, they were forced to surrender a nominal $2.8 billion devaluation "profit" to the treasury to capitalize the Exchange Stabilization Fund. The Federal Reserve was emerging as the New Deal's funder of last resort. If the recovery stalled, the reserve banks would again be called upon to ease the treasury's financing burden or underwrite a new round of state building.

THE FIGHT TO RECONSTRUCT THE FED: A NEW DEAL AFTERTHOUGHT

Many analysts agree with Friedman and Schwartz's argument that the Banking Act of 1935 effectively ended the Federal Reserve's struggle with "an almost complete shift of power from . . . New York . . . to the Board, still in control."[42] Sen. Carter Glass (D-VA) championed the system's federal design, however, and allied with reserve banks to obstruct Fed reform. This section explains how changing political times enabled Marriner Eccles to found a populist Fed despite a weak legal warrant. The 1935 Banking Act grew from compromises between Eccles, who sought to consolidate Fed power, and defenders of the status quo, yielding ambiguity. Eccles would nevertheless leverage his ties with Roosevelt to forge the Fed into an arm of the New Deal.

Marriner Eccles was a man out of place in New Deal Washington. A successful Republican banker from Utah, Eccles arrived Washington, D.C., in February 1933 with an unusual message. Of 198 experts who testified before the Senate Finance Committee, Eccles alone called for major deficit spending to cure the Depression. He laid out a five-point recovery plan, "First. Make available as a gift to the States . . . $500,000,000 to be used . . . to adequately take care of the destitute and unemployed. . . . Second. Increase . . . funds to two and a half billion dollars [for] loans to cities, counties, and States for public works. . . . Third. The adoption of the domestic allotment plan . . . to regulate production and raise prices. Fourth. Refinancing farm mortgages on a long term basis at a low rate of interest. Fifth. A permanent settlement of the interallied debts . . . cancellation being preferable."[43] Years before John Maynard Keynes's *General Theory* was published, Eccles saw an expansionary fiscal policy as necessary for recovery.[44] He argued that cheap credit alone wouldn't spur recovery, noting, "Every effort has been used to bring this about by the Reconstruction Finance Corporation and the Federal reserve banks without result. . . . Credit is the secondary offensive when there is . . . an increase in the demand for goods requiring credit."[45] Cheap credit on its own was an insufficient cure.

Eccles's bold ideas got him on Roosevelt's radar. As the early New Deal corporatist state came under judicial assault, Roosevelt embraced Eccles's 1933 call for "unification of our banking system under . . . the Federal reserve . . . a high income and inheritance tax . . . national child labor, minimum wage, unemployment insurance and old age pension laws."[46] Indeed, these 1933 calls by Eccles previewed much of what would be known as the second New Deal. Roosevelt asked Eccles to become Federal Reserve Board governor in 1934, but Eccles replied he would not "touch the position of governor with a ten-foot pole unless fundamental changes were made."[47] Eccles wanted Roosevelt to support a new Fed hierarchy which centralized power on the board. Roosevelt had previously avoided the system's power struggle, telling an advisor that Woodrow Wilson had wasted political capital on the Federal Reserve and, "[a]s a result, nothing much else on the progressive agenda had been converted into law. . . . The Federal Reserve struggle had taken most of the precious first year and just about all the credit Wilson had."[48] Impressed with Eccles's vision, however, Roosevelt agreed to take up the Fed struggle.

Early New Deal legislation built on existing trends of vesting new powers in the board (see Table 3.1). In 1933, the board was empowered to change reserve ratios, the percentage of deposits that banks were required

Table 3.1. Depression-Era Federal Reserve Legal Powers

New Power	Year	Statute	Control	Mechanism
Issue Currency against Government Bonds	1932*	Glass-Steagall Act	Reserve Banks	Bonds eligible collateral for Federal Reserve Notes.
Relaxed Discount Requirements	1932*	Glass-Steagall Act	Board	Lend against ineligible assets in "exigent circumstances."
	1932*	Emergency Relief and Construction Act	Board	Discount window open to non-banks with Board approval.
Change Reserve Requirements	1933*	Agricultural Adjustment Act	Board	Raise or lower required member bank reserve ratio.
Interest Ceilings on Time Deposits	1933	Banking Act	Board	Board sets interest rate ceilings for time deposits.
Margin Requirement for Security Loans	1934	Securities Exchange Act	Board	Board sets required capital set aside for brokers' loans.

Sources: W. R. Burgess, *The Reserve Banks and the Money Market*, 2nd ed. (New York: Harper & Brothers, 1936), 258–265; Lester V. Chandler, *American Monetary Policy, 1928–1941* (New York: Harper & Row, 1971), 304–307.

*Power first granted on a temporary basis but made permanent by later legislation.

to keep as legal reserves, with U.S. presidential approval. These ratios were previously set by law. The board was also empowered to set ceilings on interest rates banks paid out against on time deposits. This grew from of a belief that competition among banks for deposits, manifested in rising rates, fueled stock speculation in the 1920s. This accrual of powers to the board centralized control of some instruments while leaving others divided. For example, the Banking Act of 1933 gave the board power to set interest rate ceilings independently, while recognizing the Open Market Policy Conference as the Federal Open Market Committee (FOMC). The committee was finally recognized after ten years in operation.

Eccles demanded a wholesale reordering of the Fed's constituent units. Whereas reserve banks initiated open market operations and discount and bill rate changes under the inherited regime, Eccles sought a top-down board-led process. He called for abolishing the open market committee and giving the board complete power over discount rates, open market operations, and reserve requirements. Eccles's plan would have left the board's structure intact, including its ex officio members, the treasury secretary and comptroller, while adding a mandatory retirement age to purge old-timers who stood to oppose his agenda.[49] His was not a progressive plan to empower a politically insulated board. Eccles wanted the Fed remade as an arm of the New Deal.

Eccles and his assistant Lauchlin Currie considered the system's existing open market structure unworkable. Currie complained, "Decentralized control is almost a contradiction in terms." He saw the existing process as "calculated to encourage irresponsibility, conflict, friction and political maneuvering."[50] They also wanted to change the Fed's mandate. The existing charge of "accommodating commerce and business," Currie observed, was "vague to the point of meaningless."[51] Eccles instead proposed that the Fed be instructed "to mitigate by its influence unstabilizing fluctuations in the general level of production, trade, prices and unemployment."

Eccles's program faced opposition in Congress and inside the Federal Reserve. Sen. Carter Glass (D-VA) had blocked earlier attempts to change the system's structure, and was determined to stop Eccles. He stalled a vote on Eccles's Senate confirmation for five months, forcing him to serve as a recess appointment. Glass sought to sink Eccles's candidacy by pinning conflict of interest charges on him, but they didn't stick.[52] The subcommittee Glass chaired narrowly endorsed Eccles's candidacy over

Glass's objection by a four to three vote. Glass skipped a later meeting of the full committee, which approved Eccles's nomination unanimously.[53]

Eccles also faced resistance inside the Federal Reserve. The New York Fed governor led an internal committee charged with considering the system's role in the Depression and potential reforms. A committee memorandum struck a defensive tone, observing that before the 1930s central banks were not seen as responsible for stabilizing the economy, using credit levers to end market booms, or fight depressions. It was thus unfair to judge past behavior by emerging standards. The Depression's severity was blamed on banking crises brought on by declining "soundness of bank assets" and "international maladjustments that developed in the decade after the war."[54] A related New York Fed memorandum agreed that fixing "disorganization caused by the war and the peace . . . was beyond the powers of any central banking mechanism."[55]

The New York Fed governor initially invited Eccles to join the system committee. Eccles curtly replied that "one of my first acts after I'm sworn in as Governor will be to move the abolition of your committee. . . . I have accepted the post of Governor primarily for . . . carrying out an important legislative program, which you in all probability are going to oppose."[56] Eccles followed through on his threat by disbanding the committee after he was sworn in as governor.

LEGISLATIVE COMBAT AND INSTITUTIONAL COMPROMISE

Eccles's reform bill was prepared by the board staff without reserve bank input. His Fed reform program (Title II) was sandwiched between two measures popular among bankers. Title I would make deposit insurance permanent and Title III would ease loan repayment terms under the Banking Act of 1933. Title II called for consolidating open market operations control on a committee of three board members and two reserve bank governors. Eccles went farther in testimony, however, invoking a populist script to call for giving the board total control: "When the federal Reserve banks buy bills or securities in the open market, they increase the volume of the people's money and lower its cost; and when they sell in the open market, they decrease the volume of money and increase its cost. Authority over these operations, which affect the welfare of the people as a whole, must be vested in a body representing the national interest."[57]

Lawmakers remained wary of consolidating Fed power, however. One representative asked whether the "Board should have complete power [over open market operations], and no matter how much the bankers might disapprove they should be compelled to take participation?"[58] "Absolutely," replied Eccles, "the question of monetary policy is a national matter, and it cannot be dealt with regionally without having such situations as we have had in the past."[59] Southern Democrats, who experienced cotton export booms in the wake of expansionary policies in the 1920s, pushed Eccles's reform bill through the House.[60]

Glass fought tooth and nail to defeat the bill in the Senate. He first unsuccessfully tried to separate the bill's popular provisions (Titles 1 and 3) from Eccles's Fed reform (Title 2).[61] The New York Fed governor arranged for businessmen to testify against the reforms on Glass's subcommittee. Glass boasted to Harrison, "I have them badly whipped both in the subcommittee and in the big committee."[62] Glass transformed the bill by eliminating new board powers and removing administration officials from the board, confessing that when he was treasury secretary he "dominated the activities of the Board . . . and I always directed them in the interests of the Treasury."[63] Glass sought to grow the board's autonomy by reconstituting it as a seven-member body made up entirely of politically insulated appointees with fourteen-year terms and higher salaries. Glass's revised bill passed the Senate, setting the stage for a conference committee showdown.

The bill that emerged from conference was full of compromises. Glass won his more independent, seven-member board. Eccles scored a qualified victory by gaining board admission and a slight majority on a reconstituted FOMC which contained all seven board members and five reserve bank representatives.[64] At Adolph Miller's urging, the board was rechristened the Board of Governors, and each member was titled "governor" as a "matter of prestige."[65] The original governor became "chairman," a title inherited from the treasury secretary. To signify reserve banks' diminished rank, their executives were renamed "president," and the board was given a veto over president and vice-president appointments.[66] Participation in open market operations became mandatory, ending reserve bank autonomy over their investment portfolios.

The Banking Act of 1935 made permanent several powers originally granted on a provisional basis, including the use of government bonds as currency collateral, and board control over emergency lending powers and interest rate ceilings. Board authority over reserve requirements expanded. Before, changing reserve ratios had required approval by five board members and the U.S. president. Now a simple board majority could raise or lower reserve ratios up to 100 percent from their pre-1935 levels "to prevent injurious credit expansion or contraction."[67] For the next sixteen years, reserve requirements would become the system's primary credit control instrument.[68] The law clarified the board's discount primacy by requiring reserve banks to suggest rates "every 14 days, or oftener if deemed necessary by the Board."[69] National bank notes were retired from circulation, aiding the system's quest for domestic dollarization.[70] This Fed reconstruction, and the attendant thickening of the New Deal financial state, occurred over protests from Republicans and Carter Glass that a banking emergency no longer existed.

FED RECONSTITUTION AND DISEMPOWERMENT

The law gave Marriner Eccles a weak warrant for constructing a populist Fed. Despite suffering losses of power, prestige, and autonomy, the reserve banks survived as independent entities, with their sovereignty secured through representation on the open market committee. Notably, the reconstituted FOMC was incomplete. The law established a committee of seven governors and five reserve bank representatives but didn't specify who should represent the reserve banks. Some reserve banks wanted unaffiliated experts to represent the reserve banks collectively. The board blocked this plan, however, by passing a regulation requiring presidents to serve as representatives and reserve banks to hold annual elections for their five positions.[71] The New York Fed president was returned to the committee for the first five years. He also served continuously on the executive committee, an extralegal body that now contained three governors and two reserve bank presidents.[72] The FOMC considered using reserve banks other than New York to enact its investment policies, but bonds were traded primarily on Wall Street. America's financial geography dictated that New York remain the FOMC's buying agent.[73]

The law authorized the replacement of all board members. Eccles wrote a memo to Roosevelt with a slate of proposed appointments, calling to retain only himself and Roosevelt appointee M. S. Szymczak, whose main qualification lay in his role in Chicago Democratic politics.[74] Journalist Walter Lippman had wrote of Syzmczak's appointment, "It is distinctly alarming to find the President making a merely political appointment to the Federal Reserve Board."[75] Eccles's memo shows that he sought to build a Democratic board majority.[76] It would be led by himself, a "Prog. Republican." Two other Republicans made the list, but academic economist William Foster, described as an "independent" Republican, wasn't appointed.

Eccles's assault on Fed gerontocracy extended into the reserve banks. Before the new FOMC met in March 1936, the board informed the reserve banks that it would block appointments of any president more than seventy years old. Four long-serving executives departed.[77] Eccles made short work of much of the Fed old guard that stood to oppose him, except for the presidents of the New York, Boston, and St. Louis Feds, who stayed on into the new regime.

FED POLICYMAKING AS THE TREASURY'S JUNIOR PARTNER AMID A GOLDEN AVALANCHE

The Fed's geo- and macropolitical constraints limited Eccles's ability to consolidate his Fed revolution. New York's vice president of research John H. Williams told the board in December 1935 that surging gold inflows and the treasury's Exchange Stabilization Fund limited the system's power.[78] Bank reserves had risen from $2.5 billion to $6 billion since 1929 due to "the gold inflow since the devaluation of the dollar." The system's main problem was that excess reserves, those which surpassed legal minimums, could be loaned out at any moment to spark a dangerous inflation. Williams said the situation called for political solutions, "adjustment of currencies rather than an adjustment of reserves. That is outside of our sphere. . . . The second element of the problem outside of the sphere of the Federal Reserve System is the stabilization fund. That is the gold devaluation profit and the spending of it would result in a large increase in excess reserves. To get a return to more normal central banking conditions . . . it would be necessary to . . . get rid of the stabilization fund or to transfer it to the Federal Reserve."[79] Absent political action to fix these problems, Williams suggested that the system try to restore credit control by raising reserve requirements and selling bonds from the system investment account.

Before the Depression, banks had invested their deposits up to the required reserve minimum. When pushed below their required reserve minimum, banks would discount assets at the reserve banks to gain reserves. So long as member banks had outstanding discounts, the system could shape their behavior through discount rate changes and investments. This system broke down in 1933, however. As confidence in the banking system returned, Americans deposited more than two billion dollars in hoarded currency into banks.[80] Surplus reserves blunted the impact of discount rates and open market operations, making reserve requirement changes relatively more effective.[81] The board statistical director estimated that excess reserves of $3 billion in the banking system in late 1935 could support a credit expansion of $35 billion if banks returned to their traditional practice of lending out all investable resources.[82]

Treasury Secretary Henry Morgenthau secretly cheered on the Fed's reconstruction, even at the cost of his board exclusion. He hoped the "Board would be given additional powers and created . . . as a monetary authority so that they and the Treasury can share responsibility and possibly help us in case we get into a financial jam."[83] The system's determination to reduce surplus reserves would test the limits of its newfound legal autonomy. In April 1936, the New York Fed proposed that the board raise reserve requirements to mop up excess reserves. Morgenthau asked the board to wait until July, but Franklin Roosevelt wanted the hike finished before the summer's political conventions, to show that he was attuned to the inflation threat. On July 14, the board voted to raise reserve ratios by 50 percent on August 15. A press statement explained $1.9 billion in "superfluous" reserves would remain, so the move should not be interpreted as retreat from easy money.[84] Morgenthau was "furious that Eccles had not warned him about the action."[85] He combatted Fed tightening by instructing the New York Fed, in its capacity as the treasury's fiscal agent, to buy government bonds using treasury trust funds. Morgenthau offered to split these purchases with the FOMC at the end of each day. Eccles told Morgenthau the FOMC would go along, committing its support in advance of the committee's authorization. Morgenthau replied, "Well, now that's fine, Marriner, now we're partners."[86]

Morgenthau developed a plan for reducing excess reserves by having the Exchange Stabilization Fund sell short-dated bonds to buy and impound imported gold.[87] Eccles opposed the treasury gold stabilization plan because it would raise government borrowing costs and intrude on a traditional central banking sphere. The board could achieve the same outcome, he argued, at no government cost by raising reserve requirements. Morgenthau fumed, "I think there is one more issue to be settled . . . that is whether the Government through the Treasury should control . . . monetary policy . . . or whether control should be exercised through the Federal Reserve Banks who are privately owned and dominated by individuals who are banker minded."[88]

The resolution to this conflict illustrated an emergent pattern of Fed politics. Eccles and Morgenthau took their complaints to Roosevelt. Eccles shifted course and said he thought the treasury plan had merit, endorsing it over alternative board proposals to mop up excess reserves. Rather than faithfully representing the views of Fed stakeholders, Eccles undercut his colleagues by cutting a pro-treasury deal in the administration's highest ranks. With Roosevelt's approval, the treasury began sterilizing gold imports in December 1936.

The next month, the board and reserve banks agreed to raise reserve requirements by another third, using up the board's statutory authority to cumulatively double rates.[89] The board announced it would raise reserve requirements in two steps on March 6 and May 1. Treasury yields then began creeping upward. Morgenthau complained of a bond market "panic" and demanded that the FOMC intervene to stabilize the government bond market.[90] If it did not act, Morgenthau threatened to release $500 million of impounded gold. The New York Fed president told the FOMC he would not support bond purchases without an economic purpose to appease the treasury. Eccles told Morgenthau that "he could not use a club on twelve bankers, and further discussion would take time."[91] At an impasse, Eccles and Morgenthau appealed to Roosevelt.

Eccles told Roosevelt that Morgenthau's plan would signal to the public that the treasury had taken control of monetary policy, that the 1935 Fed reform had failed, and that the administration was unable to chart a steady course. He promised to try to persuade the FOMC to commit to stabilizing the government bond market. On Roosevelt's recommendation, Morgenthau attended the next FOMC meeting. He declared, "We hope and earnestly request that you use the machinery which you have and give us an orderly market. Now, if within reasonable time you don't . . . the Government will, and that's the whole story."[92] When New York Fed president George Harrison began to object, Morgenthau exploded, "You people just don't want to admit that . . . you monkeyed with the carburetor and you got the mixture too thin. . . . You give us the policy now."[93] Bowing to Morgenthau's pressure, the FOMC voted to support an "orderly" bond market and authorized new purchases. Fed policy was now to support public finance.

This sequence of episodes revealed the system's subordinate status in the New Deal order. This section has shown that the system was disempowered, in turn, by the construction of a new financial regime, the dollar's break from gold and devaluation, a "golden avalanche" from abroad fueling excess reserves, and the treasury's rise as a powerful central bank competitor and bid for Fed dominance.[94] These changes reflect this book's theoretical argument that ascendant partisan regimes empower populist reform impulses. The next section shows how World War II deepened the Fed's capture while consolidating Fed power in New York and Washington.

World War II: The New York Fed Empire Strikes Back

Americans did not want to fight another European war. Isolationist currents fueled enactment of four Neutrality Acts from 1935 to 1939, prohibiting arms exports and loans to warring nations.[95] President Roosevelt nevertheless reengaged European allies and sought to rebuild a more liberal order. This reversal was underpinned by an emergent internationalist coalition of Southern planters and Northern capital.[96] The Reciprocal Trade Agreements Act of 1935 granted Roosevelt greater authority to negotiate tariff reductions. The next year, the treasury completed the Tripartite Agreement with Britain and France, restoring trilateral currency convertibility. When Germany invaded Poland in 1939, Roosevelt persuaded Congress to repeal the arms embargo. After winning an unprecedented third term in 1940, Roosevelt gave his "Arsenal of Democracy" speech, where he urged Americans to arm European democracies with "the same sense of urgency, the same spirit of patriotism and sacrifice as we would show were we at war."[97] Japan attacked the United States one year later and Roosevelt led America to war.

Fed largesse powered America's arsenal of democracy. When war was declared, the board announced, "The System is prepared to use its powers to assure that an ample supply of funds is available at all times for financing the war effort."[98] On April 30, 1942, the board announced that the system's powers would be directed toward establishing a fixed-yield pattern on government securities. The FOMC would buy three-month Treasury bills at .375 percent, one-year notes at .875 percent, and twenty-five-year bonds at 2.5 percent, to stabilize their values.[99] Moving forward, sustaining this yield pattern, known as "the peg," would be the Fed's priority.

As they had in World War I, U.S. resources funded the Western alliance. When war broke out, Europeans went on a U.S. buying spree before exhausting their resources. Britain transferred $2.5 billion in gold and requisitioned its citizens' U.S. assets to pay for imports. By 1940, the treasury held 80 percent of the world's monetary gold.[100] Bilateral payments were suspended with enactment of the Lend-Lease Act in March 1941, which authorized arms and aid transfers to "any country whose defense the President deems vital to the defense of the United States."[101] Allies thereafter financed imports with dollar credits, further dollarizing the world economy.[102]

The wartime finance policy increased the New York Fed's responsibilities and power. It was tasked with buying and selling however many treasury bills, notes, and bonds were needed to sustain the fixed-yield pattern. In line with this book's theoretical predictions, war enhanced New York's standing within the Fed. On July 7, 1942, Congress made the New York Fed president the FOMC's ex officio vice chairman, with permanent voting rights.[103] The eleven other reserve banks would be divided into four clusters, and one bank would represent each cluster on the FOMC with rotations on an annual basis.

World War II laid waste to the Fed's old problems while paving the way for new ones. Eccles and Morgenthau called for aggressive tax hikes to fund the war, but Congress refused to deliver.[104] From June 1941 through June 1945, the national debt quadrupled from $48 to $235 billion. Outstanding Fed credit grew from $2 to $22 billion.[105] Price controls limited price level rises to 20 percent in the war, but inflation would surge when controls were lifted in 1946.

Peace Deferred? The Democratic Dilemma of Postwar Reconstruction

This book argues that the end of war portended two changes, which shaped the trajectory of the Federal Reserve's struggle. First, political authorities had opportunities to rebuild a liberal international order. Second, returns to peace unleashed centrifugal forces, which Fed leaders seized to demand restored autonomy. The last chapter showed that President Woodrow Wilson failed to secure a peace Americans would support and saw his party's internationalism repudiated. Voters returned Republicans to power, who embraced protectionism, budget surpluses, and collected European debts, thereby pushing deflationary pressures abroad. World War II's conclusion would follow a nearly opposite path. Democratic leadership led a national reimagining of America's global responsibilities. Isolationism was rejected as a failed grand strategy, and Americans spearheaded construction of an array of new international institutions.[106] This lurch toward internationalism was not without its faults, however. The next section shows that the New York Fed criticized the Bretton Woods agreements, which built a new international monetary system. Further, commitments to rebuild Germany and Japan kept the United States on a wartime footing, buttressing treasury demands to sustain wartime Fed subsidies. President Harry S. Truman's 1950 choice to lead the nation to war in Korea would weaken his party, however, bringing an end to an era of Democratic rule and paving the way for renewed Fed independence.[107]

American Support for Embedded Liberalism and New York Fed Dissent

The U.S. spearheaded the construction of an international economic regime, which aimed at moving toward freer trade while enabling countries to shield their societies from international adjustment pressures. This "embedded liberal" regime grew from a series of compromises between the U.S. and British governments which culminated in the landmark 1944 international monetary conference at Bretton Woods, New Hampshire.[108] Economist John Maynard Keynes, who negotiated on behalf of the British government, argued that the gold standard had a deflationary bias because it forced countries that ran external deficits to enact austerity to push down domestic wages and prices. This adjustment mechanism was flawed because countries that ran persistent trade surpluses, as the United States had throughout the 1930s, faced no similar pressures to stimulate their economies and raise domestic prices. Keynes called for an International Clearing Union to provide short-term financing to countries experiencing balance-of-payments deficits and to issue a reserve currency to supplement gold. Under this scheme, states would be allowed to devalue their currencies to restore external balance rather than enacting austerity. Keynes proposed that states that ran persistent surpluses should be forced to replenish the International Clearing Union shares of borrowers that depleted their reserves.

The U.S. Treasury accepted Keynes's call for a supranational fund, but it imagined a humbler one, which reflected America's interest as the world's premier creditor. The capital of the treasury's proposed fund would be one-fifth of Keynes's International Clearing Union. It would also provide short-term international payments financing, but creditors would not be forced to replenish debtors' shares. The compromise plan established two supranational agencies. An International Monetary Fund (IMF) would provide short-term balance-of-payments financing and an International Bank for Reconstruction and Development (the World Bank) would provide long-term stabilization loans to help governments engage in reconstruction. The IMF Articles of Agreement enshrined Keynes's goal of protecting states from global adjustment pressures.[109] States would be allowed to maintain capital controls in perpetuity, enabling them to reap the liberalizing benefits of a stable currency while directing monetary policy toward domestic ends. States could also devalue their currencies in circumstances of "fundamental disequilibrium," a condition that was left vaguely defined.

Inside the Federal Reserve, only New York Fed officers criticized the plan. Vice president of research John H. Williams, who was also a dean at Harvard, argued that the core problem facing the postwar world was that Great Britain was effectively bankrupt and destined to run deficits into the future.[110] This was problematic because sterling remained a global currency, used by British colonies, which kept sterling balances in London. Williams argued that the world was stuck with a major currency system. The dollar would reign supreme, backed by the bulk of the world's gold. Sterling would limp along, held up by British power over its subjects.

Williams argued that the Bretton Woods agreement pushed this problem into the future and into new, untried venues. He argued that the United States needed to exert maximal leverage to force Britain to embrace liberalization, including free trade and restoring sterling convertibility into gold, before establishing a supranational monetary agency. Williams saw an IMF tasked with providing short-term financing as prone to abuse, and as especially ineffective during a postwar transition period. As lawmakers considered the Bretton Woods Agreement Act in 1945, New York Fed president Allan Sproul testified against rushing into establishing the IMF. "We are told that unless the fund is retained there will have to be another conference . . . [which] would jeopardize international cooperation in all fields and set us back on the road toward isolation and . . . economic warfare."[111] Former New York vice president W. R. Burgess concurred, stating, "The country is now almost pathologically international-minded, so that they are not patient with even stopping to think about things, and that means we are going to pour out money too freely abroad."[112]

Some scholars see New York's opposition as rooted in a broader rejection of embedded liberalism.[113] As the world's premier financial center, New York stood to lose from a world economy characterized by pervasive capital controls. New York Fed agents' arguments reflected a Hamiltonian logic, however, because they sought to adapt a gold standard to changing times. Williams admitted that "the gold standard had a deflationary effect on some countries," while also pointing out that "currency depreciation had a deflationary effect on the outside world."[114] The solution was not "the 'exact opposite' of the gold standard, as Keynes has characterized the present agreement," Williams argued, but "two-sided cost-price adjustments. . . . There is no action which a surplus country might take which does not have its counterpart for the deficit countries. . . . Recognition of this fact is the only reasonable basis on which to proceed."

The Bretton Woods Agreements Act passed through Congress by commanding majorities, passing 349–20 in the House and 70–19 in the Senate. No House Democrat voted against the bill. Two Democratic senators voted nay. How the monetary system would come to life, however, and how embedded liberalism would be instantiated in American politics remained open questions. Franklin Roosevelt's 1945 death would make answering these questions harder.

Passing the New Deal Torch and the Dilemma of Postwar Reconstruction

Franklin Roosevelt's 1944 State of the Union Address called for a "second Bill of Rights." Roosevelt argued that "true individual freedom cannot exist without economic security and independence." He called for promising all Americans a "remunerative job" with wages to furnish "adequate food and clothing and recreation."[115] All Americans should have rights to a "decent home," "adequate medical care," "protection from the economic fears of old age, sickness, accident, and unemployment," and a "good education." "After this war is won," Roosevelt told Congress, "America's own rightful place in the world depends in large part upon how fully these and similar rights have been carried into practice for our citizens. For unless there is security here at home there cannot be lasting peace in the world."

Roosevelt died on April 12, 1945, passing the problems of completing the New Deal and ending the war to Vice President Harry S. Truman. Truman inherited a wartime economy shaped by extensive controls, including administered prices and labor repression.[116] Stimulus unleashed by the war vanquished America's depression, driving unemployment below 2 percent. Most experts held a Keynesian view that governments should continue activist fiscal and regulatory policies after the war to sustain prosperity. Central banks were assigned a low rank in the emerging embedded liberal order. The world over, central banks remained captive to heavily indebted treasuries, and all governments had incentives to sustain this arrangement.

Truman would struggle with the multifaceted challenge of ending the war, demobilizing state and society, and managing the New Deal coalition. Fighting would end in 1945, but U.S. occupations of Germany and Japan meant that war formally continued. As was the case after World War I, converting the economy back to a peacetime footing unleashed cascading problems. A wave of strikes swept across the United States and inflation surged. Answering FDR's call for new economic rights, President Truman championed the 1946 Employment Act, which declared it the government's "continuing policy and responsibility . . . to promote maximum employment, production, and purchasing power." Southern Democrats and Republicans allied to weaken the Employment Act in Congress, including removing a federal employment guarantee.[117] In coming years, Truman's plans to grow the New Deal would often be sunk by this conservative coalition.

An Engine of Inflation:
Eccles Turns on His Populist Fed Creation

This chapter has shown that Marriner Eccles leveraged Franklin Roosevelt's support to build a Washington-centered Fed. Although he failed in his bid to formally concentrate all Fed power in the board, Eccles leveraged his ties to Roosevelt to commit the system to New Deal projects, often over his Fed colleagues' objections. Eccles's political power declined with Roosevelt's death in 1945.[118] Truman had no ties to Eccles, and his treasury saw the Fed as a subordinate agency. In a context of rising postwar inflation, Eccles would earn Truman's ire by publicly warning of a coming inflation crisis and calling for ever greater fiscal restraint.[119]

Eccles began lobbying Truman for budget surpluses to fight inflation in 1946.[120] He told the House Banking and Currency Committee in

1947, "We are already in the advanced stages of inflation. Correction is overdue . . . we must continue to put our main reliance on fiscal policy, which is by far the most effective way to deal with the demand side of the equation."[121] Although Eccles made clear that he believed fiscal restraint was needed to restore price stability, he also urged the treasury to allow interest rates to rise to combat "continuing pressure toward higher prices."[122] Eccles pushed to dismantle Fed wartime subsidies. In 1947, the treasury agreed to end the ninety-day treasury bill peg in exchange for a commitment to transfer 90 percent of surplus reserve bank earnings to the treasury moving forward.[123] The treasury would not agree to end the bond peg, however. Stuck with an open-ended commitment to buy underpriced bonds, the Fed was forced to monetize public debts by creating new reserves to soak up unwanted securities.

Eccles's public campaign annoyed Truman. The administration was making steep budget cuts and would run a cumulative $8 billion surplus in fiscal years 1947–1951.[124] When Eccles's term as chair expired in January 1948, Truman chose not to reappoint him. This put Eccles in an awkward position, because he had four years remaining on his original fourteen-year board term. Truman promised to designate Eccles the board vice chairman, but the designation never came. Three months later, Eccles withdrew his name from consideration in humiliation.[125]

Freed from the burdens of Fed leadership, Eccles turned against his populist Fed creation. In 1949, Eccles and the New York Fed president called on Congress to restore Fed autonomy. Eccles told lawmakers, "The Federal Reserve System is a creature of the Congress. You can make it weak or you can make it strong. . . . So long as the Reserve System is expected to support the Government bond market . . . [it] is deprived of its only really effective instrument for curbing overexpansion of credit."[126] Sproul agreed, arguing that to be effective, monetary policy needed a capacity to tighten. "There cannot be a purposeful monetary policy unless the Federal Reserve System is able to pursue alternating programs of restraint, 'neutrality,' and ease, in a roughly contracyclical pattern. Such programs must . . . affect interest rates, not only for private credit, but for Government securities."[127] To tame inflation, Treasury borrowing costs would have to rise.

A series of government reports endorsed greater Fed autonomy. The Herbert Hoover–led 1949 Task Force Report on Regulatory Commissions observed, "A truly independent central bank, free to control the Nation's money supply counter to the wishes of the President and Congress, is unrealistic in the modern world. But a major problem remains: How to obtain the most reasoned, balanced, joint monetary-fiscal policy for the Government."[128] To fix the current power imbalance, "equal voice" should be given "to the central bank in the process of Government policy formation." A 1950 congressional panel led by Sen. Paul Douglas (D-IL) urged Congress to declare that "the primary power and responsibility for regulating the supply, availability, and cost of credit in general shall be vested in the duly constituted authorities of the Federal Reserve System, and that Treasury actions relative to money, credit, and transactions in the Federal debt shall be made consistent with the policies of the Federal Reserve."[129]

Tensions boiled over with the outbreak of the Korean War in June 1950, which "transformed the tone and the tempo of American economic life."[130] By the end of the year, consumer prices were rising at a 19 percent annualized rate.[131] So long as it remained on the peg, the Fed was on a path toward monetizing new wartime deficits. The treasury-Fed feud spilled out into the public in January 1951, after Truman took the unprecedented step of inviting the FOMC to the Oval Office.[132] Afterward, the treasury issued a statement claiming that the Fed had agreed to sustain the peg for the duration of the conflict. Acting independently, Eccles then released the board's meeting minutes to the press to show that no such promise was made.

The FOMC then began crafting a statement that would form the Treasury-Fed Accord. It agreed to gradually withdraw support for the 2.5 percent bond peg while markets adjusted. Once stabilization occurred, the Fed would chart an independent policy. Sen. Douglas urged the treasury to "yield on this issue" and counseled "the Federal Reserve [to] gird its legal loins and fulfill the responsibilities which I believe the Congress intended it to have."[133] The Treasury-Fed Accord was announced on March 2. It stated, "The Treasury and the Federal Reserve System have reached full accord with respect to debt-management and monetary policies to be pursued in furthering their common purpose to assure the successful financing of the government's requirements and, at the same time, to minimize monetization of the public debt."[134]

Progressives hail the Accord as the cornerstone of modern Fed independence.[135] Recent Fed scholarship is more circumspect, however. Binder and Spindel agree the Accord had an "existential impact" by securing a treasury "divorce," which "enabled the Fed to set interest rates independent of the Treasury, unconstrained by the administration's financing needs."[136] In their view, this did not establish independence per se, but rather "dependence on the legislature." Peter Conti-Brown is more skeptical, calling the Accord an "empty sentence."[137] In his view, the task of bringing Fed independence to life would fall to the next Fed chairman.

Conclusion: Reassessing Eccles's Fed Legacy

After the Accord, Eccles left the board and returned to Utah to run his family businesses. Scholars offer conflicting assessments of Eccles's Fed legacy. Left populists praise him as the Fed's "salvation," while Right populists cast him as a villain, seeing his 1935 reform as transferring Fed power to a mistake-prone "Board, still in control."[138] Progressives see Eccles as less transformative, scoring partial victories during his Fed rise and fall.[139] The Banking Act of 1935 laid the legal foundation of the modern Fed by remaking the Board of Governors and the FOMC, the system's central policymaking bodies. The board gained a position of primacy within the system, with reserve banks losing autonomy and influence. Board supremacy was reflected in an FOMC majority, reserve requirement discretion, and a veto over reserve bank president appointments. Progressives praise Eccles for spearheading these reforms and acting as a whistleblower in his final years, building public support for Fed autonomy promised by the law.

While Franklin Roosevelt infamously failed in bids to pack the Supreme Court and vanquish enemies from the Democratic Party, Eccles succeeded in purging old timers from the board and reserve banks, achieving the same substantive goal inside the Fed. Viewed in this light, there is an irony to progressive claims that Eccles helped build a more independent Fed. Indeed, it was Carter Glass, not Eccles, who called for making the board independent from the treasury. To the people that lived and worked inside the Federal Reserve, Eccles's arrival in 1935 and his authoritarian impulses were merely the latest in a long string of humiliations. Given this context, it is no wonder that Eccles met a conservative insurgency inside the Fed from day one.

This points toward a problem with smashing together the 1935 and 1951 reforms into a composite, linear progressive story. Eccles's public irritations in the run-up to the Accord were not the culmination of a long battle to build an independent Fed. In the 1930s he fought to forge the Fed into an arm of the New Deal. His repudiation of the Fed as an "engine of inflation" fifteen years later was an indictment of his own handiwork and institution building.[140] Changing political times fueled Eccles's Fed rise and fall. His authority peaked when he entered the Fed with Roosevelt's endorsement of a Fed makeover. He suffered a major setback when Congress refused to fully concentrate power on the board in 1935, however. Eccles was disempowered by World War II, which raised New York's power within the system. When Roosevelt died in 1945, Eccles was a man out of place in Washington. As a lifelong Republican, he had little in common with most New Dealers. His criticisms of the administration made him expendable.

So what should be made of Marriner Eccles's Fed legacy? Beyond the 1935 structural reforms, Eccles should be credited with helping unify the Fed policy regime and advancing a broader understanding of its mandate. W. R. Burgess explained that the 1935 FOMC reform "materially changed the operating mechanism in the direction of further centralization" from a "bicameral system" to a "single committee."[141] Changing the board's position from a veto player to a policy collaborator, and ending *ex post* opportunities for reserve banks to abstain from open market purchases, reduced the FOMC's veto points. It grew durably less fragmented, even as regional Fed policy influences remained. Eccles also deserves credit for broadening the Fed's mandate to include purposes beyond administering the gold standard and "accommodating commerce and business." Eccles asked lawmakers to mandate the Fed "to mitigate by its influence unstabilizing fluctuations in the general level of production, trade, prices and unemployment." Sen. Carter Glass blocked this change, permitting only an additional caveat, "with regard to the general credit situation of the country," to be added to the system's original charge. Eccles's broader vision of Fed purpose became accepted in Fed practice, however. While the system wasn't mentioned in the 1946 Employment Act, Fed officials saw themselves as bound to help "promote maximum employment, production, and purchasing power." This anticipated the Fed's modern "dual mandate" of fighting inflation and unemployment.[142]

The next chapter shows that scholars err by imagining that the Fed that emerged after 1951 mirrors the Fed of today. New chair William McChesney Martin Jr., would invoke older Fed governance traditions to build a diffuse, globally oriented Fed in the 1950s. This Fed would be challenged in the 1960s by economists who exploited changing political times and Bretton Woods's collapse to concentrate Fed power in an emergent Washington-based technocracy.

4

Economists at the Gates

The Rise and Fall of an Egalitarian Fed

> Before my appointment to the Board of Governors . . . I had spent nearly twenty years studying and teaching monetary economics. I thought I understood what the Fed did and how it affected the economy. I soon discovered how little I knew.
>
> —Sherman Maisel, Board of Governors

Progressives hail William McChesney Martin Jr. as the architect of the modern Fed. Martin is credited with negotiating the Treasury-Fed Accord on behalf of the treasury, bringing it to life in Fed practice, and rebuilding atrophied FOMC institutions.[1] Some scholars claim that Martin transformed the board into a "powerful agency . . . whose power endured long past his tenure."[2] Yet, this chapter shows Martin fought to limit the board's power and his own Fed influence. While Martin is widely praised, scholars struggle to nail down his accomplishments. This is because the egalitarian Fed order Martin crafted unraveled on his own watch. In the 1960s, Martin would wage a losing war with successive U.S. presidents to fend off a board invasion by economists who sought to consolidate Fed power and turn it toward their own ends.

This chapter uses the lens of political time to trace the Federal Reserve's struggle for power through 1970, when it durably ended. The analysis proceeds through three political moments. It begins by surveying the Fed's institutional landscape in the wake of the Accord, an era of Democratic decline and a return to peace. Martin entered a Fed that lodged open market power in New York. The system's struggle reemerged when Martin invoked Jeffersonian scripts and an idealized vision of the system's pre-1935 past to challenge inherited hierarchies, which New York president Allan Sproul defended by invoking New York's unique vantage and expertise. The two would engage in a "gentlemanly but polarizing" debate, which leveled Fed hierarchies.[3] Martin would craft an inclusive Fed, which veered from the law by encouraging all twelve reserve bank presidents to join FOMC deliberations, vacating the board's advantage.

This inclusive Fed regime would work admirably in the 1950s, an era of U.S. primacy and fiscal conservatism. The activation of the Bretton Woods fixed-exchange system in 1958 would confront the system with new problems, however, which would pull the Fed's regions and institutions apart. Reestablishment of European currency convertibility led to an outpouring of gold from the United States, calling Bretton Woods's long-term viability into question. Central banks in Europe would demand U.S. austerity to stabilize the dollar, but a rising chorus of economists on both ends of the political spectrum in the United States would call on the Fed to ignore these international adjustment pressures and instead direct monetary policy toward domestic goals.

A resurgence of Democratic electoral fortunes in the 1960s would provide a pathway to power for economists inside the Fed. President John F. Kennedy and his successors would indulge economists' demands for steady board appointments, transforming it over the course of a decade from an occupationally diverse body to an economist stronghold. As this process unfolded, a Fed old guard led by Martin and the New York Fed president, would fight to steer the Fed's powers toward stabilizing the dollar and defending Bretton Woods. The growing cohort of board technocrats rejected this goal, however, arguing that monetary policy should support domestic aims. Lyndon Johnson's choices to pass an income tax cut, launch a war on poverty, and escalate the war in Vietnam, would lock U.S. fiscal policy in an expansionary stance, stoking inflationary fires. These cumulative forces would shatter Bretton Woods, which effectively collapsed in 1968. When economist Arthur Burns replaced Martin in 1970, the board completed its technocratic conversion and seized Fed agenda-setting power, completing a migration of ideational authority inside the system from the New York Fed which began four decades earlier.

CREATIVE DEMOLITION: WILLIAM MCCHESNEY MARTIN'S
EGALITARIAN FED

The Federal Reserve Bill Martin joined in 1951 was an institution in shambles. The board was formally empowered in 1935, but World War II grew New York's power within the system. Under the wartime peg, New York's open market trading desk effectively *became* the Fed. New York president Allan Sproul explained that the Fed did not become "the supine servant of the Treasury . . . [we] lost our 'independence' . . . but we lost it to the inexorable demands of war. It was not meekly handed over to the Treasury in abdication of our responsibilities."[4] When the Accord ended this partnership, inherited institutions concentrated Fed open market power in an extralegal executive committee dominated by the New York Fed president.

This section shows how Bill Martin tore down inherited Fed hierarchies to build an egalitarian FOMC. Martin invoked childhood memories of decentralized Fed governance traditions to build a system-wide consensus in favor of a more inclusive and consensual process. Unlike in the late 1920s, fragmentation grew from an extended system-wide dialogue, not subterfuge. The protagonists in this struggle, Sproul and Martin, imagined a Fed order that adapted pre-1935 traditions to an embedded liberal age. Sproul developed a Hamiltonian defense of existing Fed hierarchies, arguing that central bankers positioned in the nation's financial capital needed flexibility to respond to destabilizing shocks.[5] Martin invoked Jeffersonian and populist scripts to call for replacing Fed hierarchies with an inclusive, democratic process. After tracing this struggle, the section ends by explaining how an alignment of domestic and global circumstances made Martin's egalitarian Fed workable in the short run.

The Struggle for the Heart of the Federal Reserve

Bill Martin and Allan Sproul agreed about a lot. Each spent early years in Fed outposts, St. Louis and New York respectively, which shaped their visions of the system's power and purpose. Both departed from contemporary Keynesian orthodoxy by believing monetary policy remained a powerful instrument in a world of large public debts. They also agreed Fed policy should counter inflationary and deflationary forces to stabilize the dollar. They also agreed, to a lesser extent, on Fed institutions. Both considered the FOMC the system's "heart" and believed it should steer all the system's policy levers, even those controlled by the board.[6] Martin and Sproul's divide lay over how the FOMC should be structured. Sproul defended an inherited process whereby the full FOMC met four times a year to write broad policy directives, which were executed by an extralegal executive committee dominated by Sproul. When Martin arrived on the Fed scene in 1951, Sproul was the Fed's "preeminent force, intellectual and political."[7]

Sproul embraced a Hamiltonian Fed construction imagined by economist Allyn Young. Sproul kept a copy of Young's 1927 *Annalist* article, which explained, "The New York Bank has come to have a position of primacy in the Federal Reserve System merely because it has not tried to shun the responsibilities which are naturally assigned to it by the structure of the national money market and" its relations with "the world market."[8] Geography vested New York with responsibilities over open market operations, international payments, and diplomacy, which rendered it "first among equals" within the Fed. It was better to concede "larger powers to the New York Bank, than to run the danger of 'unifying' the system into a cumbrous and slow-moving substitute for a single central bank, with divided authority and divided responsibilities."

Martin's experiences led him to imagine a differently configured early Federal Reserve. Martin's father, William McChesney Martin Sr., was the St. Louis Fed's founding chairman. William Jr. fondly recalled childhood visits from Fed luminaries Benjamin Strong and Carter Glass, who debated his father on Fed policy and politics over the family dinner table.[9] Martin believed that the system's 1920s strength grew from interregional dialogue and consensus. He believed policies forged through inclusive processes were equally sound and more legitimate than those chosen by powerful central bankers. Martin also saw a diffusion of Fed power as necessary to defend its newfound autonomy. The fear was that if institutional power remained lodged in New York, the system could more easily succumb once again to treasury domination.

After joining the board, Martin formed an ad hoc subcommittee composed of himself and two other system newcomers to study the system's government securities market operations. The subcommittee report was released in November 1952. To secure the system's independence, the report recommended that investments be confined to short-dated bills, rather than bonds, and be made only to advance Fed policy objectives, not to support treasury financing demands. It also called for empowering the full FOMC to make open market policy and transferring supervisory authority over the open market desk agent to the full committee, whose "unique structure . . . exemplifies the unceasing search of the American democracy for forms of organization that combine centralized direction with decentralized control."[10] Under the current regime, the report cautioned, the New York president attended FOMC meetings "not only as a contributor," but also "as a protagonist for the actual day to day operation of the account." Sproul's role as supervisor of the open market desk agent made other committee members hesitate "to scrutinize adequately the technical operations of the account" because they were "reluctant to seem critical of a colleague." To "carry out more effectively his individual statutory responsibility as a committee member," the report urged all reserve bank presidents and board governors to better acquaint themselves with technical aspects of open market operations.

The FOMC considered the report in March 1953. It voted unanimously to change the policy directive from "maintaining orderly conditions in the Government securities market" to "correcting a disorderly situation."[11] The open market desk manager was also instructed to transact in "bills-only," rather than bonds. In deference to Sproul's firm objection, Martin postponed a discussion of changing the open market desk agent's supervisory structure. In a speech to the Economic Club of Detroit, Martin explained that the reform intended to build a freer government bond market, characterized by "depth, breadth, and resiliency."[12] World War II forced the Fed "to stabilize the price of Government securities in relation to a fixed pattern of yields," causing it to feed "forces that make for inflation." A peacetime peg would be undemocratic, however. "Dictated money rates breed dictated prices all across the board. This is characteristic of dictatorships. . . . It is not compatible with our institutions." Martin thus invoked Jeffersonian themes by calling to reduce the Fed's power and grow the scope of market forces.

At the next FOMC meeting, Sproul called for rescinding bills-only and giving "the executive committee more authority than . . . correcting disorderly markets." The "present prohibition puts a premium on sluggish action which would not meet the situations that may arise."[13] In some circumstances, Sproul argued, purchases of longer-dated securities would be more effective in sustaining financial and currency stability. A "doctrinaire attitude on free markets," Sproul contended, should not result in "sacrificing credit policy to untried theory." The executive committee needed "maximum freedom to operate." Sproul insisted on voting on his proposal over Martin's objection that only nine of twelve voting FOMC members were present. The vote broke down along institutional lines, with reserve bank presidents backing Sproul, handing him a five to four victory.

Martin began the next meeting by observing, "The thing I like most about the Federal Reserve is the word 'System.' The first two words don't make much difference but 'System' does."[14] He explained that the challenge facing the committee was finding the optimal degree of delegation to the executive committee and the open market desk. When another board member proposed reinstating bills-only, Martin asked Sproul to weigh in. "What I have been objecting to as a matter of principle," Sproul explained, "is trying to write into a 'constitution' of the Open Market Committee, a prohibition against actions deemed undesirable by particular members of the Committee, holding particular views, at a particular time. We can't afford a freeze of ideas or practice. . . . It was to avoid this straitjacket . . . that I proposed the June motion to rescind the March action." The St. Louis president, who had supported Sproul at the previous meeting, then explained that his thinking had changed. While he earlier agreed "to leave the executive committee a rather large area of discretion," because it "can be . . . quickly exercised by a smaller body," he was now swayed by arguments that the full FOMC could easily assemble by telephone. When other presidents seconded some of Sproul's concerns, Martin replied that "no tablets of stone were being written." Bills-only was restored by a nine to two vote.[15]

Martin and Sproul were later forced to air their differences before Congress. Martin explained the bills-only reform was meant "to foster a stronger, more self-reliant market for Government securities." In his view, the reform was a success, with "all sectors of the market . . . characterized by great improvement with respect to their depth, breadth, and resiliency."[16] Sproul told lawmakers he "wonder[ed] whether we are talking about the same market. . . . One of the virtues of credit control is supposed to be its ability to take prompt action to head off financial disturbances. . . . If open-market operations in longer term Government securities can be used to this end, I would use them rather than wait until . . . a crisis has developed."[17]

After the hearings, Martin finished his "historic democratization" of the FOMC.[18] In March, he proposed that the FOMC consider abolishing the executive committee. From a practical standpoint, "it would mean that only three additional Presidents . . . would need to come to

Washington ... to have a meeting of the full Committee."[19] Martin told his colleagues at the next meeting that "he considered the Open Market Committee to be the heart and core of the Federal Reserve System, and that the experience of the last few months gave further indication of the desirability of having the full Open Market Committee take the responsibility."[20] While Martin saw "merit in abolishing the executive committee. He recognized, however, that there might be another side to the question." He asked other committee members to voice any "doubts as to the desirability of such action." Sproul argued the proposal reflected a populist belief "that Congress gave this great power of directing open market operations of the Federal Reserve Banks to twelve men, the twelve men gave it to five, the five gave it to one, and it ended up in the hands of Wall Street."[21] Sproul argued that the executive committee remained vital because it was "a properly constituted body ... in a position to make policy, temporarily, on behalf of the full Committee on something better than an ad hoc basis." Emergency telephone conferences would be "no substitute for a face-to-face meeting at which ideas can be developed and debated, and the reaction of your associates to those ideas can be observed and taken into account."

While "there were still only twelve votes" on the FOMC, Martin explained, he hoped "to give everybody more participation rather than less participation than they might have had in the past."[22] Commercial air travel made frequent FOMC meetings practical. Martin proposed abolishing the executive committee and holding FOMC meetings every three weeks. All reserve bank presidents would be encouraged to attend, not just those five with voting rights. Unable to persuade his colleagues, Sproul joined them in voting unanimously to abolish the committee.

Sproul did manage to mount one successful defense of the status quo. He successfully argued against the plan to transfer supervisory authority over the open market desk agent to the FOMC. Sproul identified three "overlapping weaknesses. One is its substitution of individual responsibility for institutional responsibility. The second is its attempt to separate and segregate open market operations directed by the Federal Open Market Committee, from all other forms of central banking operations in the central money market of the country. The third is ... obstacles it would place in the way of executive recruitment, training and development."[23] Sproul proposed as an alternative having the FOMC weigh in on New York's desk agent appointments. The issue was then dropped, and New York retained control over FOMC policy implementation.

Martin's Fed transformation followed the opposite track of Marriner Eccles's. Rather than appealing to outside political authorities to build a new Fed hierarchy, Martin built a broad internal consensus to tear down inherited Fed institutions. The inclusive regime Martin built, like earlier Feds, was built on norms that skirted the law. Monetary policy was forged through "go-rounds" where all twelve reserve bank presidents and seven board governors spoke in a set order. The New York president spoke first and set the agenda, in recognition of New York's unique expertise. Martin spoke last to summarize the FOMC consensus, vacating his agenda-setting role.[24] If no consensus in favor of change emerged, policy remained unchanged. Sproul warned this sprawling process would move too slowly, but his defense of inherited hierarchies could not rival the appeal of Martin's calls for a more democratic and inclusive Fed and a freer reign of market forces. Defeated but unflappable, Sproul retired the following June. Advancing secular and political time, and a weakening global monetary order, would prove Sproul's fears correct.

The Limits of Independence under Eisenhower

Some scholars see the 1951 Accord as a divorce from the treasury, but the lived reality was much murkier.[25] Martin called for a freer government bond market and thought restricting purchases to short-dated treasury bills advanced that end, but he also endorsed Sproul's view that "independence . . . does not mean independence *from* the government, but independence *within* the government."[26] The system accepted two ongoing obligations to the treasury. First, during treasury bond issues, the FOMC stabilized interest rates, a practice known as "even keel."[27] Second, when a treasury bond issue threatened to fail, the FOMC stood by as buyer of last resort. Martin believed the system had an obligation to ensure that deficits authorized by Congress were funded. These practices reflected the limits of Fed autonomy under embedded liberalism.

In the 1950s, domestic and international circumstances aligned to make Martin's Fed workable. In 1952, Americans elected Republican war hero Dwight Eisenhower as president on a promise to end the Korean War. Republicans rode his coattails to win thin majorities in both houses of Congress. Formation of a Republican administration after two decades of Democratic rule called the future of the New Deal into question. Eisenhower emerged as an unlikely New Deal defender, however, protecting Social Security, unemployment insurance, and farm subsidy programs.[28]

To pay for this welfare state while balancing the budget, Eisenhower looked to rein in America's foreign commitments. He unwound the Korean War and announced a "New Look" defense policy that promised to reduce foreign troop deployments by bringing allies under the U.S. nuclear umbrella.[29] Unlike the 1920s, the return of Republican rule did not signal a return to isolationism.[30] Eisenhower led multilateral trade negotiations, sustained alliances, and opened U.S. markets to key allies. U.S. trade surpluses were recycled into the world economy through lending by investors and the World Bank, providing needed liquidity for growing world trade.[31]

Eisenhower's fiscal conservativism and global engagement fostered a benign environment in which Martin's Fed experiment could succeed. Fiscal orthodoxy ensured that deficits remained small, lowering pressure on the Fed to support the treasury.[32] Yet, in an era before treasury auctions, the Fed was called in for extraordinary support when bond issues threatened to fail. In 1953, it stemmed an incipient panic by buying $735 million in bonds and lowering reserve requirements.[33] Two years later, amid a Fed austerity campaign, the treasury sought help with a massive refunding. Martin asked the FOMC for $400 million in purchases, while promising to "make it clear that it is an exception. . . . It would be very unwise for the Treasury to think that at any time it gets into trouble on an issue the Federal Reserve will bail it out."[34]

This revealed a weakness of the system's position in America's embedded liberal order. Martin saw the Fed's purpose as lying in charting a countercyclical policy aimed at achieving price stability.[35] He told lawmakers the Fed's mission lay in "leaning against the breezes of inflation and deflation alike."[36] Yet, recurring demands for even keel and extraordinary treasury assistance imposed an inflationary bias on Fed policy. Eisenhower's aversion to fiscal deficits also placed an outsized burden on the Fed to combat downturns in the business cycle.

These pressures converged in Eisenhower's second term, revealing tensions between embedded liberalism in the United States and the Bretton Woods monetary order. The FOMC responded to a 1957 recession by aggressively buying bills. In 1958, the FOMC bought $1.7 billion in securities in response to a treasury appeal for extraordinary support, providing what one bank called "Herculean support of the refunding."[37] These two waves of Fed stimulus pushed treasury bill yields down from 3.4 percent at the onset of recession to .88 percent a year later. Short-term rates fell across the board, and U.S. capital began flowing abroad in search of higher returns.[38] The United States exported $2.2 billion of gold in 1958, 10 percent of its total supply.

The Activation and Decay of Fixed Exchange Rates under Eisenhower

As John H. Williams predicted, the postwar world was initially plagued by a chronic dollar shortage.[39] In a world of dollar scarcity, the expansionary bias of Martin's Fed helped stabilize the global economy. Bretton Woods was initially characterized by pervasive capital controls in Europe and capital mobility in the United States. European currencies were pegged to the dollar to facilitate growing trade, but capital controls enabled states to chart autonomous macroeconomic policies. The European Payments Union was established in 1950 to settle intra-European payments in dollars to conserve gold. It was run by the Bank for International Settlements, restoring central banks' traditional role of administering the world currency regime.

Europe experienced a remarkable recovery in the 1950s. As national reserves grew, countries looked to end their exchange controls. Currency convertibility was restored throughout Europe in 1958. Moving forward, the European Payments Union would be abolished, and Europeans would settle international payments on a bilateral basis, making dollars less useful. This restored a global competitive element over access to gold reserves which had been in retreat since the 1930s.[40] As a world of dollar scarcity gave way to a dollar glut, foreigners began questioning whether the United States had the gold and willpower to redeem the vast supply of dollars in global circulation. Economist Robert Triffin observed in 1957 that the "enormous improvement of foreign countries' reserves . . . has been primarily the result of a vast redistribution of net reserves from the United States to the rest of the world . . . such a movement could not continue indefinitely without eventually undermining confidence in the dollar itself."[41]

Central bankers on both sides of the Atlantic were alarmed by this turn of events. Bill Martin warned Congress in 1958, "There was an alarming spread of the belief, not only in this country but also abroad, that creeping inflation under modern economic conditions was to be a chronic and unavoidable condition."[42] If U.S. authorities allowed inflation to erode the dollar's purchasing power, foreigners would see their dollar reserves devalued. This fear was aggravated by the U.S.'s deteriorating balance-of-payments position. The United States continued experiencing trade surpluses, but surging capital exports and government expenditures overseas, particularly costs of stationing U.S. troops in Europe, raised the external deficit to $3.5 billion in 1958.[43]

Old guard conservatives in the Fed and Eisenhower administration believed austerity was needed to defend the dollar.[44] From July 1958 through December 1959, the Federal Funds rate, the rate banks charge each other to borrow funds overnight, climbed from .68 percent to 3.99 percent, and New York's discount rate was raised three times. After fiscal year 1959 yielded a $12.5 billion deficit, equal to 15 percent of the national budget, Eisenhower announced a 1960 austerity budget forecast to achieve a small surplus.[45] This show of restraint reassured investors. The external payments deficit climbed to $4.6 billion in 1959, but gold exports fell 60 percent.[46]

In 1960, Robert Triffin identified a core tension in the dollar's dual roles under Bretton Woods.[47] The dollar served both as a reserve currency, held by central banks and governments as a store of value, and a vehicle currency used to finance international trade. Since global trade was growing faster than the world's gold, U.S. payments deficits provided the liquidity needed to support growing trade. In this sense, U.S. deficits acted as a global public good. Paradoxically, however, they also eroded confidence in the dollar's future value. Triffin predicted that a global run on the dollar would end Bretton Woods unless a new source of international liquidity was found.

Three positions would emerge in the public debate over how to respond to Triffin's dilemma. Keynesians would endorse Triffin's proposal to end the longstanding practice of each nation housing its own reserves separately, and instead transfer them to the IMF. Under Triffin's plan, the IMF would issue a new synthetic reserve to supplement gold stocks. Milton Friedman led a Right populist charge to sever the dollar's link to gold, floating it on currency markets, while requiring the Fed to grow the money supply at a constant rate.[48] Each of these economic tribes called on the Fed to turn its powers to domestic uses, instead of dollar stabilization. Bill Martin, by contrast, called for an orthodox dollar defense. He told lawmakers in 1958, austerity was needed so "savers can have confidence in the future value of their investments."[49] Under his watch, the Fed would continue "the battle against the debasement of the currency with all of its perils to free institutions." Over the next decade, Martin would lead an old guard faction in the Fed and treasury which called for trimming external deficits to save Bretton Woods.

DEMOCRATIC RESURGENCE AND THE BATTLE TO SAVE BRETTON WOODS

On the presidential campaign trail in 1960, John F. Kennedy made the unprecedented promise to raise economic growth to a 5 percent annual rate. To figure out how to achieve that goal, he surrounded himself with Keynesian surrogates.[50] As a recession broke out in early 1960 and lingered into the summer, Vice President Richard Nixon, Kennedy's opponent, struggled to separate himself from Eisenhower's austerity. With faith in the dollar waning, growing prospects of a Kennedy victory led to a surge in dollar speculation.[51] Two weeks before the election, the London gold price peaked at $40.60 an ounce, more than five dollars above the declared parity. Speculation ebbed when Kennedy promised to keep the dollar on gold, and he went on to narrowly defeat Nixon. Kennedy was joined by wide Democratic majorities in both houses of Congress, signaling the potential rise of a Democratic partisan regime.

The Left-leaning tilt of Kennedy's economic team eroded the credibility of his gold pledge. Eisenhower saw the gold-linked dollar as a cornerstone of the Western alliance, however.[52] After the election, he alerted Kennedy to the balance-of-payments problem and authorized the New York Fed to start sending a representative to monthly Bank for International Settlements meetings in Basel. Three decades after its diplomatic role was rejected, the New York Fed reemerged as America's global monetary ambassador.[53] Kennedy formed a balance-of-payments task force headed by former New York Fed president Allan Sproul.[54] Its report, submitted days before the inauguration, outlined two paths to restore international balance. It warned against a "restrictionist" course that would withdraw troops from Europe and reduce foreign aid. It recommended instead an "expansionist" path, which would aim to boost exports by lowering tariffs, promote foreign tourism inside the United States, and shift some troop deployment costs onto Europeans. The report's most urgent recommendation was to appoint a treasury secretary "who enjoys high respect and confidence in the international financial world."[55]

Like all new presidents, Kennedy faced cross-pressures while transitioning from campaigning to governing. Walter Heller, an academic Keynesian whom Kennedy appointed chair of the Council of Economic

Advisors, saw the dollar's global role as posing a "cruel dilemma."[56] He and other party-aligned economists had promised bold action to boost growth, but enactment of their expansionary schemes would widen the external payments deficit. Keynesians were placed throughout the administration, with the exception of the treasury.[57] They urged Kennedy to move forward with fiscal and monetary stimulus to boost growth while launching political negotiations to reform the world monetary system along Triffinite lines.

Keynesians were flanked by an old guard faction in the treasury and Federal Reserve. Acting on the balance of payments task force recommendation, Kennedy appointed Eisenhower holdover C. Douglas Dillon, a Wall Street regular, as treasury secretary. Dillon and Bill Martin would emerge as allies on an informal administration working group called the Quadriad, composed of the U.S. president, the treasury secretary, the director of the bureau of the budget, and chairs of the Federal Reserve Board of Governors and Council of Economic Advisors. Dillon would also cement ties with the New York Fed by recruiting its vice president of research, Robert Roosa, as the undersecretary of treasury for monetary affairs.[58]

Eisenhower's lame-duck maneuverings helped the old guard shape Kennedy's thinking. The New York Fed representative reported back from a December Bank for International Settlements meeting that "European central bankers . . . show signs of acute anxiety as to the future of the dollar . . . reflected in almost aggressive questioning as to the prospective policies of the new administration."[59] New York Fed president Alfred Hayes attended the January meeting and promised that Kennedy would not abandon U.S. commitments to free trade, capital mobility, and dollar convertibility into gold at the existing parity.[60] Hayes was warned not to "nullify European cooperative action by allowing [U.S.] interest rates to drop further." Kennedy backed up Hayes's promise two weeks after his inauguration by declaring that the "United States official dollar price of gold can and will be maintained at $35 an ounce. Exchange controls over trade and investment will not be invoked. Our national security and economic assistance programs will be carried forward. . . . Those who hope for speculative reasons for an increase in the price of gold will find their hopes in vain."[61] The speech finally quelled dollar speculation. Investors believed that the dollar's gold parity would stand, at least in the short run.[62]

This book argues that ascendant parties unleash populist forces, which penetrate the Federal Reserve and reshape its environment. Indeed, dollar speculation would flare intermittently for the rest of the decade. Under Kennedy, however, the old guard would successfully block Keynesians' expansionary schemes. This reflected Kennedy's belief, inherited from his father, that currency devaluation entailed an insufferable loss of national prestige. He often told his advisors "the two things which scared him most were nuclear war and the payments deficit."[63]

Rather than taking action to close the payments deficit or negotiate Triffinite reform, however, Kennedy greenlighted projects that pulled the Federal Reserve in opposite directions. He authorized Treasury Undersecretary Robert Roosa to work with European central banks to build linkages to combat currency speculation, but he also heeded Walter Heller's advice to use his appointment power to insert proponents of Keynesian ideas onto the Board of Governors. The rest of this section explains how these projects collided and how the introduction of a new ideological pole onto the FOMC paralyzed its policy deliberations.

THE OLD GUARD MISSION TO SAVE BRETTON WOODS

America lost nearly one-quarter of its gold reserves from 1958 to 1960. In 1961, its gold stock stood at seventeen billion dollars. Twelve billion was required to back domestic currency, so only five billion dollars' worth of gold was available to foreigners for dollar redemption (see Figure 4.1). Two views emerged among old guard officials regarding actions needed to strengthen the dollar. Treasury Secretary Dillon believed the United States needed to actively rein in its foreign expenditures and suggested withdrawing U.S. troops from abroad if European allies refused to pay the costs of stationing them.[64] Robert Roosa, by contrast, thought the external deficit could be managed in the short run and would diminish over time. The United States ran steady trade surpluses with the outside world, which Roosa believed would eventually pull its international payments back into balance. The task of mending Bretton Woods, in this view, was one of persuading Europeans to temporarily finance U.S. deficits while forging new cooperative linkages to fight currency speculation.

Roosa led the charge to strengthen Bretton Woods. Among his first treasury tasks was to ask the FOMC to end "bills only" and begin buying longer-dated bonds. This reflected the view among Keynesians in the administration that the external deficit grew from low short-term interest rates in the United States, which pushed capital abroad. "Bills-only" contributed to this problem by pushing down short-term rates across the

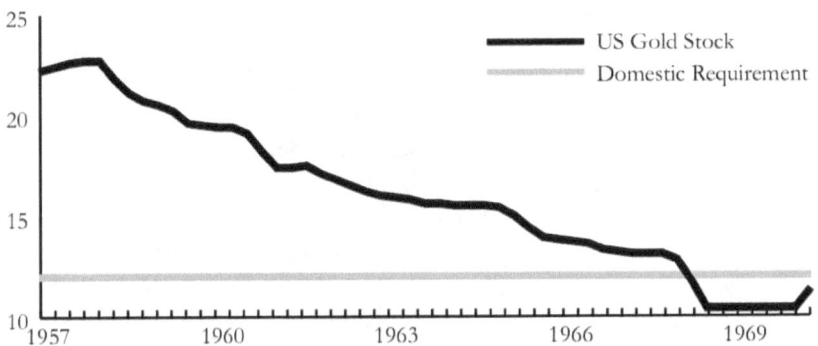

Figure 4.1. U.S. Monetary Gold Stock and Domestic Currency Collateral (billions of dollars). *Source:* Monetary Gold Stock for United States, M1476CUSM144N-NBR, National Bureau of Economics, Cambridge, MA.

credit spectrum. To foster a more appealing investment climate, the Fed was enlisted into supporting "Operation Twist," a program that sought to raise short-term rates while pushing down long-term rates. The idea was that the Fed could boost long-term investment while shrinking the external deficit by shifting its portfolio.

After Kennedy's election, Martin told the FOMC he was skeptical of the view that "all our problems—the budget, the cost-price relationship, debt management policy . . . could be solved if the System would just raise short-term interest rates and lower long-term interest rates."[65] Martin bowed to a "heavy barrage . . . from within and outside Government" after the inauguration, however, and asked the FOMC to buy bonds "to give some tangible indication of open-mindedness and willingness to experiment."[66] Citing the "delicate international situation," however, Martin stressed the contingency of Fed support. "We are confronted with an increased emphasis on experimentation in . . . fiscal policy and debt management. While we should welcome these innovations to the extent that they may relieve monetary policy from carrying the whole load of countercyclical action, we should not let an inactive or an inflexible posture on our part encourage unwise actions in these other areas of public policy."

Fed officials more readily embraced Robert Roosa's plan for building the dollar's "outer perimeter defenses."[67] Roosa enlisted European central banks to finance U.S. external deficits by marketing bonds paid for in dollars, but which paid out in Swiss francs. These "Roosa bonds" transferred currency risk to the United States.[68] The New York Fed forged the second tier of dollar defenses, new central bank linkages to repel currency speculation. European central banks were enlisted to form a gold buyers' cartel called the London Gold Pool. Under this system, the Fed and other central banks agreed to have the Bank of England act as an agent to buy and sell gold on their behalf, to prevent competition among them from bidding up gold's price. They agreed to sell up to $270 million in gold if the market price rose above $35.20.[69] The New York Fed also spearheaded the construction of a currency swap network.[70] Under this system, a country faced with a speculative currency attack could tap standing credit lines with foreign central banks to fight it. Martin enlisted Roosa to secure FOMC approval for Fed participation in the swap network. Roosa wrote, "Only the central bank can make the prompt, smooth adjustments that are called for [in a currency crisis]. The very existence of a central banking capability for coping effectively with volatile flows can give confidence to international traders and investors."[71] One scholar observed that these new central bank ties "revived in a straightforward way the day-to-day collaboration maintained in the 1920s between Governors Strong and Norman."[72]

Walter Heller's Transformative Fed Ambition

Walter Heller took over the Council of Economic Advisors in 1961 with a clear agenda. Although an economic expansion was underway, unemployment remained high at 6.8 percent.[73] Heller wanted to deploy expansionary fiscal and monetary policies to accelerate growth and lower unemployment. Conservatives in Congress and the treasury loomed as obstacles to Heller's proposed income tax cut. Heller believed Bill Martin was the main actor preventing the Fed from embracing a more expansionary monetary policy. Heller complained to Kennedy that Fed support for Operation Twist was "timid" and half-hearted," worrying that it might fail due to "the Fed's loss of conviction and heart."[74] To ensure its success, "Martin's back needs to be stiffened."[75]

When a board vacancy opened in Kennedy's first year, Heller encouraged Kennedy to appoint George Mitchell, the chief economist of the Chicago Fed. In Heller's view, Mitchell's unique combination of academic, Fed, and partisan credentials made him an excellent candidate to eventually replace Martin. Mitchell held an economics PhD and directed research at one of the system's most prominent reserve banks. He had proven his partisan chops in 1956 by working on Adlai Stevenson's failed presidential bid. Heller told Kennedy that Mitchell's "sympathy lies strongly with the president. He is not prepared to accept every move that Bill Martin makes."[76] Heller's persuasion campaign worked. Kennedy agreed to appoint Mitchell.

Heller's successful intervention weakened a pillar of Martin's consensual Fed process. Under Eisenhower, Martin had established an appointment norm whereby the Fed chair and treasury secretary jointly identified and vetted board candidates while honoring the FRA requirement that the board reflect "a fair representation of the financial, agricultural, industrial, and commercial interests, and geographical divisions of the country."[77] When Heller studied the board's ranks in 1961, he found a former comptroller, two small-town bankers, two college deans, and Martin. No economist had served as a governor since Adolph Miller retired in 1936. Board diversity helped sustain deference to New York's ideational authority. Old guard officials began and ended Martin's FOMC "go-rounds," with the New York Fed president speaking first and Martin last. With no opposing ideas between them, the old guard faction steered Martin's sprawling Fed.

The old guard would rally to block further advances of Heller's Fed makeover under Kennedy. When Martin's term as chairman was set to expire in 1963, the treasury secretary demanded he be reappointed to avoid "any foreign loss of confidence in the dollar."[78] Kennedy asked Martin to stay on. He told Heller, "I need Martin and Dillon. I need these Republicans to maintain a strong front as far as the financial community is concerned."[79] This was ironic because Martin was a lifelong Democrat. When another board vacancy opened, Heller proposed Harvard economist Seymour Harris, a vocal Fed critic. Dillon again intervened, warning that Harris's appointment would "be interpreted as . . . undermining the soundness of the Federal Reserve Board."[80] Kennedy instead backed Martin and Dillon's chosen candidate, J. Dewey Daane, a holdover from Eisenhower's treasury and former Minneapolis Fed vice president.

Monetary Policy Deadlock under Kennedy

Heller's belief that George Mitchell would tilt the Fed toward a more expansionary policy proved correct, but not in the way he expected. Rather than persuading other officials to lower interest rates, Mitchell prevented them from raising them. Previously, the FOMC raised interest rates as business expansions matured to prevent inflation from rising. When recovery began in 1958, for example, the Federal Funds rate, the rate charged by banks to one another to borrow funds overnight, rose from .25 percent to 4 percent in eighteen months. After growth returned in 1961, the Federal Funds rate took 49 months to rise from 1.5 percent to 4 percent.[81] When the FOMC agreed to begin restricting credit in December 1961, Mitchell dissented, explaining he "did not think this was the right time to start tightening."[82] In coming years, the New York Fed president and Martin would repeatedly propose rate hikes to shore up foreign confidence in the dollar, which Mitchell would oppose by citing domestic conditions.

The old guard and Mitchell bought different facts to bear on policy discussions. New York voiced the concerns of European central bankers, including alarm at the United States' balance-of-payments deficit and low interest rates. Echoing Keynesian orthodoxy, Mitchell argued that monetary restraint was powerless to improve the dollar's global position but would harm the domestic economy. He cited unused industrial capacity, unemployment, and low inflation rates, to call for keeping rates low. Two scholars observe, "On multiple occasions, the two groups deadlocked, resulting in no change in policy. Policy almost certainly would have been loosened . . . absent the importance attached by the first faction to balance-of-payments considerations."[83]

Layered atop this international/domestic divide was a creeping uptick in the system's treasury financing burden. The Kennedy administration presided over recurring fiscal deficits. A growing national debt caused the treasury to more frequently issue bonds, resulting in more demands for "even keel" stabilization of interest rates. One governor explained the FOMC's problem was one of "trying to strike a balance between the domestic situation and the international situation . . . [compounded by] the fact that a Treasury refunding [is] in the offing."[84] Martin agreed "the consensus today was essentially to maintain an even keel."[85]

The Kennedy years were marked by stalemates, which locked macroeconomic policy in a mildly expansionary stance, but broader trends offered hope for Bretton Woods's survival. A 1963 Brookings Institution study predicted that the United States would return to a balance-of-payments surplus by 1968.[86] Indeed, America's merchandise trade surplus rose from $1.1 billion in 1959 to $6.8 billion in 1964.[87] Gold exports slowed. When Kennedy died in November 1963, the United States had

$15.6 billion in gold, $3.6 billion above the legal minimum for domestic currency. Central bankers had reason for optimism that cooperation could save Bretton Woods. The ascent of Lyndon Johnson to the presidency would darken these prospects, however. Johnson's search for transformative change at home and abroad would cause the United States' fiscal and balance-of-payments deficits to explode. Johnson would empower Keynesians by pushing through an income tax cut, launching international political negotiations for Triffinite monetary reform, and greenlighting an economist takeover of the board of governors. Johnson's later choices to escalate wars in Vietnam and against domestic poverty would curb Keynesians' influence, however, and once again put the Federal Reserve in a position of monetizing deficits. In this crumbling environment, Bill Martin would rally the Fed for one last defense of the dollar.

War, Democratic Decay, and the Fed's Technocratic Makeover

After being sworn in as president, Lyndon Johnson told Walter Heller, "I'm no budget slasher . . . I am a Roosevelt New Dealer."[88] With the next presidential election a year out, Johnson prioritized passing Heller's income tax cut. In his 1964 State of the Union address, Johnson declared an "unconditional war on poverty in America," promising bold government action to raise living standards for the poor.[89] The tax cut was enacted in February, breathing life into the Keynesian fiscal experiment. Heller warned against Fed austerity in the *New York Times*, writing that a "strong upswing in the economy need not bring . . . high interest rates. It would be self-defeating to cancel the stimulus of the tax reduction by tightening money."[90] Heller had reason to worry. Martin told the FOMC months before, "If the present euphoria is translated into a tax cut into a real surge in the economy, we might be faced with the need for . . . drastic action to be taken at the first opportunity."[91] Martin feared fiscal stimulus would widen the external deficit, inviting a run on America's meager gold reserves.

In the short run, these fears were overblown. Johnson would ride a booming economy to a landslide reelection and the balance of payments stabilized. Voters handed Johnson a mandate to bring his envisioned Great Society to life by electing one of the most liberal Congresses in history. Johnson would flex partisan strength to launch wars at home and abroad, seize control of the global monetary reform agenda, and empower economists to remake the Fed.

Johnson's Wars, the Failure of the New Economics, and the Decline of Bretton Woods

Political economists contend that politicians must choose between guns and butter. Resources spent fighting wars must be paid for through taxes, social spending cuts, or inflation. Lyndon Johnson's presidency is often seen as illustrative of the perils of failing to make this choice. After cutting taxes, Johnson would steer several new social programs through Congress.[92] Johnson would also quietly escalate the war in Vietnam, fearing congressional appropriators would cut his social programs if they learned about rising troop deployments. This string of choices locked fiscal policy into a strongly expansionary stance. While Keynesians cheered on fiscal stimulus, they would soon learn that is easier to lower taxes in the United States than to raise them. Surging deficits would unleash a "great inflation" that felled Bretton Woods.[93]

The Johnson Administration started with a string of victories for Keynesians. The 1964 income tax cut was the first in history designed to accelerate growth.[94] To blunt its impact on the balance of payments, the treasury announced a "voluntary" capital export restraint program, discouraging U.S. banks and corporations from lending abroad.[95] Unwilling to sell this policy reversal to his foreign counterparts, Douglas Dillon left the treasury. His replacement, Henry Fowler, signaled the ascent of Keynesian ideas inside the treasury.[96] With his ally gone, Bill Martin sought to resign. Johnson rejected Martin's request, however, insisting he could not lose both Dillon and Martin without damaging America's reputation with the financial community.

Keynesians scored an ideational victory in 1965 when Robert Roosa endorsed the creation of a synthetic IMF-issued "Drawing Unit Reserve Asset" to supplement the world's gold stocks.[97] After working for years to fix Bretton Woods, Roosa now agreed that the fixed exchange system was doomed unless a new global reserve asset was created to remove pressure on the dollar. In July, the treasury announced that the U.S. would spearhead negotiations at the G-10 to create the new reserve.[98] The next Bank for International Settlements meeting had an atmosphere of "astonishment, puzzlement and resentment."[99] Central bankers believed their own efforts to keep Bretton Woods afloat were working, and were doubtful that U.S.-led political negotiations would yield broadly beneficial monetary reform.

These Keynesian victories would soon prove hollow, however. Board governor Sherman Maisel, the first governor appointed directly from academia, later reflected that Johnson's 1965 choice to escalate the Vietnam War "dominated most of the economic developments for the next eight years; yet . . . was never thought of as a basic economic decision."[100] By the end of 1965, however, Keynesians began to understand that the economy was overheating. Walter Heller urged Johnson "[t]o switch, temporarily, from expansion to restriction in fiscal policy," proposing a "Defense Surtax" or "Freedom Surtax" to fund the war.[101] Other Keynesians also urged Johnson to raise taxes, but he evaded the issue because he knew that conservatives in Congress would demand cuts to Great Society programs in exchange for a tax increase.

Bill Martin was quicker in recognizing rising economic dangers. Over the summer of 1965, he learned from contacts in the defense community that military spending was rising. Martin warned in a Columbia University commencement address of "disquieting similarities between our present prosperity and the fabulous twenties. . . . Then, as now, government officials, scholars, and businessmen are convinced that a new economic era has opened, an era in which business fluctuations have become a thing of the past."[102] Americans needed to consider the "international implications of national events and policies." Over the next three years, Martin would be a thorn in Johnson's side, goading him privately and publicly to raise taxes to defend the dollar.[103] Johnson would finally call for a 6 percent income tax surcharge to fund the war in his 1967 State of the Union address, but he didn't follow through.[104] In June, Martin would call for a larger 10 percent surcharge "to bring federal income and expenditures closer to balance."[105] As inflation climbed with no tax hike on the horizon, it became apparent that the Keynesian fiscal fine-tuning experiment had failed.

It would take the United States effectively crashing out of Bretton Woods to spur legislators to action. Through 1964, the London Gold Pool had ran a cumulative $1.2 billion surplus, adding gold reserves to central banks' stocks.[106] This changed after February 1965, however, when French president Charles de Gaulle announced France would begin trading its dollars for gold, observing, "The convention whereby the dollar is given a transcendent value as international currency no longer rests on its initial base, namely, the possession by America of most of the gold in the world."[107] The United States took over France's share in the London Gold Pool, but it began hemorrhaging gold. In June 1967, Bill Martin promised

Europeans that the U.S. would sell its gold "to the last bar . . . in defense of the gold price."[108] America's weakened position undermined Martin's credibility, however. The U.S. gold reserve now stood just $1 billion above the $12 billion required for domestic currency. In this precarious environment, the G-10 authorized the IMF to issue Special Drawing Rights, a new synthetic reserve, to supplement gold.[109]

Great Britain triggered a run on the London Gold Pool in October 1967 by announcing that it would devalue the pound. By March 1968, the pool had run a $3.7 billion cumulative deficit. U.S. gold stocks had fallen $1 billion below their legal minimum. The treasury announced it would leave the gold pool and Martin summoned central bankers to Washington, D.C., for an emergency conference.[110] Martin began the meeting by declaring that the United States would sustain its gold-dollar parity and called for endorsing the IMF Special Drawing Rights proposal. The central bankers reluctantly agreed and dissolved the gold pool. A two-tiered gold market was established, with official international payments carried out at official gold parities. Gold prices could fluctuate in a separate private gold market. The U.S. treasury then halted gold exports, effectively ending dollar convertibility into gold.[111]

Two weeks later, Lyndon Johnson shocked the world by announcing that he would not seek reelection. In his address, Johnson demanded "passage of a tax bill now," but Congress continued dragging its feet.[112] Two months later, Bill Martin warned in a Yale speech that if the dollar was taken off of gold, the government might be forced to implement "controls over wages, prices, and credit."[113] In June, Congress finally passed a one-year 10 percent income tax surcharge.[114] In an atmosphere of rising social and economic disorder, the Democratic Party crumbled. The year featured antiwar protests, a string of political assassinations, and riots in cities throughout the country. The social unraveling came to a head at the Democratic National Convention in Chicago, which descended into chaos when party insiders nominated vice president Hubert Humphrey as the party's presidential candidate. Humphrey would struggle to distance himself from the unpopular Vietnam war and lost the presidential contest to Republican Richard Nixon.

When Doves became Hawks:
The Board's Keynesian Invasion and Conversion

Lyndon Johnson made three Board of Governors appointments. The first two came in the wake of the Democratic 1964 landslide. When a board vacancy opened in 1965, Martin urged Johnson to appoint a banker because no other governor had banking experience. Instead, Johnson chose University of California economist Sherman Maisel, an academic economist with no Fed experience.[115] When another vacancy opened a year later, Martin urged Johnson to appoint the head of a food processing company. Instead, Johnson followed Walter Heller's advice by appointing Andrew Brimmer, a thirty-nine-year-old African American with a Harvard PhD in monetary economics.[116] Martin told Johnson that he and Kennedy had "ignored the law" by appointing "a majority from the same profession."[117] He warned that an economist-laden board "would damage confidence and gravely impair the ability of the Federal Reserve to carry out functions of vital importance to the economy and the government alike."

Martin first explained the Fed's wartime dilemma to the FOMC in November 1965. "The Treasury's financial problem . . . would either be solved by a pause in business activity . . . or else it would have to be solved . . . by an aggressively easier policy on the part of the Federal Reserve. The situation was getting . . . similar to . . . the time of the . . . accord in 1951."[118] A month before, the New York Fed president had called for raising "the discount rate [as] the most appropriate method of signaling a move toward greater firmness in monetary policy" in light of America's "serious international payments problem . . . [which] leaves us little margin for assuming inflation risk."[119] This old guard script would dominate Fed policymaking for the rest of the decade.

In December, the board voted four to three to raise the discount rate, overcoming opposition from the administration and board economists.[120] Recent appointee Sherman Maisel argued against the hike, explaining "the extra kick of Vietnam-induced demand" had helped the U.S. approach "a full-employment economy." After the vote, Martin visited Lyndon Johnson's Texas ranch and received a dose of the infamous Johnson "treatment," which on this occasion involved a tongue-lashing amid a high-speed drive across hilly dirt roads.[121] Martin refused to budge.

Two weeks later, governor George Mitchell told Congress he feared the discount hike was "interpreted by the public as a decisive shift toward more restrictive monetary policy. And it may prove to be so. A higher discount rate can influence future open market policy toward greater restrictiveness."[122] Mitchell was right, but not the way he imagined. As inflation surged and lawmakers ignored pleas for tax hikes, board economists embraced Fed austerity. To Johnson's dismay, his appointee Andrew Brimmer accelerated this process. Brimmer had previously worked in the

New York Fed research department while completing his PhD at Harvard, and previously served as a commerce department spokesperson for balance-of-payments issues.[123] Brimmer solidified a growing board majority in favor of monetary restraint to tackle inflation. Sherman Maisel wrote in his diary, "[D]oves now became hawks."[124]

Martin would lead three austerity campaigns from 1966 through 1969, each time pushing the economy to the brink of crisis. The FOMC began tightening open market policy in Spring 1966, pushing the federal funds rate above 5 percent. Martin underwent prostate surgery in June, sidelining him for two months. Brimmer led the charge for greater austerity into July, urging "as much firmness as possible . . . and an increase in the discount rate when the time is propitious."[125] No further tightening would be forthcoming, however, as a "credit crunch" enveloped the economy.[126] As market interest rates climbed above Fed Regulation Q deposit rate ceilings, depositors began withdrawing funds from commercial banks and savings and loans. This disintermediation process posed an existential threat to many financial intermediaries and slowed the flow of credit into mortgage and municipal bond markets. Contractors and local government agents complained to their congressmen, who demanded relief from the Fed. Amid a fierce political backlash, the Fed eased off the monetary brakes.

With his fourth term as chairman set to expire in March 1967, Martin sought to retire. He told Johnson he had served "too long. . . . I do not want to complicate the problems you are facing."[127] Johnson begged him to stay, however. "I desperately need you to continue. . . . If it were not for Vietnam, I would be willing to let you retire." A year before making his announcement public, Johnson had confided in Martin, "I have decided not to run again in 1968. . . . I am asking you to stay with me, if your conscience permits, until the inauguration of a new president in 1969." In exchange for Martin's agreement to stay, Johnson appointed Federal Deposit Insurance Corporation director William Sherrill to fill a board vacancy instead of another economist. This changing dynamic reflected Johnson's waning power.

Britain's devaluation in October 1967 began the next Fed tightening campaign. The FOMC voted unanimously to tighten open market policy at each subsequent meeting into April 1968.[128] The Federal Funds rate rose from 3.88 percent to 6.11 percent, and the board approved two discount hikes "to strengthen the international position of the dollar and to combat domestic inflationary pressures."[129] When Congress finally passed a tax surcharge in June, the FOMC relented. Economists warned that keeping interest rates stable amid fiscal tightening would produce "overkill," pushing the economy into recession.[130] Board Keynesians successfully demanded a quarter-of-a-point discount rate reduction. After the November elections, however, it became clear that the tax surcharge was failing to restrain growth or slow inflation. A board staff economist confessed to the FOMC that "[t]he outpouring of economic good news ... has been so overwhelming that, for a staff projecting a slowing in expansion, it has seemed almost unbearable."[131]

The old guard began its final dollar defense in December 1968, a month before Nixon took office. The New York Fed president told the FOMC that capital outflows point "to the vital need to improve the trade surplus.... There is no doubt in my mind that the major objective of monetary policy ... should be to seek an appreciably slower rate of bank credit expansion as a contribution to the long-sought slowing of the economy."[132] A directive calling for "firmer conditions in money and short-term credit markets" passed unanimously. The board also raised discount rates to "contribute to a reduction of inflationary pressures in the economy."[133]

In February, Martin told the congressional Joint Economic Committee that the Fed "was overly optimistic in anticipating immediate benefits from fiscal restraint ... but now we mean business in stopping inflation. A credibility gap exists in the business and financial community as to whether the Federal Reserve will push restraint hard enough to check inflation. The Board means to do so and is unanimous on that point."[134] When asked if higher interest rates might cause a recession, Martin replied, "You must take risks. In the last few years we have not taken real risks." In April, the board raised discount rates to 6 percent at all twelve banks, the highest level since 1929. The Federal Funds Rate surged from 6 percent in December to 8.9 percent in June.[135] The FOMC would endorse "prevailing firm conditions in money and short-term credit markets" for the rest of the year, but the hawkish Fed consensus was faltering.[136]

Martin's Egalitarian Fed Crumbles: Arthur Burns's Takeover

Richard Nixon was furious. When his economic advisers explained the April rate hikes were intended to cool the economy, he responded that a 1958 dose of Fed austerity had "cooled off the economy and cooled off

15 [Republican] Senators and 60 congressmen at the same time."[137] Nixon had an axe to grind with Bill Martin, whom he blamed for his 1960 presidential defeat. In March 1960, Council of Economic Advisors chairman Arthur Burns had warned Nixon the economy would "dip just before the elections" unless the Fed lowered interest rates.[138] Nixon asked Martin for help but felt ignored. After winning the 1968 election, Nixon asked Martin to resign so Burns could take his place. Martin declined, stating he would serve the rest of his term, which would expire in January 1970. Martin warned against appointing "another professional economist to the Board, especially one in his sixties."[139] He told Nixon, "Your administration has to deal with inflation effectively from the beginning if it is not going to get out of control."

Nixon reluctantly endorsed an extension of the expiring tax surcharge.[140] Democrats in Congress played hardball, however, and agreed to extend the 10 percent surcharge for only six months before lowering it to 5 percent for the rest of the year. In return, they extracted concessions including a capital gains tax hike and excluding low-income groups from income taxes. Whereas the first tax surcharge narrowed the budget deficit from $27.7 billion in fiscal 1968 to $500 million in 1969, the deficit would creep back up to $7 billion in 1970.

In October 1969, Nixon called Martin to the Oval Office to tell him he would announce Arthur Burns's nomination as Fed chair, rendering Martin a lame duck. At his December Senate confirmation hearing, Burns told lawmakers interest rates would soon fall. Martin bowed to the inevitable at his last FOMC meeting in January, voting with the majority to ease policy. Despite the Fed's heroic efforts, consumer prices had risen at a 6 percent rate in 1969, up from 4.7 percent two years earlier. Martin told the governors at his farewell lunch, "I've failed."[141]

Burns began his first FOMC meeting in February by declaring "a rethinking of monetary policy was in order. . . . Just as military campaigns had been lost because the generals were fighting yesterday's wars, monetary policy could go wrong if it were formulated on the basis of past rather than current and prospective conditions."[142] Burns wanted the Fed to abandon the old guard's war to stabilize the dollar. With the economy on the brink of recession, Burns called for an expansionary policy to push down rates. Burns jettisoned the preset "go-round" speaking order, allowing committee members to challenge him at their own volition. The New York Fed president did so by observing, "Now that real growth in the economy has apparently come to a stop, it is not surprising that . . . arguments are being advanced in favor of relaxing . . . [but a] rise in unemployment is a necessary condition to checking the inflationary spiral."[143] Governor Andrew Brimmer agreed: "The Committee had been trying for some time to achieve the current slowing of the economy and it should not reverse its course too soon . . . [or] lose sight of the highly unfavorable outlook for the balance of payments."[144] Afterward, Burns declared a "consensus to the effect that some movement away from the prevailing degree of restraint would be salutary at this time."[145] When the New York president challenged Burns's claim of consensus, Burns replied, "The question of whether a majority favored some move toward less firm money market conditions could . . . be readily resolved by a vote." He told the committee he had drafted his own policy directive in advance, which he insisted the committee vote on. The vote passed nine to three, signaling the fall of the Fed's old guard and the ascent of board technocrats.

Consolidating Fed Technocracy

In a series of bold reforms, Arthur Burns seized control of the Fed agenda and upended Martin's inclusive Fed regime. In his first week as chair, Burns told the board he planned to cut its meetings from five a week to three, that he would end the FOMC practice of having everyone speak in policy "go-rounds," and that he planned to replace the New York representative at the Bank for International Settlements with a board governor.[146] Unlike Martin, who vacated an agenda-setting role by speaking last in policy "go-rounds," Burns sought to wield Fed power. He would later brag in an interview, "I vote *first*. I'm willing to stick my neck out. I think it's important that I make my position known. A Chairman who sits there until everyone has made his position known and then votes with the majority—what kind of leadership is that?"[147]

Burns's brash style was off-putting, but many Board members secretly cheered on the emerging constellation of Fed power. The seeds of a more technocratic board were first laid in 1961, when Kennedy appointed George Mitchell as an ideological counterweight to Martin. Lyndon Johnson went farther in 1965 by appointing Sherman Maisel, an academic economist with no Fed experience. Maisel was shocked when he first attended FOMC meetings and learned that committee members lacked a common policy language.[148] The Fed old guard cited trends in gold stocks and the balance of payments, inflationary pressures, and market psychology, to demand policy adjustments. The Keynesian governors Maisel and

Mitchell, by contrast, invoked measures of idle industrial capacity, unemployment, and observed inflation, to argue in favor of bending monetary policy toward domestic priorities. Maisel sought to bridge this divide, and assert greater control over policy implementation, by replacing qualitative policy directives that tasked the open market desk agent with achieving greater money market "ease" or "firmness," with quantitative targets such as M1, the amount of demand deposits and currency in domestic circulation. Martin fought this change. Maisel recalled that Martin believed the FOMC "shouldn't think about the aggregates at all. It should only think about money market conditions and their impact on psychology in the financial markets and, therefore, in the real market."[149]

Martin's principled commitment to inclusivity made him amenable to another Maisel-led project, however, of growing the board's capacity and expertise. Maisel spearheaded a board project of massively growing the board's technical staff of economists, having them forge new models and forecasts, and integrating those policy tools into the monetary policy process. In Maisel's first year, the board staff began supplementing a "greenbook" it distributed before FOMC meetings which described current economic and financial conditions, with a "bluebook" that considered future prospects and contained measures of monetary aggregates.[150] Maisel led a collaboration among the Board of Governors Division of Research and Statistics and University of Pennsylvania and MIT economists to develop a new economic forecasting model.[151]

By 1968, the board staff's economic forecasts were featured in bluebook supplements and increasingly invoked as important pieces of information in FOMC policy discussions. Maisel later recalled that Martin "allowed and even encouraged the staff to explore new techniques, but . . . adhered to his belief that real quantification was impossible, that it would downgrade judgment and intuition, and therefore would lead to greater errors."[152] After the forecasts erred by predicting a sharp economic slowdown in the wake of the 1968 tax surcharge, Martin questioned whether the FOMC should continue using forecasts to shape monetary policy.[153]

While Martin opposed Maisel's plan to incorporate quantitative targets into FOMC policy directives, he allowed Maisel to lead an ad hoc committee on the directive. Its final report would not be delivered until two months after Martin retired, but the FOMC adopted one of its proposed reforms at Martin's final FOMC meeting.[154] Moving forward, the board staff would include three proposed policy directives in the bluebook supplement, alternatives A, B, and C, which would alternatively make policy tighter, easier, or leave it unchanged.

It was in this setting that this book's opening scene unfolded, when retiring Philadelphia Fed president Karl Bopp lectured his board colleagues to check their hubris. Bopp had once been in their shoes, a young economist who transitioned from academia to the Federal Reserve. But Bopp earned his position of esteem within the system through decades of hard work, often in deference to elders and inherited systems he did not always agree with. Like Martin, Bopp was skeptical of the usefulness of existing economic models and forecasts in steering monetary policy decisions. Bopp warned at his last FOMC meeting that "ignorance" of "linkages among financial and real economic variables" in existing models "was colossal."[155] Until the FOMC better understood monetary policy's impacts, it should "hesitate . . . to follow recommendations as to policy that might be provided by a computer." To remedy these ideational deficiencies, Bopp encouraged further allocation of "significant resources to developing knowledge."

Bopp also chided the board technocrats for seeking to strip autonomy from open market desk managers in New York by attaching narrow quantitative targets to policy directives. "Hold the Managers accountable? Of course!"[156] But "Governors and Presidents alike" should "concentrate on policy" and "not pretend to have—or be embarrassed to admit that it did not have—market sophistication. His own view was that the Committee's Managers had done a better job in executing its directives than the members had done in giving them directives." This advice was only partially heeded. When Maisel's committee report was released two months later, the FOMC endorsed adding monetary aggregate targets to policy directives, in addition to qualitative instructions. Moving forward, these directives would sometimes clash. Resulting ambiguity would endow the New York open market desk agent with enduring policy discretion.

The year Bopp and Martin retired, Martin wrote the introduction for a Philadelphia Fed–published edited volume called *Men, Money and Policy: Essays in Honor of Karl R. Bopp*. Martin explained their shared ambivalence about the Fed's ongoing technocratic revolution. Martin wrote, "Economists at the Board of Governors . . . are laboring . . . to isolate and measure more exactly the impact of changes in policy . . . [but for] the foreseeable future . . . the precise timing and magnitude of these effects are not subject to exact scientific, proof-positive determination. And so the meaning and direction of facts remain matters of judgement, and matters on which judgments may differ . . . central banking remains an art rather than a science . . . Economics involves moral decisions as well as abstract technical ones."[157]

Arthur Burns had no such moral quandaries about consolidating Fed power. When Burns joined the board, he took command of a burgeoning board technocracy. In the years 1965 through 1972, board salary outlays would triple from $5.7 million to $17.1 million.[158] This explosive growth made Burns the head of a well-resourced, expert-laden bureaucracy. Unlike Martin, who granted the staff autonomy to pursue innovation, Burns weaponized the staff's growing influence over the monetary policy agenda by ordering staff members to report directly to him and withhold key information from other Fed stakeholders.[159] To tamp down on leaks, Burns even asked the Federal Bureau of Investigation to investigate board staff members.[160]

Through these authoritarian tactics, Burns shattered Martin's egalitarian order and remade the Fed as his own dominion. A board staff economist later reflected that Burns "was more aggressive by far than Martin in putting forward his views. He often came in with his mind made up and there was more effort to lead the Board in the direction he decided was appropriate."[161] Burns also veered from Martin's norm of keeping the Fed out of politics. Burns was an "unabashed partisan" who "saw himself as much a politician and adviser as a central banker."[162] On the day he took office, Richard Nixon joked to reporters, "I respect [Burns's] independence. However, I hope that independently he will conclude that my views are the ones that should be followed."[163] Burns's colleagues were critical of his partisanship, but he "took over a Board all of whose members had been appointed by Presidents Kennedy and Johnson . . . a majority preferred to continue inflation rather than increase unemployment."[164] Like Marriner Eccles three decades before, Burns was willing to push his Fed colleagues into politics. Indeed, Burns is remembered today for opening the Fed's monetary floodgates in the run-up to the 1972 elections to support Nixon's reelection. This historic shift toward ease really began at Burns's first FOMC meeting. The Federal Funds rate plummeted from 8.98 percent to 3.72 percent in Burns's first year.[165] In 1971, Burns helped craft Nixon's New Economic Policy, which formally ended gold-dollar convertibility, enacted a 10 percent tariff surcharge, and implemented wage and price controls. The dollar would be formally floated on foreign exchange markets in 1973. Freed of its golden fetters, monetary policy emerged as a domestic policy domain.

Conclusion: The Old Guard's Retreat and the Birth of the Modern Fed

This book argues that the modern Fed emerged in the late 1960s and crystalized under Arthur Burns. Like earlier Fed regimes analyzed throughout this book, the modern Fed was constructed in relation to an evolving global context and layered atop an existing legal and institutional foundation. To build a new Fed order, ascendant board technocrats first built up the board's capacity and grew its agenda-setting role. Burns completed the Fed's technocratic revolution by tearing down Martin's egalitarian system of Fed norms, processes, and values.

Changing political times and global contexts catalyzed and reinforced these changes. The advent of a Democratic partisan regime early in the decade provided a pathway to power inside the Fed to Left-leaning economists. Through their control of board appointments, Democrats in the White House and Senate colluded to override a board occupational diversity requirement, effectively changing the law's meaning without changing its text. Once at work inside, economists spearheaded projects to grow the board's technical staff, forge new models and forecasts, and integrate those tools into the policy process. These changes shifted the center of ideational authority within the system from New York to Washington. The Board of Governors emerged as the most prestigious, expert-laden, and powerful agency in the federal government.

William McChesney Martin Jr. fought each of these changes, but his own limited view of Fed independence and principled embrace of inclusivity, doomed his Fed creation. Martin privately struggled with three straight U.S. presidents to prevent the board's economist onslaught. He feared Fed newcomers would not respect the system's inherited traditions and goals and would instead see it as a vehicle for testing their models and advancing their domestic projects. Like other members of the Fed old guard, Martin was skeptical of analytic lenses that sought to divide the domestic economy into its own sphere, which imagined that the reach of U.S. economic policies did not also shape the world it was embedded within.

Persistent Democratic refusals to choose between guns and butter foreclosed opportunities for reviving Bretton Woods and sustaining America's historical commitment to some version of the gold standard. While Richard Nixon is often cast as the villain who took America off gold, this chapter has shown that the forces that felled Bretton Woods were unleashed years earlier. The exchange system's fragility was first revealed as it became operational under Eisenhower, who presided over a sharp drop in U.S. gold. He left his successors a task of shoring up global faith in the dollar through diplomacy and closing America's growing international payments deficits. Under Kennedy, this project made limited headway, as the treasury and Fed advocated for orthodox responses to international deficits, namely, fiscal or monetary austerity. They also forged new cooperative linkages among central banks, recreating earlier gold standard practices. These projects were torpedoed by the Johnson administration's global ambitions. Unfunded wars in Vietnam and against poverty at home fueled exploding deficits which the Fed was forced to monetize, unleashing a great inflation which rendered attempts to save Bretton Woods futile.

Changing facts on the ground progressively weakened the Fed old guard's case that monetary policy should be aimed at dollar stabilization. Cracks in the Hamiltonian philosophy first emerged in 1965, when Robert Roosa endorsed the creation of a new IMF-issued synthetic reserve asset as a means of *sustaining* the fixed exchange rate system. Its logic became further strained during the Fed austerity campaigns of the late 1960s. Whereas the traditional view held that interest rate hikes could combat inflationary pressures, this relationship broke down in an emergent world of "Eurodollar markets." Foreign banks began accepting dollar deposits in the 1950s, which grew in the 1960s into a massive global pool of dollar liquidity.[166] In this context, Fed tightening campaigns backfired by triggering capital imports. Fed rate hikes coincided with rising inflation rates, rather than their fall. In 1970, Roosa conceded that the rise of Eurodollar markets, the proliferation of multinational corporations, and surging U.S. government overseas expenditures, made the balance of payments a less useful monetary policy indicator.[167] Today, most economists agree central banks should aim their monetary policy tools toward domestic goals such as maintaining domestic price and financial stability. The long powerful idea that an international gold standard is needed to promote global economic integration has become passé.

In an emerging world of floating currencies, Fed policymakers would look to the domestic economy alone for guidance. Milton Friedman cheered on this future development in 1967, arguing that a flexible dollar "would enable us . . . to determine our national policies on the right grounds. Monetary and fiscal policy could be directed toward pursuing internal stability without being hamstrung by the balance of payments."[168]

This echoes themes articulated by Adolph Miller and Irving Fisher in the 1920s and 1930s, namely, the primacy of domestic concerns, to justify board empowerment or requiring the system to follow a rigid policy rule.

So, what should be made Martin's Fed accomplishments? This chapter has shown that the egalitarian Fed order Martin crafted unraveled on his own watch and was repudiated by his successor. Yet Martin was respected by his colleagues at home and abroad and throughout government. Martin negotiated the Treasury-Fed Accord and brought it to life in Fed practice. He developed a public rationale for Fed independence and countercyclical policy action. This public duty was not always popular. Martin once told a group of bankers, "Action to prevent inflationary excesses is bound to have some onerous effects. . . . Those who have the task of making such policy don't expect you to applaud . . . [the Fed was] in the position of the chaperone who has ordered the punch bowl removed just when the party was really warming up."[169]

Martin's legacies were more than rhetorical, however. He established the FOMC, in his words, as "heart and core of the Federal Reserve System." He encouraged reserve banks to grow their research capacities to meaningfully participate in FOMC policy debates, reinvigorating moribund Fed institutions. Martin also presided over the Fed as it emerged as the most visible and powerful actor in the world economy. Yet, Martin was trapped within an egalitarian Fed of his own making. Democrats insisted that he remain as Fed chair to capitalize on his credibility but ate away his authority from within by steadily appointing economists. Despite Martin's incessant urgings, politicians refused to make hard choices between guns and butter to improve the United States' balance-of-payments position. In a rare 1969 board outburst, Martin complained that "the part he had to play in the gold negotiations . . . diminished his historical stature." He bitterly warned that Arthur Burns "was too inflexible . . . this was true of all the economists on the Board."[170] When the dollar was devalued in 1972, Martin described the decision as "a failure of United States economic policy . . . to restrain inflation and improve our balance of payments."[171]

In line with the braided theory of Fed development this book advances, the modern Fed emerged from Martin's tangle of institutional victories and defeats. One scholar observes that, late in Martin's term, "as its authority, influence, and historical significance became apparent, the Federal Reserve System took on a new name—'The Fed.'"[172] Martin fought this change tooth and nail, consistently describing the Federal Reserve as a system and emphasizing the importance of its constituent elements.

Reserve banks survived this evolution with their institutional sovereignty intact, but an emergent corporate Fed order was unstoppable. Arthur Burns seized onto these currents by concentrating Fed agenda-setting authority and power in a burgeoning board technocracy. This durable shift in governing authority ended the Fed's struggle for power, signaling the culmination of its political development.

Conclusion

E Pluribus Unum: The Political Development of the Fed

> I stress these limits on our knowledge in order to suggest why central banking remains an art rather than a science. And as an art, it is an art of moderation, of the balanced way. At all times, we must be aware of the risk that the economy might be undermined by either inflation or deflation. And this is a risk that involves human side effects, side effects which impinge on our polity a well as our economy. Economics involves moral decisions as well as abstract technical ones.
>
> —William McChesney Martin Jr., 1970

In 1971, construction began on a second Board of Governors building with four times the space of the Federal Reserve Building, which had opened just thirty-four years before. At the groundbreaking ceremony, Arthur Burns explained the building would offer "space for growth, if the ... Board's work load continues to grow," and announced that it would be named after William McChesney Martin Jr., who laid "the strong foundation on which our work in this new building will stand."[1] The irony of Burns announcing that the building would be made a monument to his predecessor was lost on the audience. During Martin's tenure, the board evolved from an arm of the treasury into the most powerful agency in Washington. Most of the board's staff, whose seepage into rented offices inspired the new build, were hired under Martin's watch. Martin's rare combination of expertise and humility made him a hero to the men and women who worked at the Board of Governors, even though he was ambivalent about what the board was becoming.

Yet, such was the hubris of the dawning age of the economist at the Fed that few realized how much the institution had changed just in a few years. A board-centered Fed hierarchy was layered atop Martin's diffuse Fed order. The economists who led the charge to remake the Fed showed ignorance toward the system's traditions and found Martin's inclusive FOMC puzzling. As the quotes from academics turned Fed practitioners at the start of this book's introduction and penultimate chapter suggest, economists assumed monetary policy was always forged through a technocratic battle of economic ideas, a view often at odds with Fed practice.

This book has pushed back on this narrative, showing that before 1970 the Fed policy regime's processes and goals were frequently changed. This concluding chapter summarizes the system's braided institutional development, explaining how changing times empowered certain Fed ideologies at key moments while marginalizing others. After recapping this developmental journey, a stylized portrait of the modern FOMC is offered to show how it embodies elements from each of the system's historical regimes. The last section considers the implications of the Fed's evolution for theories of American political development.

The Federal Reserve's Braided Development

"The Fed" is a heuristic used to make sense of the Federal Reserve System, a complex organization composed of thirteen separate entities. This book has argued that "the Fed" we know today crystalized in 1970 as an insular, chairman-centric, board technocracy.[2] Arthur Burns was correct in his groundbreaking ceremony remarks that the emerging Fed order was built on a foundation laid by Martin, but he neglected to tell the audience that the ascendant board faction had ripped down the walls of Martin's egalitarian Fed to make way for something new.

The 1913 FRA established a Federal Reserve Board in Washington and twelve Federal Reserve Banks spread across the country. The law failed to endorse a single ordering principle to fashion these units into a workable system. Instead, four visions were sprinkled throughout its text, lying in tension with each other. The Jeffersonian theory, championed by Carter Glass, saw the law as intending for Fed authority to be devolved among the reserve banks, which would administer the gold standard and govern their own territories independently. Hamiltonians saw New York as the system's rightful seat of power, due to its position atop America's premier money market and nexus with the world economy. Populists saw the law as endorsing a treasury-controlled bank to regulate monetary growth for domestic purposes. Progressives envisioned an independent board as the leading a system-wide collaboration to perfect U.S. capitalism.

These visions collided as the system came to life. With Democrats in command of Washington, reforms championed by progressive and Hamilton insiders to unify and strengthen the system were blocked by partisans. World War I broke the partisan obstruction. Paul Warburg later reflected that "without the [1917] amendments . . . the Federal Reserve System could never have accumulated its present imposing gold strength and reserve power."[3] Woodrow Wilson's failure to secure an equitable peace caused his Democratic regime to crumble, however. Voters rejected Wilson's internationalism, and returned Republicans promising an inward turn and trade protectionism to power. At the dawn of a new partisan era, Benjamin Strong wrote to the Republican Party chairman, "This is an age and era of people of inconsistency. We say to the nations of Europe—pay us the eleven billions that you owe us—and then we make it impossible for them to pay it by the prohibitive tariff . . . this tariff bill, if it passes, will come back some day and work the destruction of the political party that adopts it."[4]

Strong's Fed innovations and "great idea" would put off the Republican day of reckoning for another decade. Strong persuaded the reserve banks to delegate their investment powers to a central committee controlled by the leaders of the five wealthiest reserve banks. This oligarchical committee reduced the system's fragmentation by excluding the board and rural reserve banks. Strong's discretionary system-wide easing programs in 1924 and 1927 helped restore the gold standard abroad but failed to alleviate Western agricultural depression. Board member Adolph Miller linked the committee's security purchases to the surging stock market and fused progressive and Jeffersonian ideas to topple Strong's Fed. Flexing uncertain regulatory authority, Miller's revisionist board faction asserted veto authority over policy instruments, culminating in a diffusion of power on the open market committee. Miller told Congress, "Whenever the Federal Reserve System operates through the open-market committee, it operates, in effect, as a central bank. . . . You strip your regional banks of their separate control of credit in their several districts when you operate with their resources in the central money market of the country."[5]

The collapse of the Republican Party and rise of the New Deal unleashed waves of progressive and populist state building which remade the Fed and its environment. Reserve banks were empowered to issue currency against government bonds, the board gained broad new emergency powers, and an unwieldly financial state was erected. The Federal Reserve was forced to subsidize this process by buying government bonds, capitalizing national deposit insurance, nationalizing private gold holdings, and surrendering a $2.8 billion devaluation "profit" to the treasury. The simultaneous collapse of international trade and the gold standard created a world where Jeffersonian and Hamiltonian Fed philosophies no longer made sense.

Fed outsider Marriner Eccles stepped up with populist ideals to fill this ideational void. He called for refounding the Fed as an arm of the New Deal, using its monetary powers to support an unprecedented national government-led project of pulling the economy out of depression. Franklin Roosevelt endorsed Eccles's call for a new Fed hierarchy, but Eccles was forced to compromise in the Senate with Carter Glass, the architect of the original FRA. While the Banking Act of 1935 is widely understood as a progressive reform because it grew the board's legal independence by removing the treasury secretary from the board, that reform was Glass's idea. Eccles's plan would have left administration members on the board. Eccles overcame a weak legal warrant to found a populist Fed by leveraging his ties with Roosevelt. When Fed stakeholders resisted his plans, Eccles bypassed them by cutting deals with Roosevelt. Today, Eccles is often celebrated as a progressive hero due to his public irritations for greater Fed autonomy in the late 1940s. Eccles only turned on his populist Fed creation after being progressively disempowered by war, Roosevelt's death, and his own demotion by President Truman, however. Eccles's late denunciation of the Fed as an "engine of inflation" was laden with irony, because his own actions had helped secure the Fed's capture before World War II. Rather than a step toward a modern progressive Fed, Eccles's reign is better understood as a populist detour.

William McChesney Martin Jr. negotiated the 1951 Treasury-Fed Accord on behalf of the treasury and was chosen by President Truman afterward to chair the Board of Governors. Truman chose Martin, a fellow Democrat from his home state of Missouri, because he hoped Martin would sustain treasury dominance. Truman was sorely disappointed, however, when Martin emerged as an articulate defender of Fed autonomy. The FOMC process Martin inherited veered from the law by concentrating power and authority in a New York–dominated executive committee. Martin invoked childhood memories of a more inclusive Fed and

Jeffersonian and populist scripts to repudiate and dismantle this de facto central bank. Martin established an egalitarian FOMC process wherein nineteen FOMC principals, twelve reserve bank presidents, and seven board governors participated in "go-rounds" to collectively make monetary policy decisions. This order pushed the boundaries of the law, as FOMC voting was limited to twelve members. While championing deliberative processes, Martin's vision of Fed purpose leaned Hamiltonian. In public speeches and before Congress, Martin argued that the Fed was tasked with safeguarding the dollar's purchasing power to protect dollar holders around the globe. More broadly, he urged Americans to consider the impact of their policies on the outside world, and to preserve a fixed exchange rate system. While Martin's reforms reduced New York's power, its place as "first among equals" was built into FOMC go-rounds, which started with the New York president explaining the status of the system account and his views on the state of the economy.

Routinization of FOMC meetings paved the way for emergence of a unified Fed culture. By regularly speaking in public forums as a forceful advocate for traditional central banking values, Martin became the face of an institution increasingly understood as America's central bank. Near the end of Martin's Fed tenure, "as its authority, influence, and historical significance became apparent, the Federal Reserve System took on a new name—"The Fed."[6] This change was more than rhetorical; it reflected the eclipse of Martin's diffuse Fed regime by an emergent board technocracy. Martin fought this institutional transformation, urging U.S. presidents throughout the 1960s to honor the board's occupational diversity requirements. Before 1961, Adolph Miller was the only PhD economist ever appointed to the board. Economists aligned with the ascendant Democratic Party plotted to use partisan control of the board appointment process to overturn the occupational diversity requirement through fiat. This project made limited headway under President Kennedy but was greenlighted fully by Lyndon Johnson. Democrats saw the Fed as a convenient vehicle for avoiding painful decisions between guns and butter. Board appointments were made with an eye toward empowering economists who would oppose Martin's old guard faction, which called for stabilizing the dollar to save Bretton Woods.

This technocratic movement reached its moment of triumph inside the Fed as the hubris of Democratic leaders was revealed and rejected by voters. When Republican Richard Nixon became president in 1969, most governors now held economics PhDs. A swelling board staff was developing new models and forecasts, which were incorporated into the monetary policy process. In Martin's last year, he mobilized the FOMC behind a monetary restraint program to fight inflation and preserve the dollar's link to gold. This plan failed, however, and inflation surged despite monetary austerity. The Nixon administration and new Fed chair Arthur Burns pushed the Fed to end its tight money campaign, and the Fed's old guard collapsed as Martin and other members retired. Burns ripped apart Martin's inclusive norms to consolidate Fed power. While board economists lamented Burns's autocratic instincts, many agreed that the Fed should turn its gaze inward and abandon dollar stabilization as a monetary policy goal. The board was reimagined as a problem-solving technocracy whose expertise-based ability to learn justified its Fed primacy. Because the outlines of such an order were enshrined in the law in 1935, economists saw the board's rise to power as rectifying a historical anomaly, rather than smashing traditions.

The modern Fed is best understood as a hybrid of vestiges of the Feds that came before. Fed regime builders left behind durable legacies forged in both victories and defeats.[7] The next section ties the different strands of Fed culture together by showing how the modern FOMC embodies elements from each of earlier Feds and the ideologies that informed them.

A Stylized Portrait of the Modern Fed

Every day, tens of thousands of employees travel to Federal Reserve Banks across the country, and the Board of Governors convenes in Washington, D.C., where they surveil and regulate the financial system and measure the economy. The process of building metrics and central banking expertise began at the New York Fed in the 1910s. In the 1920s, the board started its own research division in Washington. In the 1950s, William McChesney Martin Jr. encouraged all the reserve banks to grow their own research capacities. In the 1960s, the board invested massively in growing its own technical capacity and emerged as the system's locus of ideational authority.

The Board of Governors chair is the center of the Fed drama. Chairs differ in their leadership postures. Some follow Arthur Burns's lead of dominating the Fed.[8] Others follow Bill Martin's path of fostering inclusivity.[9] Regardless of their leadership styles, modern Fed chairmen share several roles, which were cemented by 1970. Eccles pioneered a practice of Fed chairmen acting in a political advisory role, providing counsel beyond the Fed's immediate orbit. Under Martin, the chair became the Fed's public spokesperson and congressional liaison, decades before biannual testimony was mandated by Congress. Since 1970, the board chair and staff have shaped the FOMC agenda. In 1973, governor Sherman Maisel, who spearheaded procedural reforms, estimated that the chairman and staff together exercised 70 percent control over policy decisions.[10] Peter Conti-Brown has shown that this extralegal Fed order endures.[11]

Monetary policy today is forged in two long-standing venues. The Board of Governors retains formal control over discount rates and reserve requirements.[12] These instruments have long been eclipsed by open market operations, however, purchases and sales of government securities, which expand or contract bank reserves. The open market committee was first established by a reserve bank agreement in 1922. Congress recognized the FOMC formally in 1933 and restructured it in 1935 to give the board a voting majority. The FOMC's formal structure was finalized in 1942, when Congress named the New York Fed president the FOMC's *ex officio* vice chairman. One of William McChesney Martin's enduring reforms was a norm that all twelve reserve bank presidents and seven board governors attend FOMC meetings.

Every six to eight weeks, these nineteen Fed stakeholders gather around a table at the board's headquarters in Washington.[13] Meetings begin with a report from the manager of the system open market account, a New York Fed employee, who explains how the open market desk fared in meeting the Federal Funds rate target set at the last meeting.[14] Next up are the directors of the Board of Governors Research and Statistics and International Finance divisions, who give presentations based on staff forecasts. Afterward, monetary policy is forged through two "go-rounds," another durable Martin procedural innovation. In the first go-round, each committee member weighs in on economic conditions in the system's districts and the country at large.[15] The director of the board's division of monetary affairs then begins the policy debate by laying out three alternative directives compiled by the staff in the bluebook, a legacy of Sherman Maisel. All nineteen committee members then debate whether the Federal Funds rate should be raised, lowered, or left unchanged. The chair ends the second go-round by proposing an action program and a statement explaining the policy to the public. Once phrasing is agreed upon, the policy is put up for a vote by the twelve voting members. Once a policy is chosen, it is enacted by the New York Fed's open market desk, continuing a tradition started in the 1920s. Through this delegation of operating authority to the New York Fed, and its president's role as the FOMC's vice chairman, its place as "first among equals" endures.

In forging policy, the Fed advances a "dual mandate" of maximizing domestic employment and price stability. This mandate was legally codified in 1977, but its roots lie in the 1946 Employment Act's charge to pursue "maximum employment, production, and purchasing power."[16] In the 1970s, many Fed policymakers believed there was a tradeoff between inflation and unemployment, and preferred lower unemployment at the cost of higher inflation.[17] Milton Friedman argued that higher inflation would only temporarily lower unemployment, however, because agents care about real (inflation-adjusted) rather than nominal wages.[18] Simultaneous rises in inflation and unemployment in the 1970s tilted this debate in favor of Friedman.[19] In an environment of rising political support to tackle inflation, the Fed reinterpreted its mandate to prioritize domestic price stability.[20] In its deliberations, Fed officials emphasized the need to rebuild credibility with market participants.[21] These ideas, that the Fed needed to actively fight inflation to maintain credibility and prevent rising structural unemployment, represented a return to Bill Martin's "lean against the wind" central banking philosophy.[22]

While the Fed normally directs monetary policy toward macroeconomic stabilization, in crises it draws upon an arsenal of emergency powers pioneered in the Great Depression. During the 2008 global financial crisis, it invoked FRA Section 13(3) authority to extend loans directly to domestic and foreign corporations.[23] In ensuing years, it engaged in three rounds of so-called quantitative easing, creating trillions of reserves to inject liquidity into the banking system. While the scale of this practice was new, it was tried before in 1932.[24] Bold Fed responses kept the world financial system afloat, and arguably avoided another Depression.[25] Benjamin Strong recognized this capacity in 1928, writing "we have the power to deal with an . . . emergency instantly by flooding the street with money, but I think the country is well aware of this and probably places reliance upon the common sense and power of the System."[26]

This stylized portrait has shown that the Fed's institutional order, mandate, and emergency powers, were settled by 1970. The modern Fed emerged at the dawn of a new era of flexible exchange rates, which left it free to pursue domestic goals. Social forces later aligned in support of an aggressive Fed inflation-fighting posture, but this change reflected an emerging consensus that central banks should prioritize domestic price stability over other goals, not a reordering of Fed institutions.[27] Those skeptical of the claim that the Fed's development ended in 1970 can rightfully point out that Fed communication strategies have since evolved. This claim is correct insofar as the Fed has grown its transparency by making the public aware of its policy decisions right after FOMC meetings and even providing forward guidance regarding how its members think interest rates will move in the future.[28] This change has not resulted in "a durable shift in governing authority," however.[29] The technocratic Fed built in 1970 still stands.

We can now consider how different ideologies are braided into the fabric of the modern Fed. Jeffersonianism occupies the most subordinate strand in modern Fed culture. Its vision of a decentralized system of autonomous reserve banks mechanistically enacting the gold standard was repudiated in the 1930s, when reserve banks were stripped of autonomy, the gold standard collapsed, and a hierarchical Fed formed in Washington. Lingering reserve bank sovereignty and policy influence, and board diversity requirements were vestiges of this vision, but the latter fell in the 1960s. The Hamiltonian Fed ideology occupies the next higher strand in the Fed's braided culture. Like Jeffersonianism, support for this vision's Fed purpose and structure is linked to its environment. Its project of directing monetary policy externally toward promoting international monetary stability makes sense only in settings where U.S. adherence to a fixed exchange regime is viable. This has never been the case since the modern Fed was born. New York's position as "first among equals" within the Fed is nevertheless still reflected in its control over open market policy implementation and its president's *ex officio* FOMC vice chairmanship.

The modern Fed's constellation of power accords higher rank to populist and progressive ideologies. In a world of flexible exchange rates, monetary policy can be directed solely toward domestic projects, as U.S. populists have advocated since Edward Kellogg. One of Milton Friedman's great intellectual victories lay in persuading scholars and policymakers that the Fed's purpose lies in regulating monetary growth to stabilize the domestic macroeconomy.[30] Yet, the modern Fed is more often imagined as a model progressive agency, separated from its Washington counterparts by its unusual autonomy, power, and expertise. The modern Fed marries populist purposes of regulating monetary growth to a progressive technocratic process.

Whether this Fed stands aloof from politics, or bends to pressures to sustain an entrenched elite, is an empirical question of immense practical importance. Yet, most analysts arrive at their answer to this question in advance by adopting ideological frames of what the Fed should be and do and judging its past performance by that standard. This book sees the modern Fed as more plastic, bending in response to changing winds in Washington. The result is a Fed that deeply institutionalized Friedman's call to grow the money supply in response to economic downturns and financial panics to avoid crises from spiraling. This has fostered a growing dependency in Washington on Fed power to sustain American prosperity. As the Fed has emerged as the nation's economic stabilizer of first resort, it has abandoned the oppositional stance toward elected officials imagined by Hamilton in times of crisis. Instead of goading politicians to tackle looming challenges and reconcile ends with means, the Fed now follows what Hamilton considered lawmakers' worst instincts, by printing money to throw at problems.

Implications of the Fed's Rise for American Political Development

This last section examines the implications of this book's argument for debates in American Political Development (APD). It first calls on APD scholars to pay greater heed to the array of international forces which shape American domestic politics, as well as the long shadow of American domestic policies on the global environment. It then considers how integrating international factors into APD analytic frameworks allows for a more nuanced understanding of the interplay of structure and agency in political time. Finally, it argues that the Fed's evolution into a globally powerful, domestic economy stabilizer has blunted the impact of political time.

Situating American Politics in a Global Setting

Nearly two decades ago, Ira Katznelson and Martin Shefter called on APD scholars to better incorporate international structures and variables into their analyses.[31] APD scholars responded with a flurry of analyses on the role of war on American state building, but made less headway incorporating other global elements into their analyses. Peter Trubowitz's *Politics and Strategy* made an important inroad in this direction by recognizing the Janus-faced nature of American grand strategy.[32] Trubowitz argues that presidents forge foreign policies in relation to the combination of global threats and opportunities they are confronted with, but with an eye toward pleasing their partisan allies at home to ensure their political survival.

This book builds on this insight by situating the struggle to shape the Federal Reserve within national and global contexts. The analysis incorporates several systemic-level factors, including wars, international regimes, and societal interests vis-à-vis the world economy, to offer a richer understanding of the Fed's struggle for power. It shows that war was an important catalyst for growing Fed power, both its legal warrants and its control over globally valuable resources. It also shows that in the wake of wars, America's uneven integration into the world economy repeatedly acted as a spark for Fed policy conflicts and spiraling debates about the system's normative structure and purpose. New York would call to look outward and deploy the Fed's power toward fostering international monetary order, while officials located elsewhere in the system would view Fed powers and responsibilities through parochial lenses. These debates were nested within larger national conversations over whether the United States rebuild liberal world orders. The outcomes of these broader debates shaped both the problems Fed agents would face and the range of viable policy options the system could pursue to address those problems. A theme that emerges throughout this book is that historically the Fed has often played a key role of mitigating tensions that grow from incongruences between U.S. domestic and foreign policies.

This points toward a second problem APD scholars must grapple with: the constitutive impact of American grand strategic decisions (and nondecisions) on global regimes. International Political Economists (IPEs) are outpacing APD scholars on this score. Recent works analyze the interaction of war and congressional fragmentation to explain patterns of war-debt-fueled bubbles followed by financial crises; the role of America's structural power in global financial markets as a magnet for fueling its 2000s housing bubble; and how American choices to fight wars wholly on credit prolong conflicts and obscure their costs from voters.[33] IPE also has a long tradition of analyzing how America's grand strategic decisions shape or destabilize the world economy.[34] APD theorists must consider how the global reach of U.S. policies shapes its internal politics, and how those political processes in turn shape the outside world.

Intersections of Political Time and Agency

Political time is often conceived as cyclical, with regimes naturally forming and governing for an era before collapsing in the face of new crises, and then being supplanted by a new regime. Such theories are often structural and insular, with regimes conceived as born with predetermined half-lives, impervious to environmental shocks. This logic is juxtaposed against historical institutionalist theories of critical junctures, whereby shocks reveal institutional vulnerabilities, which agents and lawmakers remedy. While the latter school sees reform as a generative process wherein incremental reforms rationalize institutions through time, political time theories emphasize the destructive elements of institutional change. Regimes and policies that came before must be repudiated and torn down in order to pave the way to build something new.

The agent-centered theory developed in this book is compatible with each of these logics. On the one hand, the four political moments this book identifies can be thought of as critical juncture-opening shocks, as is emphasized in the historical institutionalist literature. This book's argument varies in two crucial ways, however. Rather than conceiving of shocks as exogenous, this book shows that political moments flow from agency-laden choices, such as whether to join a war, or when to attack a ruling party and on what grounds. Once these decisions are made, however, they set in motion state-building sequences which work at contradictory purposes. War inspires Hamiltonian state building, but peace invites Jeffersonian attacks on war-swollen states. A collapsing partisan regime builds independent agencies, meant to be sealed off from politics, which the next ascendant party seeks to invade and turn toward partisan ends. Broadening the political time clock to incorporate war and peace calls attention to the crucial role of agency in shaping the resilience and duration of partisan regimes. Three times in the twentieth century, Democratic presidents led the nation to unpopular wars which ended with their parties being ousted from power. Likewise, acts of agency by central banks that steer the economy away from crises can prolong partisan ascendancy. By drawing from a well of global power to stabilize the domestic economy, the modern Fed contributes to the "waning of political time."[35]

The Fed's Role in the Waning of Political Time

Stephen Skowronek argues that the United States has experienced a "waning of political time" due to "institutional thickening."[36] In this view, the rise of an enduring welfare and regulatory state blunts all presidents' capabilities to destroy existing policies, programs, and institutions, the essence of "reconstructive" power wielded by a regime-founding president. Skowronek argues that Ronald Reagan is the architect of the current partisan regime, but sees his reconstruction as "more rhetorical than institutional" due the New Deal state's entrenchment.[37] Others have problematized the waning of the political time thesis. Curt Nichols argues that Reagan repurposed agencies to advance his deregulatory agenda.[38] Jacob Hacker and Paul Pierson argue that the Reagan revolution's fruits emerged gradually through "drift."[39] Republicans flexed their power across decades by preventing welfare benefits from being updated to account for inflation, and through endless demands for tax cuts and deregulation, which eroded the social safety net. Christopher Adolph argues the Fed's success in preventing recessions from spiraling into broader crises makes it complicit in preempting the formation of Keynesian countercyclical fiscal capacity.[40]

This book argues that the Fed contributes to the "waning of political time" by wielding global power, derived from a monopoly over dollar production, to stabilize America's domestic economy. This influence is direct, through Fed interventions, which avoid crises, and indirect, through the Fed's emergence as a major source of government revenue. The system began transferring 90 percent of its investment earnings to the treasury in 1947.[41] Figure C.1 shows that treasury remittances began rising in the 1960s and fluctuated between $20 and $40 billion constant dollars until

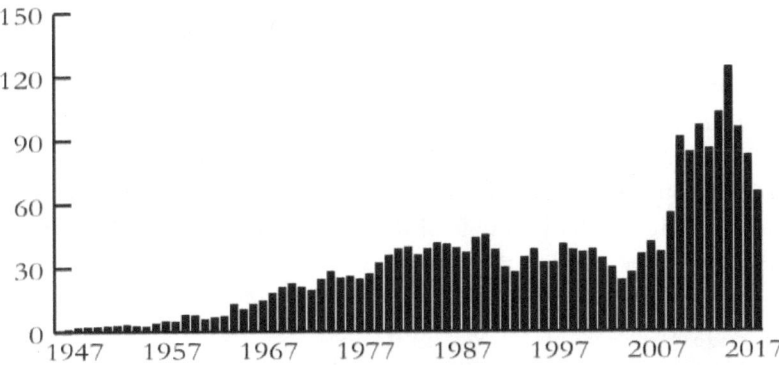

Figure C.1. Federal Reserve Payments to the U.S. Treasury (billions of 2018 dollars). *Source:* Federal Reserve Board of Governors, Annual Reports of the Board of Governors of the Federal Reserve System (1947–2019), Washington, DC.

the mid-2000s. In March 2008, the Fed's balance sheet stood at $900 billion. Three rounds of "quantitative easing" to combat the Great Recession then exploded it to $4.5 trillion by December 2014.[42] As the Fed's investment portfolio grew, so did its treasury remittances, which peaked in 2015 at $124.1 billion. If not for the Fed's payment that year, the deficit would have been 28 percent higher. These transfers mask the true size of deficits and subsidize debt servicing costs. They make it easier for politicians to avoid hard choices of reconciling means with ends, pushing the nation's mounting debts and problems into the future.

Because the modern Fed follows Milton Friedman's call to print dollars whenever the economy stumbles, it has vacated the oppositional approach to government that Alexander Hamilton thought was necessary to spur government energy. This book has focused on currency stability as a proxy for the Hamiltonian vision of Fed purpose. While dollar stabilization is no longer a viable policy goal, Hamilton's broader central bank philosophy remains useful in a world characterized by flexible exchange rates and dollar primacy. Hamilton's New York Fed descendants believed the system had a critical role to play in sustaining a classical liberal order, including stable currencies, free trade, balanced budgets, and minimal domestic regulation.

A Hamiltonian standard for evaluating central bank behavior includes questions of whether, in times of crisis, central bank support is conditioned on the development of credible congressionally endorsed plans to tackle underlying problems within a framework of budgetary constraints. Is the central bank a consistent advocate for classical liberal policies, including free trade, balanced budgets, and American leadership of a liberal world order? And finally, when lawmakers adopt myopic policies, does the central bank allow politicians to bear the electoral consequences of imprudent policies? Or does it flex its powers to put off the day of reckoning?

Judging by these standards, none of the Fed regimes surveyed in this book come out with a clean bill of health. At the system's origin, Benjamin Strong feared that its federal design would channel politics inside and paralyze the system in times of crisis. A decade later, Strong partially fixed this problem by erecting an exclusionary open market committee, which critics deemed a de facto central bank, atop the system's fragmented structure. Strong wanted America to seize the mantle of hegemonic leadership from Great Britain and spearheaded reconstruction of a liberal world order. Americans rejected internationalism, however, and installed a Republican regime committed to pushing adjustment costs overseas. Strong called out the incoherence of Republican protectionism, but soon found himself championing "experimental" system-wide easing policies to promote gold restoration abroad. These policies did not address the underlying cause of global disorder, America's neomercantilism, but rather pushed a global crisis into the future. In this way, Strong helped the ruling party evade the consequences of its myopic policies. When Herbert Hoover doubled down on irresponsibility by ratcheting up protectionism in 1930, the gold standard tumbled along with the world economy.

Such was, and remains, the temptation and peril of Fed power. In Strong's era, Fed strength grew from the reserve bank's immense gold reserves. This condition was altered in the 1930s through nationalization of private gold holdings and dollar devaluation but continued on a global level due to America's accumulation of most of the world's monetary gold. Marriner Eccles's Fed was explicitly crafted to support the New Deal. It did so by promising to maintain an "orderly" government securities market in the 1930s, which hardened into a commitment to sustain a security market yield pattern in World War II. The Fed's subordinate rank in the New Deal order continued after the war, making it what Eccles colorfully described as an "engine of inflation." In these years, Fed largesse helped forestall a widely feared return of global depression, but it also made it easier for lawmakers to put off thorny questions of how to pay for war debts and convert the economy to a peacetime footing.

William McChesney Martin Jr.'s inclusive Fed was crafted in reaction to this legacy. Martin's tenure began with a push to restore the system's independence. The spirit of an embedded liberal age shaped his egalitarian Fed, but it also limited its practical autonomy. Martin's Fed stabilized interest rates during treasury financing operations and stepped in as buyer of last resort when treasury bond issues threatened to fail. These commitments grew more onerous in the 1960s, when an ascendant Democratic Party slashed taxes before launching unfunded wars against poverty at home and communism in Vietnam. Throughout the decade, Martin was a public irritant in favor of traditional central banking values. In private correspondence and public speeches, Martin urged presidents and lawmakers to make tough choices between guns and butter and sustain America's liberal foreign economic policy commitments, to help stabilize the dollar and preserve Bretton Woods. Changing political times worked to disempower him inside the Fed, however, and the institution was soon repurposed.

While Benjamin Strong, Marriner Eccles, and Bill Martin all used their bully pulpit to plead for policies they considered prudent in the worlds they occupied, their calls were ignored by politicians and the Fed ultimately bowed to political pressures. By the 1970s, when the Fed abandoned its dollar stabilization objective, it had once again been transformed into an engine of inflation. At the end of the decade, during the Jimmy Carter presidency, which marked the twilight of the New Deal Democratic regime, new Fed chair Paul Volcker boldly reasserted the Fed's independence. He built a Fed consensus in favor of using austerity, even to the point of inducing a recession, to break entrenched inflationary expectations.[43]

This austerity campaign carried on into the Reagan administration, but reflecting this book's theoretical expectations, it was progressively weakened by a reconstructive president's board appointment choices. Looking for relief from a relentless tight money campaign, which clouded his electoral prospects, Reagan steadily appointed dovish members to the board. By 1987, Volcker was outnumbered on the board by a countervailing coalition that blocked his attempt to raise the discount rate. Volcker was replaced later that year by "conservative Republican" Alan Greenspan, who had for the past year "worried aloud at many public forums about the weakened state of the economy and the need to avert a recession at all costs."[44]

Greenspan would rule the Fed for a generation, building a steeper hierarchy than Arthur Burns.[45] In the process, he embroiled the Fed in politics by championing financial deregulation and supporting tax cuts in the early 2000s to end fiscal surpluses. Greenspan decided the Fed should not use monetary restraint to pop asset bubbles but should lower interest rates after major stock market falls. This became known as the "Greenspan put," which investors priced into their calculations. The Fed's response to the 2008 financial crisis reflected the culmination of this policy, as it boldly injected funds into the financial system and lent funds to dollar-starved firms around the world. Bold Fed interventions fended off a global collapse, but they also preempted the repudiation of the ruling Republican Party's antitax and deregulatory agenda.

Some political scientists have asked why the global meltdown, which originated in America's poorly regulated mortgage markets, did not cause political time to advance. Andrew Polsky has suggested that the timing of the onset of the financial crisis, which occurred just two months before

Democrat Barack Obama won the presidency, foreclosed opportunities for Obama to pin that crisis on the myopic Republican drive to deregulate the economy at all costs.[46] This book offers a more ambivalent diagnosis. Since the Fed swooped in and prevented the crisis from spiraling into a broader catastrophe, the Republican ideology of endless tax cuts and deregulation was not repudiated. Obama was also elected in response to a backlash against ongoing wars in Iraq and Afghanistan, which he promised to end. In a world with only soft budgetary constraints, however, the promise was deferred, and America's global wars continued.

At the time of this book's writing in 2019, the Fed finds itself in an uncomfortable position. It is under attack by a U.S. president who claims that Fed restraint is suffocating the economy, even while interest and unemployment rates are near historic lows. Simultaneously, the president invokes national security threats to raise tariffs on America's trading partners, eroding the foundations of the liberal world order the United States has fostered since World War II. Citing a weakening global economy, explained as a result of the president's reckless trade policies, the Fed recently began lowering interest rates. In response to this accommodation, former New York Fed president Bill Dudley went rogue by invoking a Hamiltonian script, proposing that Fed officials "state explicitly that the central bank won't bail out an administration that keeps making bad choices on trade policy, making it abundantly clear that Trump will own the consequences of his actions. . . . If the goal of monetary policy is to achieve the best long-term economic outcome, then Fed officials should consider how their decisions will affect the political outcome in 2020."[47]

The Fed establishment quickly distanced itself from Dudley's comments. Chair Jerome Powell declared, "Political factors play absolutely no role in our process, and my colleagues and I would not tolerate any attempt to include them in our decision-making or our discussions. We are going to act as appropriate to sustain the expansion."[48] Dudley's thinking reflects the vestiges of a Hamiltonian tradition forged at the New York Fed by Benjamin Strong a century ago. Hamilton wanted a central bank to act as a governing ally for the political class that would goad lawmakers into making hard choices between guns and butter. The modern Fed has vacated this role, imagining itself as a guardian of a distinct economic realm, accommodating political pressures without seriously pushing back. The result is widespread ambivalence about the Fed's awesome power, and its culpability in propping up reckless partisan regimes.

Notes

Introduction

1. Federal Open Market Committee, minutes, February 10, 1970, 53–56, Federal Open Market Committee Meeting Minutes, Transcripts, and Other Documents, 1933–2020, FRASER (hereafter Federal Open Market Committee, minutes), https://fraser.stlouisfed.org/title/677.

2. Karl Bopp, "Confessions of a Central Banker," in *Essays in Monetary Policy in Honor of Elmer Wood*, ed. Pinkney C. Walker (Columbia: University of Missouri Press, 1965), 12.

3. Milton Friedman and Anna J. Schwartz, *A Monetary History of the United States, 1867–1960* (Princeton: Princeton University Press, 1963).

4. Sherman J. Maisel, *Managing the Dollar* (New York: W. W. Norton, 1973); Eleanor Stockwell, ed. *Working at the Board: 1930s–1970s* (Washington, DC: Board of Governors of the Federal Reserve System, 1989); Stephen Axilrod, *Inside the Fed* (Cambridge: MIT Press, 2011).

5. Robert P. Bremner, *Chairman of the Fed: William McChesney Martin Jr., and the Creation of the Modern American Financial System* (New Haven: Yale University Press, 2004); Allan Meltzer, *A History of the Federal Reserve, Volume 2* (Chicago: University of Chicago Press, 2009); Robert L. Hetzel and Ralph Leach, "After the Accord: Reminiscences on the Birth of the Modern Fed," *FRB Richmond Economic Quarterly* 87, no. 1 (2001): 57–64.

6. Federal Reserve Act, Public Law 63-43, 63d Cong., 2d sess. (December 23, 1913), section 10.

7. W. R. Burgess, "What the Federal Reserve System Is Doing to Promote Business Stability," *Proceedings of the Academy of Political Science in the City of New York* 12, no. 3 (1927): 139–47; W. R. Burgess, *The Reserve Banks and the Money Market*, 2nd ed. (New York: Harper and Brothers, 1936); Carl Snyder, *Capitalism the Creator: The Economic Foundations of Modern Industrial Society* (New York: Macmillan, 1940); John H. Williams, *Post-War Monetary Plans: And Other Essays*

(London/Oxford: Basil Blackwell, 1949); Lester V. Chandler, *Benjamin Strong, Central Banker* (Washington, DC: The Brookings Institution, 1958); Arthur Bloomfield, *Monetary Policy under the Gold Standard: 1880–1914* (New York: Federal Reserve Bank of New York, 1959); Stephen Clarke, *Central Bank Cooperation: 1924–31* (New York: Federal Reserve Bank of New York, 1967); Charles Kindleberger, *The World in Depression, 1929–1939* (Berkeley: University of California Press, 1973).

8. Allyn Young, "Position of the New York Bank in the Reserve System," *The Annalist*, May 13, 1927, Allan Sproul Papers, FRB-Corr, 1927–1958, Federal Reserve Bank of New York.

9. James Forder, "'Independence' and the Founding of the Federal Reserve," *Scottish Journal of Political Economy* 50, no. 3 (2003): 297–310.

10. Stephen Skowronek, *The Politics Presidents Make: Presidential Leadership from John Adams to Bill Clinton*, 2nd ed. (Cambridge: Harvard University Press, 1997).

11. Karen Orren and Stephen Skowronek, *The Search for American Political Development* (New York: Cambridge University Press, 2004), 123.

12. Jeffrey K. Tulis and Nicole Mellow, *Legacies of Losing in American Politics* (Chicago: University of Chicago Press, 2018).

13. Robert C. West, *Banking Reform and the Federal Reserve, 1863–1923* (Ithaca: Cornell University Press, 1977), 215.

14. Paul M. Warburg, *Federal Reserve System, Its Origin and Growth*, vol. 1 (New York: Macmillan, 1930), 166.

15. Friedman and Schwartz, *A Monetary History*, 414.

16. Lester Chandler shows that most original committee members opposed stimulus after 1929. Lester V. Chandler, *American Monetary Policy, 1928–1941* (New York: Harper and Row, 1971).

17. Michael D. Bordo, "Could the United States Have Had a Better Central Bank? An Historical Counterfactual Speculation," *Journal of Macroeconomics* 34, no. 3 (2012): 597–607; Michael D. Bordo and David Wheelock, "The Promise and Performance of the Federal Reserve as Lender of Last Resort 1914–1933," in *A Return to Jekyll Island: The Origins, History, and Future of the Federal Reserve*, ed. Michael D. Bordo and William Roberds (New York: Cambridge University Press, 2013).

18. Barry Eichengreen, *Golden Fetters: The Gold Standard and the Great Depression, 1919–1939* (New York: Oxford University Press, 1992); Barry Eichengreen and Peter Temin, "The Gold Standard and the Great Depression," *Contemporary European History* 9, no. 2 (2000): 183–207.

19. Robert L. Hetzel and Ralph Leach, "The Treasury-Fed Accord: A New Narrative Account," *FRB Richmond Economic Quarterly* 87, no. 1 (2001): 33–56.

20. Bremner, *Chairman of the Fed*; Meltzer, *A History of the Federal Reserve*, Volume 2.

21. Peter Conti-Brown, *The Power and Independence of the Federal Reserve* (Princeton: Princeton University Press, 2016), 23.

22. Sarah Binder and Mark Spindel, *The Myth of Independence: How Congress Governs the Federal Reserve* (Princeton: Princeton University Press, 2017).

23. They claim that Martin "became a legendary advocate for the Fed, forcefully articulating its positions and expanding its capacity." Lawrence R. Jacobs and Desmond King, *Fed Power: How Finance Wins* (New York: Oxford University Press, 2016), 78.

24. Conti-Brown, *Power and Independence*, 70–93.

25. Jacobs and King, *Fed Power*, 30.

26. Juan Acosta and Beatrice Cherrier, "The Transformation of Economic Analysis at the Federal Reserve During the 1960s," Center for the History of Political Economy at Duke University Working Paper Series 4 (Durham: Duke University, 2019), 2. For the first point, see Maisel, *Managing the Dollar*; Stockwell, ed. *Working at the Board*; Axilrod, *Inside the Fed*.

27. Bernard Shull, *The Fourth Branch: The Federal Reserve's Unlikely Rise to Power and Influence* (Westport: Praeger, 2005), 14.

28. See, for example, Alberto Alesina and Lawrence H. Summers, "Central Bank Independence and Macroeconomic Performance: Some Comparative Evidence," *Journal of Money, Credit and Banking* 25, no. 2 (1993): 151–62; Alex Cukierman, Steven B. Webb, and Bilin Neyapti, "Measuring the Independence of Central Banks and Its Effect on Policy Outcomes," *The World Bank Economic Review* 6, no. 3 (1992): 353–98.

29. See, for example, Allan H. Meltzer, *A History of the Federal Reserve, Volume 1* (Chicago: University of Chicago Press, 2003); Meltzer, *A History*, vol. 2; Robert Hetzel, *The Monetary Policy of the Federal Reserve: A History* (New York: Cambridge University Press, 2008).

30. See, for example, Richard H. Timberlake, *Monetary Policy in the United States: An Intellectual and Institutional History* (Chicago: University of Chicago Press, 1993); Ron Paul, *End the Fed* (New York: Grand Central Publishing, 2009); John H. Wood, *Central Banking in a Democracy: The Federal Reserve and Its Alternatives* (New York: Routledge, 2014).

31. Shull, *The Fourth Branch*; Binder and Spindel, *Myth of Independence*.

32. Friedman and Schwartz, *Monetary History*. Scholars have returned to this theme by analyzing how committee structures shape policy outcomes. See Henry Chappell Jr., Rob R. McGregor, and Todd A. Vermilyea, *Committee Decisions on Monetary Policy: Evidence from Historical Records of the Federal Open Market Committee* (Cambridge: MIT Press, 2004); Alan S. Blinder and John Morgan, "Are Two Heads Better than One? Monetary Policy by Committee," *Journal of Money, Credit and Banking* 37, no. 5 (2005): 789–811; Anne Sibert, "Central Banking by Committee," *International Finance* 9, no. 2 (2006): 145–68.

33. Adolph shows that central bankers from the private sector have more hawkish views toward inflation than bureaucrats from the public sector. Christopher Adolph, *Bankers, Bureaucrats, and Central Bank Politics: The Myth of Neutrality* (New York: Cambridge University Press, 2015).

34. Barry Eichengreen, *Golden Fetters*; Gianni Toniolo, *Central Bank Cooperation at the Bank for International Settlements, 1930–1973* (New York: Cambridge University Press, 2005); Rodney Bruce Hall, *Central Banking as Global Governance: Constructing Financial Credibility* (New York: Cambridge University Press, 2008); Liaquat Ahamed, *Lords of Finance: The Bankers Who Broke the World* (New York: Random House, 2009); Wesley Widmaier, *Economic Ideas in Political Time* (New York: Cambridge University Press, 2016).

35. George Tsebelis, "Decision Making in Political Systems: Veto Players in Presidentialism, Parliamentarism, Multicameralism and Multipartyism," *British Journal of Political Science* 25, no. 3 (1995): 289–325.

36. This is akin to historical institutionalist understandings which see the United States' many veto points and complexity as barriers to state capacity. See Sven H. Steinmo, "American Exceptionalism Reconsidered: Culture or Institutions," in *The Dynamics of American Politics: Approaches and Interpretations*, ed. Lawrence C. Dowd and Calvin Jillison (Boulder: Westview, 1994), 106–31; Margaret M. Weir, "When Does Politics Create Policy? The Organizational Politics of Change," in *Rethinking Political Institutions: The Art of the State*, ed. Ian Shapiro, Stephen Skowronek, and Daniel Galvin (New York: New York University Press, 2006), 171–86.

37. Paul M. Warburg, "Defects and Needs of Our Banking System." *Proceedings of the Academy of Political Science in the City of New York* 4, no. 4 (1914): 7–22; Paul M. Warburg, "A United Reserve Bank of the United States." *Proceedings of the Academy of Political Science in the City of New York* 1, no. 2 (1911): 302–42.

38. Edward Kellogg forged financial populism in the 1840s. See Edward Kellogg, *Labor and Other Capital: The Rights of Each Secured and the Wrongs of Both Eradicated* (New York: Published by the Author, 1849). Kellogg's ideas informed nineteenth-century populist movements. See Gretchen Ritter, *Goldbugs and Greenbacks: The Antimonopoly Tradition and the Politics of Finance in America, 1865–1896* (New York: Cambridge University Press, 1999).

39. Jeffry Frieden, "Sectoral Conflict and Foreign Economic Policy, 1914–1940," *International Organization* 42, no. 1 (1988): 59–90; Peter Trubowitz, *Defining the National Interest: Conflict and Change in American Foreign Policy* (Chicago: University of Chicago Press, 1998).

40. J. L. Broz, *The International Origins of the Federal Reserve System* (Ithaca: Cornell University Press, 1997).

41. Elizabeth Sanders, *Roots of Reform: Farmers, Workers, and the American State, 1877–1917* (Chicago: University of Chicago Press, 1999).

42. Richard Bensel, *The Political Economy of American Industrialization, 1877–1900* (New York: Cambridge University Press, 2000).

43. Scott C. James, *Presidents, Parties, and the State: A Party System Perspective on Democratic Regulatory Choice, 1884–1936* (New York: Cambridge University Press, 2000), 124; Alan Ware, *The Democratic Party Heads North, 1877–1962* (New York: Cambridge University Press, 2006).

44. Irving Fisher, "The Mechanics of Bimetallism," *The Economic Journal* 4, no. 15 (1894): 527–37; Irving Fisher, "A Compensated Dollar," *The Quarterly Journal of Economics* 27, no. 2 (1913): 213–35; Milton Friedman, "The Case for Flexible Exchange Rates," in *Essays in Positive Economics* (Chicago: University of Chicago Press, 1953), 157–203.

45. Warburg, "Defects and Needs."

46. Federal Reserve Act, Public Law 63-43, 63d Cong., 2d sess. (December 23, 1913), section 10.

47. Susan Hoffmann, *Politics and Banking: Ideas, Public Policy, and the Creation of Financial Institutions* (Baltimore: John Hopkins University Press, 2001), 120–27; Ritter, *Goldbugs and Greenbacks*, 276–79.

48. Albert Clifford, *The Independence of the Federal Reserve System* (Philadelphia: University of Pennsylvania Press, 1965); Gyung-Ho Jeong, Gary Miller, and Andrew Sobel, "Political Compromise and Bureaucratic Structure: The Political Origins of the Federal Reserve System," *Journal of Law, Economics, and Organization* 25, no. 2 (2009): 472–98.

49. Timberlake, *Monetary Policy in the United States*, 255.

50. Federal Reserve Act, Public Law 63-43, 63d Cong., 2d sess. (December 23, 1913), section 10.

51. Alexander Hamilton, "Report on a National Bank, December 13, 1790," in *Writings*, ed. Joanne B. Freeman (New York: Library of America, 2001), 585.

52. Ibid.

53. Ibid., 592.

54. Carter Glass, *An Adventure in Constructive Finance* (Garden City: Doubleday, Page, 1927), 173–74.

55. Benjamin Strong to Theodore Burton, December 5, 1913, Papers of Benjamin Strong, Jr., Folder 021.2, Federal Reserve Bank of New York.

56. Allyn Young, "Position of the New York Bank in the Reserve System."

57. Elmus Wicker, *Federal Reserve Monetary Policy, 1917–1933* (New York: Random House, 1966), vii.

58. Eichengreen, *Golden Fetters*, 11.

59. Jeffry Frieden, "Economic Integration and the Politics of Monetary Policy in the United States," in *Internationalization and Domestic Politics*, ed. Robert Keohane and Helen Milner, 108–36 (New York: Cambridge University Press, 1996).

60. The macroeconomic trilemma holds that states cannot simultaneously maintain stable exchange rates, capital controls, and monetary independence. See J. M. Fleming, "Domestic Financial Policies under Fixed and under Floating Exchange Rates," *IMF Staff Papers* 9, no. 3 (1962): 369–80; Robert A. Mundell, "Capital Mobility and Stabilization Policy under Fixed and Flexible Exchange

Rates," *Canadian Journal of Economic and Political Science* 29, no. 4 (1963): 475–85; Benjamin Cohen, "The Triad and the Unholy Trinity: Lessons for the Pacific Region," in *Pacific Economic Relations in the 1990s: Conflict or Cooperation*, ed. Richard Higgott, Richard Leaver, and John Ravenhill, 133–58 (Boulder: Lynne Rienner, 1993.

61. Jeffry Frieden, "Invested Interests: The Politics of National Economic Policies in a World of Global Finance," *International Organization* 45, no. 4 (1991): 425–51.

62. Stefanie Walter, *Financial Crises and the Politics of Macroeconomic Adjustments* (New York: Cambridge University Press, 2013).

63. Kindleberger, *The World in Depression*; Frieden, "Sectoral Conflict"; Trubowitz, *National Interest*; Broz, *International Origins*.

64. Bloomfield, *Monetary Policy under the Gold Standard*, 47, observes, "The concept of the rules of the game . . . was first developed in the *post*-1914 literature . . . by Keynes in the early twenties."

65. Barry Eichengreen, *Globalizing Capital: A History of the International Monetary System* (Princeton: Princeton University Press, 1996), 30–35.

66. David Bearce and Mark Hallerberg, "Democracy and de facto Exchange Rate Regimes," *Economics & Politics* 23, no. 2 (2011): 172–94.

67. Skowronek, *Politics Presidents Make*.

68. Widmaier, *Economic Ideas in Political Time*.

69. Peter Trubowitz, *Politics and Strategy: Partisan Ambition and American Statecraft* (Princeton: Princeton University Press, 2011).

70. Frieden, *Invested Interests*.

71. Andrew J. Polsky, "Partisan Regimes in American Politics," *Polity* 44, no. 1 (2011): 1–30; Nicolas Jabko and Adam Sheingate, "Practices of Dynamic Order," *Perspectives on Politics* 16, no. 2 (2018): 312–27.

72. Polsky, "Partisan Regimes," 6, argues that after a "partisan coalition secures control of national policymaking institutions, the regime becomes a causal force or independent variable." This logic is compatible with rational choice veto player theory, which sees partisan government as reducing legislative veto points. See Tsebelis, "Decision Making in Political Systems."

73. James A. Morone, *The Democratic Wish: Popular Participation and the Limits of American Government* (New York: Basic Books, 1990).

74. Keith Whittington has shown that the rise of a new partisan regime leads to a waning of Supreme Court judicial authority, as presidents assert their own constitutional interpretations and fill the bench with like-minded jurists. Keith E. Whittington, *Political Foundations of Judicial Supremacy: The Presidency, the Supreme Court, and Constitutional Leadership in US History* (Princeton: Princeton University Press, 2009).

75. Polsky, "Partisan Regimes," 24.

76. David Lewis, *The Politics of Presidential Appointments: Political Control and Bureaucratic Performance* (Princeton: Princeton University Press, 2008).

77. Polsky, "Partisan Regimes," 24.

78. Stephen Skowronek, *Building a New American State: The Expansion of National Administrative Capacities, 1877–1920* (Cambridge University Press, 1982).

79. Terry M. Moe, "Political Institutions: The Neglected Side of the Story," *Journal of Law, Economics, & Organization* 6 (1990): 213–253; Jeong, Miller, and Sobel, "Political Compromise and Bureaucratic Structure."

80. Shull, *Fourth Branch*; Binder and Spindel, *Myth of Independence*.

81. A growing APD literature emphasizes the role of war in growing U.S. state capacity. See Richard Bensel, *Yankee Leviathan: The Origins of Central State Authority in America, 1859–1877* (New York: Cambridge University Press, 1990); Bartholomew H. Sparrow, *From the Outside In: World War II and the American State* (Princeton: Princeton University Press, 1996); Sheldon D. Pollack, *War, Revenue, and State Building: Financing the Development of the American State* (Ithaca: Cornell University Press, 2009); Robert P. Saldin, *War, the American State, and Politics since 1898* (New York: Cambridge University Press, 2010).

82. Jeffrey W. Taliaferro, "State Building for Future Wars: Neoclassical Realism and the Resource-Extractive State," *Security Studies* 15, no. 3 (2006): 464–95.

83. Meltzer, *A History*, vol. 1, 85, observes, "Wartime changes [in World War I] made the System more like a central bank, as in World War II." Meltzer fails to develop this insight, however, because his study focuses on the Fed's ideational development.

84. Samuel P. Huntington, *American Politics: The Promise of Disharmony* (Cambridge: Harvard University Press, 1981).

85. Aaron Friedberg, "Why Didn't the United States Become a Garrison State?" *International Security* 16, no. 4 (1992): 109–42.

86. Thomas Oatley, *A Political Economy of American Hegemony* (New York: Cambridge University Press, 2015).

87. Kindleberger, *The World in Depression*; G.J. Ikenberry, *After Victory: Institutions, Strategic Restraint, and the Rebuilding of Order after Major Wars* (Princeton: Princeton University Press, 2000); Jeffrey W. Legro, *Rethinking the World: Great Power Strategies and International Order* (Ithaca: Cornell University Press, 2005).

88. Williams, *Post-War Monetary Plans*; Benjamin Cohen, *Organizing the World's Money: The Political Economy of International Monetary Relations* (New York: Basic Books, 1977).

89. David Bearce, *Monetary Divergence: Domestic Policy Autonomy in the Post–Bretton Woods Era* (Ann Arbor: University of Michigan Press, 2009).

90. Eric Schickler, *Disjointed Pluralism: Institutional Innovation and the Development of the US Congress* (Princeton: Princeton University Press, 2001).

91. Ibid., 15; Robert C. Lieberman, "Ideas, Institutions, and Political Order: Explaining Political Change," *American Political Science Review* 96, no. 4 (2002): 697–712.

92. Mark Blyth, *Great Transformations: Economic Ideas and Institutional Change in the Twentieth Century* (New York: Cambridge University Press, 2002), 37–45.

93. Gerald Berk and Dennis Galvan, "How People Experience and Change Institutions: A Field Guide to Creative Syncretism," *Theory and Society* 38, no. 6 (2009): 543–80.

94. Craig Parsons, "Ideas and Power: Four Intersections and How to Show Them," *Journal of European Public Policy* 23, no. 3 (2016): 447.

95. Mark Blyth, "Structures Do not Come with an Instruction Sheet: Interests, Ideas, and Progress in Political Science," *Perspectives on Politics* 1, no. 4 (2003): 695–706.

96. Legro, *Rethinking the World*.

97. Burgess, "What the Federal Reserve System Is Doing to Promote Business Stability."

98. Lawrence S. Ritter, "Allan Sproul, 1896–1978. 'A Tower of Strength,'" in *Selected Papers of Allan Sproul*, ed. Lawrence S. Ritter (New York: Federal Reserve Bank of New York, 1980), 11; Meltzer, *A History*, vol. 1, 13.

99. John G. Ruggie, "International Regimes, Transactions, and Change: Embedded Liberalism in the Postwar Economic Order," *International Organization* 36, no. 2 (1982): 379–415; Eric Helleiner, *States and the Reemergence of Global Finance: From Bretton Woods to the 1990s* (Ithaca: Cornell University Press, 1996); Rawi Abdelal, *Capital Rules: The Construction of Global Finance* (Cambridge: Harvard University Press, 2007).

100. Friedman and Schwartz, *Monetary History*, 415.

101. Ben Bernanke, "Remarks," Conference to Honor Milton Friedman, University of Chicago, Chicago, Illinois, November 8, 2002, https://www.federalreserve.gov/boarddocs/Speeches/2002/20021108/default.htm.

102. Goldenweiser memorandum on Banking Reform to Committee, September 6, 1934, 2. Quoted in Meltzer, *A History*, vol. 1, 471.

103. Allan Sproul, memorandum, 1934, Papers of Allan Sproul, Folder 4380, Federal Reserve Bank of New York.

104. Chandler, *American Monetary Policy*, 10–11.

105. Friedman and Schwartz, *Monetary History*, 379.

106. Kindleberger, *The World in Depression*, 20–24.

107. Allan Sproul to William Carson, February 27, 1962, Allan Sproul Papers, Folder 4017, Federal Reserve Bank of New York.

108. Richard Sylla, "Financial Foundations: Public Credit, the National Bank, and Securities Markets," in *Founding Choices: American Economic Policy in the 1790s*, ed. Douglas Irwin and Richard Sylla (Chicago: University of Chicago Press, 2011), 70.

109. Shull, *The Fourth Branch*; Binder and Spindel, *Myth of Independence*; Jacobs and King, *Fed Power*.

110. Legro, *Rethinking the World*; Helleiner, *States and the Reemergence of Global Finance*; Herman M. Schwartz, *Subprime Nation: American Power, Global Capital, and the Housing Bubble* (Ithaca: Cornell University Press, 2009); Jonathan Kirshner, *American Power after the Financial Crisis* (Ithaca: Cornell University Press, 2014); Oatley, *A Political Economy of American Hegemony*.

111. Kindleberger, *The World in Depression*; Theodore J. Lowi, *The End of Liberalism: The Second Republic of the United States* (New York: W. W. Norton, 1979), 128–45; Fareed Zakaria, *From Wealth to Power: The Unusual Origins of America's World Role* (Princeton: Princeton University Press, 1999); Michael Mastanduno, "System Maker and Privilege Taker: U.S. Power and the International Political Economy," *World Politics* 61, no. 1 (1999): 121–54; Louis Pauly, "Woodrow Wilson's Problem in Reverse: The Continuing Challenge of Making American Democracy Safe for the World," in *Political Science as Public Philosophy: Essays in Honor of Theodore J. Lowi*, ed. Benjamin Ginsberg and Gwendolyn Mink (New York: W. W. Norton, 2010), 113–32.

112. Benjamin Cohen, "The Macrofoundations of Monetary Power," in *International Monetary Power*, ed. David M. Andrews, 31–50 (Ithaca: Cornell University Press, 2006).

113. Christopher Adolph, "The Missing Politics of Central Banks," *PS: Political Science & Politics* 51, no. 4 (2018): 737–42.

114. Skowronek, *Politics Presidents Make*, 33–52, 442.

115. Sarah Kreps makes a similar argument that war finance has shifted from a mix of taxes and borrowing to relying wholly on credit to mask costs. Sarah Kreps, *Taxing Wars: The American Way of War Finance and the Decline of Democracy* (New York: Oxford University Press, 2018).

116. James Mahoney and Kathleen Thelen, "A Theory of Gradual Institutional Change," in *Explaining Institutional Change: Ambiguity, Agency, and Power*, ed. James Mahoney and Kathleen Thelen, 1–37 (New York: Cambridge University Press, 2009); Giovanni Capoccia and Daniel Kelemen, "The Study of Critical Junctures: Theory, Narrative, and Counterfactuals in Historical Institutionalism," *World Politics* 59, no. 3 (2007): 341–69; Wolfgang Streeck and Kathleen Thelen, "Introduction: Institutional Change in Advanced Political Economies," in *Beyond Continuity: Institutional Change in Advanced Political Economies*, ed. Wolfgang Streeck and Kathleen Thelen, 1–39 (New York: Oxford University Press, 2005).

117. Conti-Brown, *Power and Independence*, 15–44.

118. Tulis and Mellow, *Legacies of Losing*.

Chapter 1

1. See, for example, G. Griffin, *The Creature from Jekyll Island: A Second Look at the Federal Reserve* (Westlake Village, CA: American Media, 1998).

2. Elmus Wicker, *The Great Debate on Banking Reform: Nelson Aldrich and the Origins of the Fed* (Columbus: Ohio State University Press, 2005); Eichengreen, *Exorbitant Privilege*, 24.

3. Bensel, *Yankee Leviathan*, 293–97.

4. For the political impacts of deflation in the United States, see Ritter, *Goldbugs and Greenbacks*; Bensel, *The Political Economy of American Industrialization*; Jeffry Frieden, *Global Capitalism: Its Fall and Rise in the Twentieth Century* (New York: W. W. Norton, 2006), 13–19, 43–45.

5. Eichengreen, *Globalizing Capital*, 41.

6. Bensel, *The Political Economy of American Industrialization*.

7. This regulatory competition is analyzed in Eugene N. White, *The Regulation and Reform of the American Banking System, 1900–1929* (Princeton: Princeton University Press, 1983), 10–62.

8. Richard Sylla, "Federal Policy, Banking Market Structure, and Capital Mobilization in the United States, 1863–1913," *The Journal of Economic History* 29, no. 4 (1969): 657–86.

9. Eichengreen, *Globalizing Capital*, 40–41.

10. Howard Bodenhorn, *A History of Banking in Antebellum America: Financial Markets and Economic Development in an Era of Nation-Building* (New York: Cambridge University Press, 2000), 169–78.

11. Sanders, *Roots of Reform*, 239.

12. Richard H. Timberlake, "Mr. Shaw and His Critics: Monetary Policy in the Golden Era Reviewed," *The Quarterly Journal of Economics* 77, no. 1 (1963): 40–54.

13. Contagion's logic is explained in Douglas W. Diamond and Philip H. Dybvig, "Bank Runs, Deposit Insurance, and Liquidity," *The Journal of Political Economy* 91, no. 3 (1983): 401–19.

14. Richard H. Timberlake, "The Central Banking Role of Clearinghouse Associations," *Journal of Money, Credit and Banking* 16, no. 1 (1984): 1–15; Gary Gorton, "Clearinghouses and the Origin of Central Banking in the United States," *The Journal of Economic History* 45, no. 2 (1985): 277–83.

15. Warburg, "Defects and Needs," 9–10, saw this an improvement over practices of relying "on the willingness and the ability of a few . . . bankers to use their own credit by drawing their own long bills on Europe . . . a costly and most unscientific mode of procedure."

16. Jon R. Moen and Ellis W. Tallman, "New York and the Politics of Central Banks, 1781 to the Federal Reserve Act," Working Paper 2003-42. Atlanta: Federal Reserve Bank of Atlanta, 2003.

17. Robert F. Bruner and Sean Carr, *The Panic of 1907: Lessons Learned from the Market's Perfect Storm* (Hoboken: John Wiley and Sons, 2008).

18. It also included Harvard economist A. Piatt Andrew and two *ex officio* representatives from the New York and Chicago banking communities. Broz, *International Origins*, 175.

19. Richard T. McCulley, *Banks and Politics during the Progressive Era* (New York: Garland, 1992), 226.

20. McCulley, *Banks and Politics*, 227–28.

21. Broz, *International Origins*, 180.

22. Power was diffused by apportioning 60 percent of votes for bank directors under a one-bank, one-vote rule, and distributing the rest by stock holdings. Broz, *International Origins*, 181.

23. Warburg, "Defects and Needs"; Charles Goodhart, *The Evolution of Central Banks* (Cambridge: MIT Press, 1988), 105–11.

24. Quoted in McCulley, *Banks and Politics*, 257–58.

25. Louis Brandeis, *Other People's Money and How the Bankers Use It* (New York: Frederick A. Stokes Company, 1914).

26. Scott C. James, *Presidents, Parties, and the State*, 124; Ware, *The Democratic Party*, 130.

27. *National Democratic Platform: Progress in Every Plank*, Democratic National Committee (Baltimore, Maryland: 1912), http://www.presidency.ucsb.edu/ws/index.php?pid=29590.

28. Roger Lowenstein, *America's Bank: The Epic Struggle to Create the Federal Reserve* (New York: Penguin, 2015), 174.

29. Quoted in Broz, *International Origins*, 195.

30. Arthur S. Link, *The New Freedom* (Princeton: Princeton University Press, 1956), 203.

31. Glass, *An Adventure*.

32. Quoted in Shull, *Fourth Branch*, 44.

33. Wilson campaigned against the "money monopoly." He warned in a 1911 speech, "Our system of credit is concentrated. The growth of the nation . . . [is] in the hands of a few men who . . . destroy genuine economic freedom." Quoted in McCulley, *Banks and Politics*, 270.

34. Quoted in ibid., 295.

35. William McAdoo to Colonel House, June 18, 1913. Quoted in Link, *The New Freedom*, 211.

36. Louis D. Brandeis to Woodrow Wilson, June 14, 1913. Quoted in McCulley, *Banks and Politics*, 297.

37. Quoted in Lowenstein, *America's Bank*, 213.

38. Link, *The New Freedom*, 213.

39. Quoted in ibid., 220.

40. Democrats were required to support bills endorsed by two-thirds of the Democratic House caucus on the House floor, a party discipline mechanism borrowed from Republicans. See Glass, *An Adventure*, 146–55; West, *Banking Reform*, 115; McCulley, *Banks and Politics*, 298–301.

41. Link, *The New Freedom*, 227.

42. West, *Banking Reform*, 125–29.

43. Vanderlip asked Wilson to discuss the proposal. He replied that doing so would be "useless . . . I could in no circumstances accept or recommend it." Quoted in Sanders, *Roots of Reform*, 253.

44. Ibid., 251–56.

45. Binder and Spindel argue that this design provided "an economic shot in the arm for Democratic constituencies in the region." See Sarah Binder and Mark Spindel, "Monetary Politics: Origins of the Federal Reserve," *Studies in American Political Development* 27, no. 1 (2013): 7.

46. Clifford, *Independence*, 51.

47. Quoted in Donald Kettl, *Leadership at the Fed* (New Haven: Yale University Press, 1986), 24.

48. Federal Reserve Act, Public Law 63-43, 63d Cong., 2d sess. (December 23, 1913), section 10.

49. The Independent Treasury System provided the Treasury Secretary patronage opportunities and interest income on public funds deposited in commercial banks. Meltzer, *A History*, vol. 1, 8.

50. James N. Primm, *A Foregone Conclusion: The Founding of the Federal Reserve Bank of St. Louis* (St. Louis: Federal Reserve Bank of St. Louis, 1989), 50.

51. Quoted in Link, *The New Freedom*, 452.

52. Primm, *A Foregone Conclusion*, 51.

53. Warburg, *Federal Reserve System*, 147.

54. West, *Banking Reform*, 214.

55. Warburg, *Federal Reserve System*, 184–86.

56. Federal Reserve Act, Public Law 63-43, 63d Cong., 2d sess. (December 23, 1913), section 2.

57. White, *Regulation and Reform*, 61–62; Broz, *International Origins*, 51–53.

58. Incentives included allowing banks to manage estates and separate time and demand deposits. Competition among regulators is explored in White, *Regulation and Reform*, 10–62.

59. Federal Reserve Act, Public Law 63-43, 63d Cong., 2d sess. (December 23, 1913), sections 16 and 19.

60. Nelson Aldrich, "Banking Reform in the United States," *Proceedings of the Academy of Political Science* 4, no. 1 (1913): 59, 85.

61. Benjamin Strong to Theodore Burton, December 5, 1913, Papers of Benjamin Strong, Jr., Folder 021.2, Federal Reserve Bank of New York.

62. Warburg, *Federal Reserve System*, 105.

63. Paul M. Warburg, "The Owen-Glass Bill as Submitted to the Democratic Caucus: Some Criticisms and Suggestions," *The North American Review* 198, no. 695 (1913): 541.

64. Ibid., 552.

65. Paul Warburg to Benjamin Strong, November 3, 1913, Papers of Benjamin Strong, Jr., Folder 211.2, Federal Reserve Bank of New York.

66. Warburg, *Federal Reserve System*, 172.
67. Wicker, *Federal Reserve Monetary Policy*, 6–7; Kettl, *Leadership at the Fed*, 24–25.
68. William G. McAdoo, *Crowded Years: The Reminiscences of William G. McAdoo* (New York: Houghton Mifflin, 1931), 288.
69. Quoted in Wicker, *Federal Reserve Monetary Policy*, 7.
70. Charles Hamlin, Diaries, Volume III, 53, Library of Congress. Quoted in Kettl, *Leadership at the Fed*, 24.
71. Member banks would elect three bankers as Class A directors and three Class B directors "engaged in their district in commerce, agriculture or some other industrial pursuit." The board would appoint three Class C directors to represent the public interest. Federal Reserve Act. Federal Reserve Act, Public Law 63-43, 63d Cong., 2d sess. (December 23, 1913), section 4.
72. Warburg, *Federal Reserve System*, 172.
73. Primm, *A Foregone Conclusion*, 55.
74. Chandler, *Benjamin Strong*, 67.
75. Federal Reserve Board, *First Annual Report of the Federal Reserve Board* (Washington, DC, 1914), 75, https://fraser.stlouisfed.org/title/117/item/2472.
76. W. P. G. Harding, *The Formative Period of the Federal Reserve System: During the World Crisis* (London: Constable, 1925), 10.
77. Federal Reserve Act, Public Law 63-43, 63d Cong., 2d sess. (December 23, 1913), section 10.
78. Federal Reserve Board, *First Annual Report*, 54–57.
79. Quoted in Wicker, *Federal Reserve Monetary Policy*, 8.
80. Warburg, "The Owen-Glass Bill," 541–42.
81. Ibid., 541.
82. Paul Warburg to Carter Glass, December 23, 1913. Reprinted in Warburg, *Federal Reserve System*, 137–38.
83. Federal Reserve Act, Public Law 63-43, 63d Cong., 2d sess. (December 23, 1913), section two.
84. Federal Reserve Board, Committee on Redistricting, *Revised Report*, reprinted in Warburg, *Federal Reserve System*, 767–74.
85. Warburg wanted to merge the Richmond, Atlanta, and Philadelphia Feds. The organization would be "administered substantially" as before, "by three bank boards . . . united by one stock capital instead of three and forming one district." This plan was "too radical," however, because it would lead to only "five or six districts," violating the legal minimum of eight districts. Paul Warburg, "Memorandum Concerning Mr. Broderick's Report on Federal Reserve Bank of Philadelphia," February 7, 1916, Paul M. Warburg File, Box 264, Folder 5, Records of the Federal Reserve System, Record Group 82, United States, National Archives and Records Administration, College Park, MD (hereafter Record Group 82), https://fraser.stlouisfed.org/archival/1344#473063|540510|540517|540524|540529.

86. Harding, *The Formative Period*, 36.

87. Letter from Subcommittee on Redistricting to the Federal Reserve Board, November 29, 1915. Paul M. Warburg File, Box 264, Folder 5, Records of the Federal Reserve System, Record Group 82, https://fraser.stlouisfed.org/archival/1344#473063|540510|540517|540524|540529.

88. Federal Reserve Board, *Second Annual Report of the Federal Reserve Board* (Washington, 1915), 19, https://fraser.stlouisfed.org/title/117/item/2473.

89. West, *Banking Reform*, 215; Meltzer, *A History*, vol. 1, 78–81.

90. Federal Reserve Act, Public Law 63-43, 63d Cong., 2d sess. (December 23, 1913), section 14. West, *Banking Reform*, 220, observes, "The interpretation placed on this passage depended on two factors: first, belief about the intent of the law; and second, one's location in the organizational structure of the system."

91. Meltzer, *A History*, vol. 1, 77.

92. Chandler, *Benjamin Strong*, 71.

93. West, *Banking Reform*, 216; Chandler, *Benjamin Strong*, 72–74.

94. Warburg, *Federal Reserve System*, 175.

95. Paul Warburg to Benjamin Strong, October 29, 1914, Papers of Benjamin Strong, Jr., Folder 211.2, Federal Reserve Bank of New York.

96. Paul Warburg to Benjamin Strong, January 27, 1915, Papers of Benjamin Strong, Jr., Folder 211.2, Federal Reserve Bank of New York.

97. Benjamin Strong, "The Federal Reserve System," speech, Atlantic City, May 14, 1915, https://fraser.stlouisfed.org/files/docs/historical/frbny/presidents/strong/strong_19150514.pdf.

98. Federal Reserve Board, *Third Annual Report of the Federal Reserve Board* (Washington, DC, 1916), 135, https://fraser.stlouisfed.org/title/117/item/2474.

99. Allan Sproul, "Policy Norms in Central Banking," in *Men, Money, and Policy: Essays in Honor of Karl R. Popp*, edited by David P. Eastburn (Philadelphia: Federal Reserve Bank of Philadelphia, 1970), 69.

100. Warburg, "Defects and Needs," 11, claimed dollar-denominated bills would "create a new and most powerful medium of international exchange—a new defense against gold shipments."

101. Benjamin Strong to Paul Warburg, April 12, 1915, Papers of Benjamin Strong, Jr., Folder 211.2, Federal Reserve Bank of New York.

102. Benjamin Strong to Paul Warburg, February 24, 1915, and August 2, 1915, Papers of Benjamin Strong, Jr., Folder 211.2, Federal Reserve Bank of New York.

103. Paul Warburg to Benjamin Strong, March 18, 1915, Papers of Benjamin Strong, Jr., Folder 211.2, Federal Reserve Bank of New York.

104. William Silber, *When Washington Shut Down Wall Street: The Great Financial Crisis of 1914 and the Origins of America's Monetary Supremacy* (Princeton: Princeton University Press, 2007), 2–17.

105. Eugene Gholz and Daryl G. Press, "The Effects of Wars on Neutral Countries: Why It Doesn't Pay to Preserve the Peace," *Security Studies* 10, no. 4 (2001): 1–57.

106. Benjamin Strong to Paul Warburg, October 25, 1916, Papers of Benjamin Strong, Jr., Folder 211.3, Federal Reserve Bank of New York.

107. Paul Warburg to Benjamin Strong, January 11, 1916, Papers of Benjamin Strong, Jr., Folder 211.3, Federal Reserve Bank of New York.

108. Paul Warburg to Benjamin Strong, November 16, 1916, Papers of Benjamin Strong, Jr., Folder 211.3, Federal Reserve Bank of New York.

109. Benjamin Strong to Paul Warburg, October 30, 1916, Papers of Benjamin Strong, Jr., Folder 211.3, Federal Reserve Bank of New York.

110. Benjamin Strong to Paul Warburg, September 6, 1916, Papers of Benjamin Strong, Jr., Folder 211.3, Federal Reserve Bank of New York.

111. Federal Reserve Board, *Third Annual Report*, 22–24, explains, "When the [FRA] was drafted its principal object was to deal with internal problems of banking and currency. Since its enactment . . . conditions . . . have undergone far-reaching changes which were not foreseen. . . . The United States has attained to world influence in financial affairs and it seems necessary that the Act, which has proved of such great value in the treatment of our domestic problems, should be amended in order to enable us to deal effectively with the international problems which now confront us and which seem destined to play so important a part in our economic life."

112. Paul Warburg to Benjamin Strong, July 18, 1916, Papers of Benjamin Strong, Jr., Folder 211.3, Federal Reserve Bank of New York.

113. Paul Warburg to Benjamin Strong, August 26, 1916, Papers of Benjamin Strong, Jr., Folder 211.3, Federal Reserve Bank of New York.

114. Benjamin Strong to Paul Warburg, September 6, 1916, Papers of Benjamin Strong, Jr., Folder 211.3, Federal Reserve Bank of New York.

115. Benjamin Strong to Paul Warburg, October 11, 1916, Papers of Benjamin Strong, Jr., Folder 211.3, Federal Reserve Bank of New York.

116. Paul Warburg to Benjamin Strong, August 26, 1916, Papers of Benjamin Strong, Jr., Folder 211.3, Federal Reserve Bank of New York.

117. Adam Tooze, *The Deluge: The Great War, America, and the Remaking of the Global Order, 1916–1931* (New York: Penguin, 2014), 51.

118. Quoted in Conti-Brown, *Power and Independence*, 30.

119. Quoted in Clifford, *Independence*, 41.

120. Conti-Brown, *Power and Independence*, 13.

Chapter 2

1. U.S. Congress, House, Committee on Banking and Currency, *Banking Act of 1935*, 517–20.

2. Federal Reserve Act, Public Law 63-43, 63d Cong., 2d sess. (December 23, 1913), section 14.

3. Friedman and Schwartz, *A Monetary History*, 240.

4. Burgess, "What the Federal Reserve System Is Doing to Promote Business Stability."

5. William Greider, *Secrets of the Temple: How the Federal Reserve Runs the Country* (New York: Simon and Schuster, 1989), 293.

6. Bordo, "Could the United States Have Had a Better Central Bank?"; Bordo and Wheelock, *The Promise and Performance of the Federal Reserve*; Binder and Spindel, *Myth of Independence*.

7. Clarke, *Central Bank Cooperation*; Kindleberger, *The World in Depression*.

8. As commerce secretary, Hoover lobbied the U.S. president to block Fed bond purchases but "Coolidge, a strict legalist . . . insisted that the Reserve Board had been created by the Congress entirely independent of the Executive." After Hoover was elected president in 1928, he "conferred several times" with the Board governor, urging him "to use the full powers of the Board to strangle the speculative movement." Herbert Hoover, *The Memoirs of Herbert Hoover: The Great Depression 1929-1941* (New York: The MacMillan Company, 1952), 9-16.

9. Benjamin Strong to Henry Towne, November 8, 1916. Quoted in Chandler, *Benjamin Strong*, 101.

10. Benjamin Strong to Pierre Jay, April 22, 1917. Quoted in Chandler, *Benjamin Strong*, 105.

11. Ibid., 107; Meltzer, *A History*, vol. 1, 85.

12. Warburg, *Federal Reserve System*, 155.

13. Harding, *The Formative Period*, 82; Warburg, *Federal Reserve System*, 155-57.

14. Burgess, "What the Federal Reserve System Is Doing to Promote Business Stability," 140.

15. Harding, *The Formative Period*, 83-84, explains that this appeal took the form of a Wilson-signed letter, which the board distributed to nonmember banks and trust companies.

16. Burgess, *The Reserve Banks*, 15.

17. Chandler, *Benjamin Strong*, 91; Eichengreen and Flandreau, "The Federal Reserve, the Bank of England, and the Rise of the Dollar as an International Currency, 1914-1939," *Open Economies Review* 23, no. 1 (2012): 57-87.

18. Paul Warburg to Woodrow Wilson, May 18, 1918. Reprinted in Warburg, *Federal Reserve System*, 802-804.

19. Harding, *The Formative Period*, 127-29.

20. Andrew J. Polsky, *Elusive Victories: The American Presidency at War* (New York: Oxford University Press, 2012), 121-29.

21. John M. Keynes, *The Economic Consequences of the Peace* (New York: Harcourt, Brace and Howe, 1920).

22. Robert Johnson, *The Peace Progressives and American Foreign Relations* (Cambridge: Harvard University Press, 1995); Legro, *Rethinking the World*, 62.

23. Milton Cooper, *Pivotal Decades* (New York: W. W. Norton, 1990), 343–56.

24. Benjamin Strong to R. H. Treman, September 12, 1919. Cited in Chandler, *Benjamin Strong*, 148.

25. Quoted in ibid., 138–39.

26. Quoted in Jane D'Arista, *Federal Reserve Structure and the Development of Monetary Policy: 1915–1935*, Staff Report of the Subcommittee on Domestic Finance, Committee on Banking and Currency. 92nd Cong., 1st Sess., 1971. Committee Print 68-574, 32.

27. Chandler, *Benjamin Strong*, 163.

28. The opinion is reprinted in Warburg, *Federal Reserve System*, 820–22.

29. Wicker, *Federal Reserve Monetary Policy*, 45; Meltzer, *A History*, vol. 1, 104.

30. Chandler, *Benjamin Strong*, 168.

31. Cooper, *Pivotal Decades*, 356.

32. Warren G. Harding, "Back to Normal," speech, Home Market Club of Boston, May 14, 1920, https://millercenter.org/the-presidency/presidential-speeches/may-14-1920-readjustment.

33. The price level doubled from 1915 to 1920. Bureau of the Census, 1975, Series Y 335–38.

34. Eichengreen, *Golden Fetters*, 194; Hetzel, *The Monetary Policy of the Federal Reserve*, 14.

35. Kindleberger, *The World in Depression*; Peter A. Gourevitch, *Politics in Hard Times: Comparative Responses to International Economic Crises* (Ithaca: Cornell University Press, 1986), 148.

36. Trubowitz, *National Interest*, 101.

37. Calculated from NBER Macrohistory database, National Bureau of Economic Research, https://data.nber.org/databases/macrohistory/contents/.

38. Chandler, *Benjamin Strong*, 139–45. For analyses of Strong's central bank diplomacy, see Clarke, *Central Bank Cooperation*; Ahamed, *Lords of Finance*.

39. Benjamin Strong to Will H. Hays, July 1, 1921, Papers of Benjamin Strong, Jr., Folder 16.0, Federal Reserve Bank of New York.

40. Kindleberger, *The World in Depression*, 295.

41. Chandler, *American Monetary Policy*, 149. See also, Burgess, "What the Federal Reserve System Is Doing to Promote Business Stability"; Eichengreen, *Golden Fetters*, 194.

42. In April 1920, Congress passed the Phelan Act authorizing reserve banks to charge penalty rates for heavy borrowers. This power was exercised by rural reserve banks, eliciting a backlash and then policy abandonment. See Meltzer, *A History*, vol. 1, 105; Shull, *Fourth Branch*, 72.

43. Meltzer, *A History*, vol. 1, 115; Shull, *Fourth Branch*, 71–82.

44. Charles Hamlin, Diaries, Volume VI, 412, Library of Congress.

45. Meltzer, *A History*, vol. 1, 112–13.

46. U.S. Congress, *Agricultural Inquiry: Hearing before the Joint Commission of Agricultural Inquiry*, 67th Cong, 1st sess., 1921, 20–43, https://fraser.stlouisfed.org/title/959/item/37518.

47. George L. Harrison to James H. Case, August 12, 1921. Quoted in Chandler, *Benjamin Strong*, 179.

48. U.S. Congress, Joint Commission of Agricultural Inquiry, *The Agricultural Crisis and its Causes: Report of the Joint Commission of Agricultural Inquiry*, 67th Cong., 1st sess., 1922, H. Rep. 408, Part 2, 15, https://hdl.handle.net/2027/pst.000057629179?urlappend=%3Bseq=5.

49. Federal Reserve Board, *Ninth Annual Report of the Federal Reserve Board* (Washington, DC, 1922), 36.

50. Harding, *The Formative Period*, 242, warned, "There would be more talk and less action."

51. *New York Times*, May 12, 1922. Quoted in Kettl, *Leadership at the Fed*, 28.

52. Kettl, *Leadership at the Fed*, 28; Meltzer, *A History*, vol. 1, 156.

53. Governors Conference, minutes, October 27, 1921. Cited in Meltzer, *A History*, vol. 1, 126.

54. Joint Conference of the Chairmen and Governors of the Federal Reserve Banks, minutes, October 25–28, 1921. Quoted in D'Arista, *Federal Reserve Structure*, 62.

55. Montagu Norman to Benjamin Strong, February 27, 1922. Cited in Clarke, *Central Bank Cooperation*, 34.

56. Ibid., 36–40.

57. Quoted in Eichengreen, *Globalizing Capital*, 62.

58. Benjamin Strong to Montagu Norman, July 14, 1922, Papers of Benjamin Strong, Jr., Folder 1116.2, Federal Reserve Bank of New York.

59. Benjamin Strong to Montagu Norman, February 22, 1923. Cited in Clarke, *Central Bank Cooperation*, 31.

60. Chandler, *Benjamin Strong*, 205–12; Wicker, *Federal Reserve Monetary Policy*, 64.

61. Governors Conference, minutes, May 2, 1922. Cited in Chandler, *Benjamin Strong*, 212.

62. Ibid., 221; Wicker, *Federal Reserve Monetary Policy*, 71.

63. Quoted in Meltzer, *A History*, vol. 1, 150.

64. Benjamin Strong to James H. Case, April 21, 1923, Papers of Benjamin Strong, Jr., Folder 320.226, Federal Reserve Bank of New York.

65. Herbert Feis, *The Diplomacy of the Dollar: First Era, 1919–1932* (Baltimore: John Hopkins University Press, 1950); Trubowitz, *National Interest*, 99.

66. Clarke, *Central Bank Cooperation*, 47–57.

67. W. R. Burgess to James H. Case, November 30, 1923. Cited in John H. Wood, *A History of Central Banking in Great Britain and the United States* (New York: Cambridge University Press, 2005), 187.

68. Wicker, *Federal Reserve Monetary Policy*, 81.

69. Burgess, "What the Federal Reserve System Is Doing to Promote Business Stability," 146.

70. Frieden, "Sectoral Conflict"; Trubowitz, *National Interest*, 108–109.

71. Benjamin Strong to Montagu Norman, March 3, 1924, Papers of Benjamin Strong, Jr., Folder 1116.4, Federal Reserve Bank of New York.

72. Charles Hamlin, Diaries, Volume VIII, 129, Library of Congress.

73. Benjamin Strong to Andrew Mellon, May 27, 1924. Cited in Chandler, *Benjamin Strong*, 266–67.

74. Burgess, "What the Federal Reserve System Is Doing to Promote Business Stability," 146–47.

75. Clarke, *Central Bank Cooperation*, 89–90.

76. Chandler, *Benjamin Strong*, 241; Wicker, *Federal Reserve Monetary Policy*, 77.

77. U.S. Congress, House, Committee on Banking and Currency, *Stabilization: Hearings before the Committee on Banking and Currency*, 69th Cong., 1st sess., 1926, 508–13, https://fraser.stlouisfed.org/title/108/item/1271.

78. Keynes pointed out that indexes used by financiers for currency valuation measured prices determined in global markets, whereas the prices that would need to fall were domestic wages. Keynes argued sterling remained overvalued by 10 percent. John M. Keynes, *The Economic Consequences of Mr. Churchill* (London: L. and V. Woolf, 1925).

79. Burgess, "What the Federal Reserve System Is Doing to Promote Business Stability," 147.

80. French citizens repatriated foreign balances in anticipation of a revaluation when the gold standard was legalized. If the lower rate instead enshrined, exporters would benefit from a cheap currency. Clarke, *Central Bank Cooperation*, 110–12; Eichengreen, *Golden Fetters*, 210–16.

81. Clarke, *Central Bank Cooperation*, 140.

82. Chandler, *Benjamin Strong*, 375; Wicker, *Federal Reserve Monetary Policy*, 111; Kindleberger, *The World in Depression*, 69.

83. Clarke, *Central Bank Cooperation*, 126.

84. Benjamin Strong to Daniel Crissinger, August 19, 1927. Cited in Meltzer, *A History*, vol. 1, 222.

85. James McDougal to Benjamin Strong, August 24, 1927. Cited in Chandler, *Benjamin Strong*, 445.

86. Benjamin Strong to James MacDougal, August 26, 1927. Cited in ibid., 445.

87. Charles Hamlin, Diaries, Volume XIV, 12–13, Library of Congress.

88. Federal Reserve Board, minutes, September 6, 1927. Platt, Hamlin, and Miller cast dissenting votes. See discussions in Wicker, *Federal Reserve Monetary Policy*, 112–13; Kettl, *Leadership at the Fed*, 32; Eichengreen, *Golden Fetters*, 26; Meltzer, *A History*, vol. 1, 222–23.

89. Charles Hamlin, Diaries, Volume XIV, 31, Library of Congress.

90. Benjamin Strong to Newton Baker, September 19, 1927. Cited in Chandler, *Benjamin Strong*, 448–49.

91. Benjamin Strong to Carter Glass, October 5, 1927, Papers of Benjamin Strong, Jr., Folder 21.1, Federal Reserve Bank of New York.

92. Quoted in Kettl, *Leadership at the Fed*, 33.

93. Charles Hamlin, Diaries, Volume XIV, 2–3, Library of Congress.

94. Friedman and Schwartz, *A Monetary History*, 255, 418.

95. Meltzer, *A History*, vol. 1, 289.

96. Eichengreen, *Golden Fetters*, 252.

97. National Bureau of Economic Research, Raw Cotton Exports for United States, M0743AUSM149NNBR, https://fred.stlouisfed.org/series/M0743AUSM149NNBR.

98. Richard Bensel, *Sectionalism and American Political Development, 1880–1980* (Madison: University of Wisconsin Press, 1984), 137.

99. This figure excludes Michigan's upper peninsula which is also part of the district. Federal Reserve Board of Governors, *Federal Reserve Bulletin*, September 1937, 868, https://fraser.stlouisfed.org/title/62/item/21220.

100. The pro–New York faction also included Charles Hamlin (Boston), Edward Platt (New York), and the comptroller of the currency. D'Arista, *Federal Reserve Structure*, 62.

101. McFadden Act, Public Law 69-639, 69th Cong., 2d sess. (February 25, 1927), https://fraser.stlouisfed.org/title/976.

102. "Changes Impending in Reserve System," *Wall Street Journal*, February 25, 1927. New York deputy governor George Harrison reported that Charles Hamlin told him the article was written by another board member. George L. Harrison to Benjamin Strong, March 15, 1927, George L. Harrison Papers, Folder 2320.211, Federal Reserve Bank of New York.

103. Young, "Position of the New York Bank in the Reserve System."

104. Hoover, *Memoirs*, 16, recalled that after being elected president in 1928, he "conferred several times with [the board governor who] agreed to use the full powers of the Board to strangle the speculative movement."

105. Clarke, *Central Bank Cooperation*, 148.

106. U.S. Congress, House, Committee on Banking and Currency, *Stabilization: Hearings before the Committee on Banking and Currency*, 70th Cong., 1st sess., 1928, 164–92, https://fraser.stlouisfed.org/title/754.

107. U.S. Congress, House, Committee on Banking and Currency, *Stabilization*, 16–21.

108. Chandler, *Benjamin Strong*, 455.

109. Adolph Miller and George James dissented. Federal Reserve Board, minutes, August 16, 1928, Records of the Federal Reserve System, Record Group 82, Volume 15, Part 2, https://fraser.stlouisfed.org/title/821/item/32961.

110. Federal Advisory Council, "Meeting documents," September 27–28, 1928, Records of the Federal Reserve System, Record Group 82, Box 1, Volume 1921–1930, https://fraser.stlouisfed.org/title/1152/item/1660.

111. Federal Reserve Board, minutes, November 15, 1928, Records of the Federal Reserve System, Record Group 82, Volume 15, Part 2, https://fraser.stlouisfed.org/title/821/item/32570.

112. Charles Hamlin, Diaries, Volume XV, 74–77, Library of Congress.

113. Ibid., 121.

114. Clarke, *Central Bank Cooperation*, 152; Eichengreen, *Golden Fetters*, 219.

115. Federal Reserve Board, minutes, February 5, 1929, Records of the Federal Reserve System, Record Group 82, Volume 16, Part 1, https://fraser.stlouisfed.org/title/821/item/32010.

116. Charles Hamlin, Diaries, Volume XIV, 49, Library of Congress.

117. Wicker, *Federal Reserve Monetary Policy*, 137; Meltzer, *A History*, vol. 1, 235; Wood, *A History of Central Banking*, 190.

118. Cited in Clarke, *Central Bank Cooperation*, 157.

119. The Board approved follow-up requests to reduce its discount rate, respectively, to 5 percent and 4.5 percent. Charles Hamlin, Diaries, Volume XVI, 187–91, Library of Congress. See Wicker, *Federal Reserve Monetary Policy*, 145; Wood, *A History of Central Banking*, 197.

120. Montagu Norman cable to George Harrison, October 24, 1929. Quoted in Clarke, *Central Bank Cooperation*, 160.

121. These purchases ultimately reached $132 million. Wood, *A History of Central Banking*, 197.

122. Friedman and Schwartz, *A Monetary History*, 335–39.

123. Charles Hamlin, Diaries, Volume XVI, 187–91, Library of Congress.

124. Only Edmund Platt voted no. Federal Reserve Board, minutes, November 5, 1929, Records of the Federal Reserve System, Record Group 82, Volume 16, Part 2, https://fraser.stlouisfed.org/title/821/item/31844.

125. Open Market Investment Committee, minutes, November 12, 1929, Records of the Federal Reserve System, Record Group 82, File 333.-b-2, https://fraser.stlouisfed.org/title/5187/item/22613.

126. George L. Harrison, memorandum, November 15, 1929, George L. Harrison Papers, Folder 2210.1, Federal Reserve Bank of New York.

127. Miller, James, and Cunningham dissented. Federal Reserve Board, minutes, November 25, 1929, Records of the Federal Reserve System, Record Group 82, Volume 16, Part 2, https://fraser.stlouisfed.org/title/821/item/32227.

128. Federal Reserve Board, minutes, January 16, 1930, Records of the Federal Reserve System, Record Group 82, Volume 17, Part 1, https://fraser.stlouisfed.org/title/821/item/31408.

129. Open Market Policy Conference, Organization of, Records of the Federal Reserve System, Record Group 82, Box 1437, Folder 1, File 333.-c, https://fraser.stlouisfed.org/archival/1344/item/469080.

130. Kindleberger, *The World in Depression*, 128–9; Eichengreen, *Golden Fetters*, 249.

131. Clarke, *Central Bank Cooperation*, 170–71.

132. Eichengreen, *Golden Fetters*, 259; Toniolo, *Central Bank Cooperation*, 45–48.

133. John Calkins to George Harrison, October 8, 1929, Records of the Federal Reserve System, Record Group 82, Box 1435, Folder 4, File 333.-b-1.

134. Chandler, *American Monetary Policy*, 150.

135. Quoted in Wicker 1966, 150.

136. Kindleberger, *The World in Depression*, 137; Meltzer, *A History*, vol. 1, 297–98; Shull, *Fourth Branch*, 98.

137. Open Market Policy Conference, minutes, May 21, 1930. Cited in Meltzer, *A History*, vol. 1, 301.

138. Federal Reserve Bank of New York, Board of Directors, minutes, May 29, 1930. Cited in Meltzer, *A History*, vol. 1, 305.

139. Dallas, Philadelphia, Chicago, and San Francisco disapproved. St. Louis posed no objection. Federal Reserve Board, minutes, June 3, 1930, Records of the Federal Reserve System, Record Group 82, Volume 17, Part 2, https://fraser.stlouisfed.org/title/821/item/26399.

140. Quoted in Meltzer, *A History*, vol. 1, 307.

141. Federal Reserve Board, minutes, January 30, 1930, Records of the Federal Reserve System, Record Group 82, Volume 17, Part 1, https://fraser.stlouisfed.org/title/821/item/31254.

142. The governor admitted that he "hesitated to vote favorably on the New York application . . . because of the position of the governors at the OMPC meeting on March 25." Open Market Policy Conference, minutes, May 21, 1930. Cited in Meltzer, *A History*, vol. 1, 301.

143. Open Market Policy Conference, Executive Committee, minutes, June 23, 1930, Records of the Federal Reserve System, Record Group 82, Box 1437, File 333.-c-2, https://fraser.stlouisfed.org/title/5188/item/22617/content/pdf/rg82_ompcminutes_19300623.

144. Federal Reserve Bank of New York, Board of Directors, minutes, June 26, 1930. Cited in Wicker, *Federal Reserve Monetary Policy*, 154; Chandler, *American Monetary Policy*, 152.

145. Open Market Policy Conference, minutes, September 25, 1930. Cited in Wicker, *Federal Reserve Monetary Policy*, 161.

146. Wicker, *Federal Reserve Monetary Policy*, 157; Kindleberger, *The World in Depression*, 136; Meltzer, *A History*, vol. 1, 319, 408.

147. Kindleberger, *The World in Depression*, 133.

148. Eichengreen, *Golden Fetters*, 252; Meltzer, *A History*, vol. 1, 289.

149. From October 1929 through October 1930, the system bought $448 million in government securities. These purchases were surpassed by a contraction of New York Fed investments, including a 77.8 percent fall in discount loans and a 44.8 percent contraction of its bill portfolio. Calculated from Federal Reserve Economic Database, https://fred.stlouisfed.org/.

150. Benjamin Strong to Will H. Hays, July 1, 1921, Papers of Benjamin Strong, Jr., Folder 16.0, Federal Reserve Bank of New York.

151. Burgess, *The Reserve Banks*, 245.

152. Board of Directors of the Federal Reserve Bank of New York, minutes, August 20, 1931. Cited in Friedman and Schwartz, *A Monetary History*, 380.

153. Adolph C. Miller, "The Banking Bill Considered in the Light of 1927–1929," released for newspaper publication on June 24, 1935, https://fraser.stlouisfed.org/title/457/item/475524.

Chapter 3

1. Open Market Policy Conference, minutes, April 27, 1931. Cited in Chandler, *American Monetary Policy*, 164; Kindleberger, *The World in Depression*, 148–52.

2. Open Market Policy Conference, Executive Committee, minutes, June 21, 1931, Records of the Federal Reserve System, Record Group 82, Box 1437, File 333.-c-2, https://fraser.stlouisfed.org/title/5188/item/22620.

3. Kindleberger, *The World in Depression*, 156–57.

4. Montagu Norman cable to George Harrison, July 4, 1931. Cited in Chandler, *American Monetary Policy*, 165.

5. Kindleberger, *The World in Depression*, 159.

6. Chandler, *American Monetary Policy*, 167.

7. Wicker, *Federal Reserve Monetary Policy*, 163–66; Chandler, *American Monetary Policy*, 177.

8. Wicker, *Federal Reserve Monetary Policy*, 169.

9. Clarke, *Central Bank Cooperation*, 219.

10. Chandler, *American Monetary Policy*, 175.

11. Blyth, *Great Transformations*, 53; Eichengreen and Temin, "The Gold Standard and the Great Depression."

12. Barry Eichengreen, *Hall of Mirrors: The Great Depression, the Great Recession, and the Uses-and Misuses-of-History* (New York: Oxford University Press, 2014), 156–57.

13. Timberlake, *Monetary Policy in the United States*, 275.

14. Eichengreen, *Hall of Mirrors*, 250.

15. Walker F. Todd, *The Federal Reserve Board and the Rise of the Corporate State, 1931–1934* (Great Barrington: American Institute for Economic Research, 1995).

16. Burgess, *The Reserve Banks*, 50; Shull, *Fourth Branch*, 98.

17. Burgess, *The Reserve Banks*, 65; Jacobs and King, *Fed Power*, 75.

18. Eichengreen, *Hall of Mirrors*, 158–59.

19. For analyses that explain reserve bank opposition through varied interests or ideas, see, Gerald Epstein and Thomas Ferguson, "Monetary Policy, Loan

Liquidation, and Industrial Conflict: The Federal Reserve and the Open Market Operations of 1932," *The Journal of Economic History* 44, no. 4 (1984): 957–83; Christina D. Romer and David H. Romer, "The Most Dangerous Idea in Federal Reserve History: Monetary Policy Doesn't Matter," *American Economic Review* 103, no. 3 (2013): 55–60.

20. Blyth, *Great Transformations*, 53.

21. Chandler, *American Monetary Policy*, 209–24; Meltzer, *A History*, vol. 1, 427; Eichengreen, *Hall of Mirrors*, 165.

22. Hoover, *Memoirs*, 210; Meltzer, *A History*, vol. 1, 383–84; Eichengreen, *Hall of Mirrors*, 225–26.

23. Quoted in Meltzer, *A History*, vol. 1, 383.

24. Meltzer, *A History*, vol. 1, 386–89; Eichengreen, *Hall of Mirrors*, 229–33.

25. Chandler, *American Monetary Policy*, 263–71.

26. Burgess, *The Reserve Banks*, 67; Chandler, *American Monetary Policy*, 244.

27. Kindleberger, *The World in Depression*, 219.

28. Meltzer, *A History*, vol. 1, 450, observes, "By rejecting the London agreement, Roosevelt freed policy from the gold standard and kept the Federal Reserve in the backseat."

29. Foreign government–owned gold remained exportable. Eichengreen, *Hall of Mirrors*, 229–33; Kindleberger, *The World in Depression*, 202; Meltzer, *A History*, vol. 1, 442.

30. Timberlake, *Monetary Policy in the United States*, 276.

31. Franklin D. Roosevelt, "Executive Order 6102—Requiring Gold Coin, Gold Bullion and Gold Certificates to Be Delivered to the Government," April 5, 1933, The American Presidency Project, Gerhard Peters and John T. Woolley, https://www.presidency.ucsb.edu/node/208042.

32. Roosevelt endorsed the Thomas amendment contingent on making presidential powers discretionary. It authorized (1) reserve banks to buy up to $3 billion in government bonds from the treasury, (2) the U.S. president to issue up to $3 billion in greenbacks if the reserve banks chose not to buy bonds, (3) the president to devalue the dollar by up to 50 percent in terms of gold and silver, and (4) Federal Reserve Board, with presidential approval, to declare a state of emergency and raise or lower member bank reserve requirement ratios.

33. In the event of a currency devaluation, debtors were required to pay the sum of gold specified when the contract was signed. See Richard H. Timberlake, *Constitutional Money: A Review of the Supreme Court's Monetary Decisions* (New York: Cambridge University Press, 2013), 183–84.

34. Quoted in Meltzer, *A History*, vol. 1, 451.

35. Montagu Norman to George L. Harrison, November 2, 1933, George L. Harrison Papers, Folder 3115.4, Federal Reserve Bank of New York.

36. Burgess, *The Reserve Banks*, 125; Chandler, *American Monetary Policy*, 244; Timberlake, *Monetary Policy in the United States*, 279.

37. Quoted in Meltzer, *A History*, vol. 1, 457.

38. Creditors sought to defend gold clauses. See Timberlake, *Constitutional Money*, 182–205.

39. Chandler, *American Monetary Policy*, 260–71, 304–305.

40. Burgess, *The Reserve Banks*, 139.

41. Chandler, *American Monetary Policy*, 244.

42. Friedman and Schwartz, *A Monetary History*, 255. See also, David C. Wheelock, "National Monetary Policy by Regional Design: The Evolving Role of the Federal Reserve Banks in Federal Reserve System Policy," in *Regional Aspects of Monetary Policy in Europe*, ed. Jurgen von Hagen and Christopher J. Waller, 241–74 (New York: Kluwer Academic Publishers, 2000); Meltzer, *A History*, vol. 1, 415.

43. U.S. Congress, Senate, Committee on Finance, *Investigation of Economic Problems: Hearings Before the Committee on Finance*, 72nd Cong., 2nd sess., 1933, 710–13, https://fraser.stlouisfed.org/title/176.

44. Eccles's proto-Keynesian views made him an outlier in the Roosevelt administration. See Chandler, *American Monetary Policy*, 251; Kettl, *Leadership at the Fed*, 47.

45. U.S. Congress, Senate, Committee on Finance, *Investigation of Economic Problems*, 709.

46. U.S. Congress, Senate, Committee on Finance, *Investigation of Economic Problems*, 730.

47. Quoted in Mark Nelson, *Jumping the Abyss: Marriner S. Eccles and the New Deal, 1933–1940* (Salt Lake City: University of Utah Press, 2017), 178.

48. Quoted in Shull, *Fourth Branch*, 103.

49. Binder and Spindel, *Myth of Independence*, 115.

50. Lauchlin Currie to Marriner Eccles, April 1, 1935. Quoted in Conti-Brown, *Power and Independence*, 29.

51. Quoted in Kettl, *Leadership at the Fed*, 48–49.

52. U.S. Congress, Senate, Committee on Banking and Finance, Nomination of Marriner S. Eccles to be a Member of the Federal Reserve Board: Hearings before a Subcommittee of the Committee on Banking and Currency, 74th Cong., 1st sess., 1935, 11, https://fraser.stlouisfed.org/archival/1343/item/468253.

53. Kettl, *Leadership at the Fed*, 50.

54. Goldenweiser memorandum on Banking Reform to Committee, September 6, 1934, 2. Quoted in Meltzer, *A History*, vol. 1, 471.

55. Allan Sproul, memorandum, 1934, Papers of Allan Sproul, Folder 4380, Federal Reserve Bank of New York.

56. Marriner S. Eccles, *Beckoning Frontiers* (New York: Alfred A. Knopf, 1951), 192.

57. U.S. Congress, House, Committee on Banking and Currency, *Banking Act of 1935*, 181.

58. Ibid., 367.

59. Chandler, *American Monetary Policy*, 11.

60. Binder and Spindel, *Myth of Independence*, 118, see this as reflecting support for the New Deal, but the last chapter showed that 1920s bond purchases stimulated Southern cotton exports.

61. Meltzer, *A History*, vol. 1, 479.

62. Harrison Telephone Conversation with Senator Glass, June 15, 1935. Quoted in Meltzer, *A History*, vol. 1, 483.

63. Cited in Timberlake, *Monetary Policy in the United States*, 285.

64. Eccles signaled that he would accept a compromise where reserve banks remained on the FOMC if the board was given a voting majority. Binder and Spindel, *Myth of Independence*, 120.

65. Quoted in Meltzer, *A History*, vol. 1, 482.

66. Chandler, *American Monetary Policy*, 306, observes the change to reserve bank president was "meant to imply a lowering of their status relative to that of the governors on the new Board."

67. Federal Reserve Board of Governors, *Twenty-Third Annual Report of the Board of Governors of the Federal Reserve System* (Washington, D.C., 1936), 14, https://fraser.stlouisfed.org/title/117/item/2494.

68. David C. Wheelock and Mark A. Carlson, "Navigating Constraints: The Evolution of Federal Reserve Monetary Policy, 1935–1959," in *The Federal Reserve's Role in the Global Economy: A Historical Perspective*, ed. Michael D. Bordo and Mark A. Wynne, 50–83 (New York: Cambridge University Press, 2016).

69. Chandler, *American Monetary Policy*, 306, observes "ambiguity was removed . . . clumsily."

70. Emanuel Goldenweiser, *American Monetary Policy* (New York: McGraw-Hill, 1951), 284.

71. Meltzer, *A History*, vol. 1, 480.

72. Federal Open Market Committee, "Regulations Packet," Records of the Federal Reserve System, Record Group 82, Box 2760, Folder 6, https://fraser.stlouisfed.org/archival/1344/item/469189.

73. The regulation states that "transactions for the System . . . shall be executed by a Federal Reserve bank selected by the Committee," Federal Open Market Committee, "Regulations Packet," 3.

74. *New York Times*, "Close Friend of Cermak," June 3, 1933.

75. Walter Lippman, "The First Roosevelt Program Completed," *New York Herald Tribune*, June 14, 1933.

76. Marriner Eccles, "List of Suggested Appointments to the Federal Reserve Board along with Biographical Information," January 11, 1936, Marriner S. Eccles papers, MS 0178, Box 3, Folder 2, Special Collections and Archives, University

of Utah, J. Willard Marriott, Salt Lake City, Utah, https://fraser.stlouisfed.org/archival/1343/item/464040.

77. Meltzer, *A History*, vol. 1, 501.

78. Clifford, *Independence*, 125; Chandler, *American Monetary Policy*, 244; Shull, *Fourth Branch*, 117.

79. "Notes on Statement Made by Mr. J. H. Williams at the Meeting of the Board on December 17, 1935," Records of the Federal Reserve System, Record Group 82, Box 1450, Folder 4.

80. Clifford, *Independence*, 158.

81. Chandler, *American Monetary Policy*, 244; Wheelock and Carlson, *Navigating Constraints*.

82. Goldenweiser, *American Monetary Policy*, 175.

83. Quoted in John Blum, *From the Morgenthau Diaries: Years of Crisis, 1928–1938* (Boston: Houghton Mifflin, 1959), 352.

84. Quoted in Meltzer, *A History*, vol. 1, 502–503.

85. Blum, *Morgenthau Diaries*, 356.

86. Quoted in Clifford, *Independence*, 152–53.

87. Sidney Hyman, *Marriner S. Eccles, Private Entrepreneur and Public Servant* (Palo Alto: Stanford University Graduate School of Business, 1976), 221–22.

88. Quoted in Blum, *Morgenthau Diaries*, 363.

89. Meltzer, *A History*, vol. 1, 509.

90. Blum, *Morgenthau Diaries*, 369.

91. Quoted in Clifford, *Independence*, 156.

92. Ibid., 157.

93. Quoted in Meltzer, *A History*, vol. 1, 516.

94. Clifford, *Independence*, 138–62; Chandler, *American Monetary Policy*, 255; Meltzer, *A History*, vol. 1, 574; Binder and Spindel, *Myth of Independence*, 122–23.

95. Trubowitz, *National Interest*, 119–21; Legro, *Rethinking the World*, 66–73; Polsky, *Elusive Victories*, 136–42.

96. Frieden, "Sectoral Conflict"; Trubowitz, *National Interest*.

97. Franklin D. Roosevelt, "Fireside Chat," radio address, December 29, 1940, The American Presidency Project, Gerhard Peters and John T. Woolley, https://www.presidency.ucsb.edu/node/209416.

98. Quoted in Clifford, *Independence*, 173.

99. Ritter, *Allan Sproul*, 6–7; Meltzer, *A History*, vol. 1, 594.

100. Meltzer, *A History*, vol. 1, 547.

101. An Act to Promote the Defense of the United States, Public Law 77-11, 77th Cong., 1st sess. (March 11, 1941), http://www.loc.gov/law/help/statutes-at-large/77th-congress/session-1/c77s1ch11.pdf.

102. Eric Rauchway, *The Money Makers: How Roosevelt and Keynes Ended the Depression, Defeated Fascism, and Secured a Prosperous Peace* (New York:

Basic Books, 2015). Also see Meltzer, *A History*, vol. 1, 548; Polsky, *Elusive Victories*, 146.

103. Federal Reserve Board of Governors, *Twenty-Ninth Annual Report of the Board of Governors of the Federal Reserve System* (Washington, D.C., 1942), 56, https://fraser.stlouisfed.org/title/117/item/2500.

104. Kettl, *Leadership at the Fed*, 59; Meltzer, *A History*, vol. 1, 589.

105. Wood, *A History of Central Banking*, 226.

106. Legro, *Rethinking the World*, 68–72.

107. Jonathan Kirshner, *Appeasing Bankers: Financial Caution on the Road to War* (Princeton: Princeton University Press, 2007), 122–53.

108. Ruggie, "International Regimes"; Helleiner, *States and the Reemergence of Global Finance*; Rawi Abdelal, *Capital Rules: The Construction of Global Finance* (Cambridge: Harvard University Press, 2007); Kirshner, *American Power*, 37–44.

109. Helleiner, *States and the Reemergence of Global Finance*, 25; Eichengreen, *Globalizing Capital*, 136; Blyth, *Great Transformations*, 128; Abdelal, *Capital Rules*.

110. John H. Williams, "The Postwar Monetary Plans," *The American Economic Review* 34, no. 1 (1944): 372–84; John H. Williams, "International Monetary Plans: After Bretton Woods," *Foreign Affairs* 23, no. 1 (1944): 38–56.

111. U.S. Congress, Senate, Banking and Currency Committee, *Bretton Woods Agreements Act: Hearings Before the Committee on Banking and Currency*, 79th Cong., 1st sess., 1945, 310, https://fraser.stlouisfed.org/title/767.

112. U.S. Congress, Senate, Banking and Currency Committee, *Bretton Woods Agreements Act*, 476.

113. Helleiner, *States and the Reemergence of Global Finance*, 39–44.

114. John H. Williams, "The Bretton Woods Agreements," address, Academy of Political Science meeting on "World Organization—Economic, Political, and Social," April 4–5, 1945.

115. Franklin D. Roosevelt, "Annual Message to Congress," January 11, 1944. In *The Public Papers and Addresses of Franklin D. Roosevelt*, ed. Samuel I. Rosenman, 40–42 (New York: Harper and Bros., 1950).

116. Binder and Spindel, *Myth of Independence*, 144.

117. Ibid., 145–50.

118. Kettl, *Leadership at the Fed*, 79; Conti-Brown, *Power and Independence*, 33.

119. Clifford, *Independence*, 210.

120. Kettl, *Leadership at the Fed*, 62–63.

121. U.S. Congress, House, Committee on Banking and Currency, *Economic Stabilization Aids: Hearings before the Committee on Banking and Currency*, 80th Cong., 1st sess., 1947, 280, https://hdl.handle.net/2027/uc1.a0004770376?urlappend=%3Bseq=1.

122. Marriner Eccles to John Snyder, October 14, 1947. Quoted in Kettl, *Leadership at the Fed*, 63.

123. Clifford, *Independence*, 203–204.
124. Meltzer, *A History*, vol. 1, 714.
125. Kettl, *Leadership at the Fed*, 65.
126. U.S. Congress, Joint Committee on the Economic Report, Monetary, Credit, and Fiscal Policies: Hearings before the Subcommittee on Monetary, Credit, and Fiscal Policies of the Joint Committee of the Economic Report, 81st Cong., 1st sess., 1950, 216, https://fraser.stlouisfed.org/title/3615.
127. U.S. Congress, Joint Committee on the Economic Report, *Monetary, Credit, and Fiscal Policies*, 430.
128. United States, Commission on Organization of the Executive Branch of the Government, Task Force Report on Regulatory Commissions, Appendix N, Marriner S. Eccles Papers, Box 8, Folder 12, Item 2, Special Collections, J. Willard Marriott Library, University of Utah, Salt Lake City, UT, https://fraser.stlouisfed.org/archival/1343/item/464292.
129. U.S. Congress, Joint Committee on the Economic Report, *Report of the Joint Committee on the Economic Report on the January 1950 Economic Report of the President*, 81st Cong., 2nd sess., 1950, S. Rep. 1843, 19, https://fraser.stlouisfed.org/title/1250/item/536769.
130. Federal Reserve Bank of New York, *Thirty-Sixth Annual Report*, 1950, 5, https://fraser.stlouisfed.org/title/467/item/17995.
131. Meltzer, *A History*, vol. 1, 698.
132. Allan Sproul, "The 'Accord'—A Landmark in the First Fifty Years of the Federal Reserve System," *Monthly Review: Federal Reserve Bank of New York* 58, no. 11 (1964): 227–36, https://fraser.stlouisfed.org/title/1170/item/2991.
133. Quoted in ibid., 232.
134. Quoted in Conti-Brown, *Power and Independence*, 35.
135. See, for example, Hetzel and Leach, "The Treasury-Fed Accord."
136. Binder and Spindel, *Myth of Independence*, 124–25, 162.
137. Conti-Brown, *Power and Independence*, 37.
138. Quoted, respectively, in Greider, *Secrets of the Temple*, 310; Friedman and Schwartz, *A Monetary History*, 255.
139. Conti-Brown, *Power and Independence*, 28–39.
140. Quoted in Ritter, *Allan Sproul*, 11.
141. Burgess, *The Reserve Banks*, 245.
142. Binder and Spindel, *Myth of Independence*, 125.

Chapter 4

1. Bremner, *Chairman of the Fed*; Meltzer, *A History*, vol. 2; Hetzel and Leach, "After the Accord."
2. Kettl, *Leadership at the Fed*, 81.

3. Bremner, *Chairman of the Fed*, 102.

4. Allan Sproul, address, New York State Bankers Association, January 25, 1954. Quoted in Clifford, *Independence*, 185.

5. These themes are also developed in Allan Sproul, "Reflections of a Central Banker," *The Journal of Finance* 11, no. 1 (1956): 1–14; Sproul, "Policy Norms in Central Banking."

6. Clifford, *Independence*, 216–22.

7. Quote from Kettl, *Leadership at the Fed*, 85.

8. Young, "Position of the New York Bank in the Reserve System."

9. Bremner, *Chairman of the Fed*, 13; Conti-Brown, *Power and Independence*, 43.

10. Reprinted in U.S. Congress, Joint Committee on the Economic Report, *United States Monetary Policy, Recent Thinking and Experience: Hearings before the Subcommittee on Economic Stabilization*, 83rd Cong., 2nd sess., 1954, 281–83, https://fraser.stlouisfed.org/title/763.

11. Federal Open Market Committee, minutes, March 4, 1953, *Federal Open Market Committee Meeting Minutes, Transcripts, and Other Documents*, FRASER, Federal Reserve Bank of Saint Louis (hereafter Federal Open Market Committee, minutes), https://fraser.stlouisfed.org/title/677/item/22732/content/pdf/19530305Minutesv.

12. William McChesney Martin Jr., "The Transition to Free Markets," speech, Economic Club of Detroit. Reprinted in Federal Reserve Board of Governors, *Federal Reserve Bulletin*, April 1953, 330–335, https://fraser.stlouisfed.org/title/62/item/21220.

13. Federal Open Market Committee, minutes, June 11, 1953, 27, https://fraser.stlouisfed.org/title/677/item/22733/content/pdf/19530611Minutesv.

14. Federal Open Market Committee, minutes, September 24, 1953, https://fraser.stlouisfed.org/title/677/item/22734/content/pdf/19530924Minutesv.

15. Sproul (New York) and Powell (Minneapolis) dissented.

16. U.S. Congress, Joint Committee on the Economic Report, *United States Monetary Policy*, 15–25.

17. U.S. Congress, Joint Committee on the Economic Report, *United States Monetary Policy*, 224.

18. Bremner, *Chairman of the Fed*, 112.

19. Federal Open Market Committee, minutes, March 2, 1955, 36, https://fraser.stlouisfed.org/title/677/item/22739/content/pdf/19550302Minutes1v.

20. Federal Open Market Committee, minutes, June 22, 1955, 3, https://fraser.stlouisfed.org/title/677/item/22741/content/pdf/19550622Minutesv.

21. Ibid., 7.

22. Ibid., 10–15.

23. Allan Sproul to Special Committee, June 6, 1955. In William McChesney Martin, Jr., Papers, Box 20, Folder 12, Missouri History Museum, https://fraser.stlouisfed.org/archival/1341/item/472998.

24. Bremner, *Chairman of the Fed*, 103.

25. Binder and Spindel, *Myth of Independence*, 162, describe the accord as a treasury "divorce."

26. Quoted in Kettl, *Leadership at the Fed*, 76.

27. Meltzer, *A History*, vol. 2, 478.

28. Blyth, *Great Transformations*, 94–95.

29. Hal Brands, *What Good Is Grand Strategy? Power and Purpose in American Statecraft from Harry S. Truman to George W. Bush* (Ithaca: Cornell University Press, 2014), 17–59; Francis J. Gavin, *Gold, Dollars, and Power: The Politics of International Monetary Relations, 1958-1971* (Chapel Hill: University of North Carolina Press, 2004).

30. Lowi, *The End of Liberalism*, 154; Legro, *Rethinking the World*.

31. Jeffrey Chwieroth, "International Liquidity Provision: the IMF and the World Bank in the Treasury and Marshall Systems, 1942–1957," in *Orderly Change: International Monetary Relations since Bretton Woods*, ed. David Andrews, 52–77 (Ithaca: Cornell University Press, 2008).

32. Meltzer, *A History*, vol. 2, 251–52.

33. Bremner, *Chairman of the Fed*, 105.

34. Quoted in ibid., 115.

35. Unlike modern economists, who view low levels of inflation as beneficial, Martin strove for total price stability. See Christina D. Romer and David H. Romer, "A Rehabilitation of Monetary Policy in the 1950's," *American Economic Review* 92, no. 2 (2002): 121–27.

36. U.S. Congress, Joint Economic Committee, *Monetary Policy 1955-1956: Hearings Before the Subcommittee on Economic Stabilization of the Joint Economic Committee*, 84th Cong., 2nd sess., 1956, 73, https://fraser.stlouisfed.org/title/388.

37. Bremner, *Chairman of the Fed*, 135.

38. Harold James, *International Monetary Cooperation since Bretton Woods* (New York: Oxford University Press, 1996), 180.

39. Williams, "The Postwar Monetary Plans."

40. Cohen, *Organizing the World's Money*, 98–99; Eichengreen, *Globalizing Capital*, 106–13; Toniolo, *Central Bank Cooperation*, 423; David Andrews, "Kennedy's Gold Pledge and the Return of Central Bank Collaboration: The Origins of the Kennedy System, 1959-1962," in *Orderly Change: International Monetary Relations since Bretton Woods*, ed. David Andrews (Ithaca: Cornell University Press, 2008), 105–108.

41. Robert Triffin, *Europe and the Money Muddle: From Bilateralism to Near-Convertibility, 1947-1956* (New Haven: Yale University Press, 1957), 296–97.

42. U.S. Congress, Joint Economic Committee, *January 1958 Economic Report of the President: Hearings Before the Joint Economic Committee*, 85th Cong., 2nd sess., 385, https://www.jec.senate.gov/reports/85th%20Congress/January%201958%20Economic%20Report%20of%20the%20President%20(109).pdf.

43. Andrews, *Kennedy's Gold Pledge*, 106.

44. Gavin, *Gold, Dollars, and Power*, 38.
45. Bremner, *Chairman of the Fed*, 137.
46. James, *International Monetary Cooperation*, 154.
47. Robert Triffin, *Gold and the Dollar Crisis: The Future of Convertibility* (New Haven: Yale University Press, 1960).
48. Friedman, "The Case for Flexible Exchange Rates"; Milton Friedman, *A Program for Monetary Stability* (New York: Fordham University Press, 1960); Milton Friedman and Robert V. Roosa, *The Balance of Payments: Free versus Fixed Exchange Rates* (Washington: American Enterprise Institute for Public Policy Research, 1967).
49. U.S. Congress, Joint Committee on the Economic Report, *January 1959 Economic Report of the President: Hearings before the Joint Economic Committee*, 86th Cong., 1st sess., 467, https://www.jec.senate.gov/reports/86th%20Congress/Hearings/January%201959%20Economic%20Report%20of%20the%20President%20(154).pdf.
50. James, *International Monetary Cooperation*, 178; Bremner, *Chairman of the Fed*, 149.
51. Toniolo, *Central Bank Cooperation*, 369; Andrews, *Kennedy's Gold Pledge*, 107.
52. Gavin, *Gold, Dollars, and Power*, 33–58.
53. Toniolo, *Central Bank Cooperation*, 364; Andrews, *Kennedy's Gold Pledge*, 110–13.
54. Ritter, *Allan Sproul*, 19.
55. Gavin, *Gold, Dollars, and Power*, 56–57, 62.
56. Quoted in Gavin, *Gold, Dollars, and Power*, 71.
57. Kennedy appointed Walter Heller chairman of the Council of Economic Advisors along with James Tobin and Kermit Gordon. Paul Samuelson became a presidential adviser. John Kenneth Galbraith was named ambassador to India.
58. This position was created in 1954 and originally filled by New York Fed alum W. R. Burgess.
59. Quoted in Toniolo, *Central Bank Cooperation*, 371. New York Fed vice president Charles Coombs recounts his experiences at the Bank for International Settlements in Charles A. Coombs, *The Arena of International Finance* (New York: John Wiley and Sons, 1976).
60. Toniolo, *Central Bank Cooperation*, 372.
61. Quoted in Andrews, *Kennedy's Gold Pledge*, 111.
62. Meltzer, *A History*, vol. 2, 327; Toniolo, *Central Bank Cooperation*, 374.
63. Quoted in James, *International Monetary Cooperation*, 158.
64. Dillon negotiated an offset agreement with West Germany, but other European states were reluctant to pay for protection. To reduce overseas expenditures, U.S. agencies were also tasked with forming a "gold budget" to minimize the balance-of-payments impact of their purchases. Gavin, *Gold, Dollars, and Power*, 47–52, 68–80; Andrews, *Kennedy's Gold Pledge*, 111–17.

65. Federal Open Market Committee, minutes, November 22, 1960, 42, https://fraser.stlouisfed.org/title/677/item/22830/content/pdf/fomchistmin19601122.

66. Federal Open Market Committee, minutes, February 7, 1961, 45, 17. https://fraser.stlouisfed.org/title/677/item/23397/content/pdf/19610207Minutesv.

67. Robert Roosa, "Reconciling Internal and External Financial Policies," *Journal of Finance* 17, no. 1 (1962): 1–16.

68. Toniolo, *Central Bank Cooperation*, 388; Michael D. Bordo and Barry Eichengreen, "Bretton Woods and the Great Inflation," in *The Great Inflation: The Rebirth of Modern Central Banking*, ed. Michael D. Bordo and Athanasios Orphanides, 449–89 (Chicago: University of Chicago Press, 2013).

69. The U.S., Switzerland, Britain, West Germany, France, Italy, Belgium, and the Netherlands participated in the London Gold Pool. See James, *International Monetary Cooperation*, 160; Gavin, *Gold, Dollars, and Power*, 60; Toniolo, *Central Bank Cooperation*, 375–81.

70. James, *International Monetary Cooperation*, 162; Toniolo, *Central Bank Cooperation*, 387.

71. Letter included in Federal Open Market Committee, minutes, December 19, 1961, 85–86, https://fraser.stlouisfed.org/title/677/item/22846/content/pdf/19611219Minutesv.

72. James, *International Monetary Cooperation*, 160.

73. Bremner, *Chairman of the Fed*, 155.

74. Quoted in Kettl, *Leadership at the Fed*, 99.

75. Quoted in Bremner, *Chairman of the Fed*, 159.

76. Ibid., 161.

77. This legal clause remains. See, https://www.federalreserve.gov/about-thefed/section10.htm.

78. Quoted in Bremner, *Chairman of the Fed*, 174.

79. Walter Heller, "Council of Economic Advisers Oral History Interview– JFK#1," August 1, 1964, 194–95, John F. Kennedy Oral History Collection, John F. Kennedy Presidential Library, Boston, MA, https://www.jfklibrary.org/asset-viewer/archives/JFKOH.

80. Quoted in Meltzer, *A History*, vol. 2, 340.

81. Discount rates tell a parallel story. They rose from 2 to 4 percent in eighteen months during the first recovery and from 3 to 4 percent over forty-nine months in the second. Data from FRASER.

82. Federal Open Market Committee, minutes, December 19, 1961, 78, https://fraser.stlouisfed.org/title/677/item/22846/content/pdf/19611219Minutesv.

83. Bordo and Eichengreen, *Bretton Woods and the Great Inflation*, 457.

84. Federal Open Market Committee, minutes, January 23, 1962, 27, https://fraser.stlouisfed.org/title/677/item/22847/content/pdf/19620123Minutesv.

85. Ibid., 32.

86. Walter S. Salant, "Competitiveness and the US Balance of Payments," In *The US Balance of Payments in 1968* (Washington: The Brookings Institution, 1963).

87. James, *International Monetary Cooperation*, 157.

88. Cited in Bremner, *Chairman of the Fed*, 187.

89. Lyndon B. Johnson, "Annual Message to the Congress on the State of the Union," January 8, 1964, The American Presidency Project, Gerhard Peters and John T. Woolley, https://www.presidency.ucsb.edu/node/242292.

90. Walter Heller, "The President's Economic Report for 1964," *New York Times*, January 26, 1964.

91. Federal Open Market Committee, minutes, December 17, 1963, 55, https://fraser.stlouisfed.org/title/677/item/22876/content/pdf/19631217Minutesv.

92. Julian E. Zelizer, *The Fierce Urgency of Now: Lyndon Johnson, Congress, and the Battle for the Great Society* (New York: Penguin, 2015).

93. Ronald McKinnon, *The Unloved Dollar Standard: from Bretton Woods to the Rise of China* (New York: Oxford University Press, 2013), 43–45.

94. Herbert Stein, *The Fiscal Revolution in America: Policy in Pursuit of Reality*, 2nd ed. (Washington: American Enterprise Institute Press, 1996).

95. James, *International Monetary Cooperation*, 160; McKinnon, *The Unloved Dollar Standard*, 45.

96. Bremner, *Chairman of the Fed*, 161–62; Meltzer, *A History*, vol. 2, 441.

97. Robert Roosa, *Monetary Reform for the World Economy* (New York: Harper and Row, 1965); John S. Odell, *US International Monetary Policy: Markets, Power, and Ideas as Sources of Change* (Princeton: Princeton University Press, 1982), 147; Meltzer, *A History*, vol. 2, 364.

98. Odell, *US International Monetary Policy*, 79; Gavin, *Gold, Dollars, and Power*, 82.

99. Toniolo, *Central Bank Cooperation*, 408.

100. Maisel, *Managing the Dollar*, 13.

101. Walter Heller to Lyndon Johnson, memorandum, "Subject: Pros and Cons of a Tax Increase in 1966," December 22, 1965, Papers of Lyndon B. Johnson, CF, Box 44, LBJ Presidential Library, Austin, TX, https://fraser.stlouisfed.org/archival/1172/item/3340.

102. William McChesney Martin Jr., "Does Monetary History Repeat Itself?" Commencement Day Luncheon of the Alumni Federation of Columbia University, June 1, 1965, New York City, https://fraser.stlouisfed.org/title/448/item/7898.

103. Bremner, *Chairman of the Fed*, 221.

104. Kettl, *Leadership at the Fed*, 109.

105. Quoted in Bremner, *Chairman of the Fed*, 235.

106. Toniolo, *Central Bank Cooperation*, 381.

107. Quoted in James, *International Monetary Cooperation*, 169.

108. Quoted in Toniolo, *Central Bank Cooperation*, 414.

109. Odell, *US International Monetary Policy*, 171–73.

110. Bremner, *Chairman of the Fed*, 243–45.

111. A two-tiered gold market was established, where official payments were settled at existing parities while gold prices could fluctuate in private markets.

Robert Collins, "The Economic Crisis of 1968 and the Waning of the 'American Century,'" *The American Historical Review* 101, no. 2 (1996): 412; Gavin, *Gold, Dollars, and Power*, 182; McKinnon, *The Unloved Dollar Standard*, 44.

112. Tom Wicker, "Johnson Says He Won't Run," *New York Times*, April 1, 1968.

113. H.E. Heinemann, "Economic 'Abyss' Seen by Martin," *New York Times*, June 12, 1968.

114. Meltzer, *A History*, vol. 2, 538.

115. Bremner, *Chairman of the Fed*, 200.

116. Ibid., 212.

117. William McChesney Martin Jr., to Lyndon Johnson, February 2, 1966. Cited in Meltzer, *A History*, vol. 2, 491.

118. Federal Open Market Committee, minutes, November 2, 1965, 52, https://fraser.stlouisfed.org/title/677/item/23380/content/pdf/19651102Minutesv.

119. Federal Open Market Committee, minutes, October 12, 1965, 25, https://fraser.stlouisfed.org/title/677/item/22903/content/pdf/19651012Minutesv.

120. Federal Reserve Board of Governors, minutes, December 3, 1965, Records of the Federal Reserve System, Record Group 82, Volume 52, Part 12, https://fraser.stlouisfed.org/title/821/item/516663.

121. Bordo and Eichengreen, *Bretton Woods and the Great Inflation*, 463.

122. U.S. Congress, Joint Economic Committee, *Federal Reserve Action and Economic Policy Coordination: Hearings before the Joint Economic Committee*, 89th Cong., 1st sess., 1965, 24, https://hdl.handle.net/2027/mdp.39015077929266?urlappend=%3Bseq=7.

123. Bremner, *Chairman of the Fed*, 213.

124. Sherman Maisel, diary, February 9, 1966. Cited in Meltzer, *A History*, vol. 2, 494.

125. Federal Open Market Committee, minutes, July 26, 1966, 77, https://fraser.stlouisfed.org/title/677/item/22914/content/pdf/19660726Minutesv.

126. Wood, *A History of Central Banking*, 256; Hetzel, *The Monetary Policy of the Federal Reserve*, 71.

127. William McChesney Martin Jr., "Memorandum of a Conversation with President Lyndon B. Johnson," March 14, 1967, William McChesney Martin Jr. Papers, Box 60, Missouri History Museum, St. Louis, Missouri. Quoted in Bremner, *Chairman of the Fed*, 230–32.

128. Similarly, the board raised discount rates three times and reserve requirements once.

129. Federal Reserve Board of Governors, *Fifty-Fifth Annual Report of the Board of Governors of the Federal Reserve System* (Washington, DC, 1968), 4, https://fraser.stlouisfed.org/title/117/item/2423.

130. Meltzer, *A History*, vol. 2, 542–43.

131. Federal Open Market Committee, minutes, December 17, 1968, 34, https://fraser.stlouisfed.org/title/677/item/22948/content/pdf/fomcmod19681217.

132. Ibid., 49.

133. Federal Reserve Board of Governors, *Fifty-Sixth Annual Report of the Board of Governors of the Federal Reserve System* (Washington, DC, 1969), 10, https://fraser.stlouisfed.org/title/117/item/2424.

134. "Text of Martin Statement to Congress on Economic Problems," *New York Times*, February 27, 1969.

135. Meltzer, *A History*, vol. 2, 560–61.

136. Federal Reserve Board of Governors, *Fifty-Sixth Annual Report of the Board of Governors of the Federal Reserve System* (Washington, DC, 1969), 11.

137. Quoted in Bremner, *Chairman of the Fed*, 264–65.

138. Richard Nixon, *Six Crises* (New York: Doubleday, 1962), 309–11.

139. Quoted in Bremner, *Chairman of the Fed*, 260–61.

140. He did so at Martin's prodding. Meltzer, *A History*, vol. 2, 560.

141. Quoted in Bremner, *Chairman of the Fed*, 277.

142. Federal Open Market Committee, minutes, February 7, 1970, 3, https://fraser.stlouisfed.org/title/677/item/22961/content/pdf/fomcmod19700210.

143. Ibid., 45–46.

144. Ibid., 59.

145. Ibid., 83–84.

146. Meltzer, *A History*, vol. 2, 585 n152.

147. Lawrence Malkin, "A Practical Politician at the Fed," *Fortune Magazine*, May 1971, 151.

148. Meltzer, *A History*, vol. 2, 477.

149. Sherman Maisel, diary, February 16, 1970. Quoted in Meltzer, *A History*, vol. 2, 572 n135.

150. Federal Open Market Committee, minutes, November 2, 1965, https://fraser.stlouisfed.org/title/677#22905; Bremner, *Chairman of the Fed*, 252–54; Meltzer, *A History*, vol. 2, 594.

151. Roger Backhouse and Beatrice Cherrier, "The Ordinary Business of Macroeconometric Modeling: Working on the Fed-MIT-Penn Model, 1964–74," *History of Political Economy* 51, no. 3 (2019): 425–47.

152. Maisel, *Managing the Dollar*, 170.

153. Meltzer, *A History*, vol. 2, 546.

154. The committee wouldn't issue its report for two months, but its proposal to task the staff with forming policy directives was authorized at Martin's final meeting. Federal Open Market Committee, minutes, January 15, 1970, 82, https://fraser.stlouisfed.org/title/677/item/23368/content/pdf/fomcmod19700115.

155. Federal Open Market Committee, minutes, February 7, 1970, 53–56.

156. Ibid., 55.

157. Martin, *Introduction*, 36.

158. Federal Reserve Board of Governors, *Annual Reports* (Washington, DC, 1965–1972).

159. Maisel, *Managing the Dollar*, 121.

160. Meltzer, *A History*, vol. 2, 584.
161. Quoted in Kettl, *Leadership at the Fed*, 119.
162. Ibid., 113, 119.
163. Ibid., 116.
164. Meltzer, *A History*, vol. 2, 677.
165. Effective Federal Funds Rate, FRED database, Federal Reserve Bank of St. Louis, https://fred.stlouisfed.org/.
166. Helleiner, *States and the Reemergence of Global Finance*, traces the rise of Eurodollars.
167. Robert Roosa, "Capital Movements and Balance-Of-Payments Adjustment," in *Men Money & Policy: Essays in Honor of Karl R. Bopp*, ed. David P. Eastburn, 171–94 (Philadelphia: Federal Reserve Bank of Philadelphia, 1970).
168. Milton Friedman and Robert V. Roosa, *The Balance of Payments: Free versus Fixed Exchange Rates* (Washington, DC: American Enterprise Institute for Public Policy Research, 1967), 17.
169. William McChesney Martin Jr., "Address before the New York Group of the Investment Bankers Association of America," October 19, 1955, Waldorf Astoria Hotel, New York City, https://fraser.stlouisfed.org/title/448/item/7800.
170. Sherman Maisel, diary, January 24, 1969. Quoted in Meltzer, *A History*, vol. 2, 563 n124.
171. Quoted in Bremner, *Chairman of the Fed*, 290.
172. Shull, *Fourth Branch*, 14.

Conclusion

1. Arthur Burns, "Possible Remarks at Ground-Breaking for New Federal Reserve Building," April 5, 1971, https://fraser.stlouisfed.org/title/449/item/7966.
2. Federal Open Market Committee, minutes, January 15, 1970, 82.
3. Warburg, *Federal Reserve System*, 149.
4. Benjamin Strong to Will H. Hays, July 1, 1921, Papers of Benjamin Strong, Jr., Folder 016.0, Federal Reserve Bank of New York.
5. U.S. Congress, Senate, Banking and Currency Committee, *Operation of the National and Federal Reserve Banking Systems*: Hearings Before a Subcommittee of the Banking and Currency Committee, 71st Cong., 3rd sess., 1931, 140, https://fraser.stlouisfed.org/title/675/item/22457.
6. Shull, *Fourth Branch*, 14.
7. Tulis and Mellow, *Legacies of Losing*.
8. Domineering chairmen include Marriner Eccles, Arthur Burns, and Alan Greenspan. See Maisel, *Managing the Dollar*, 113–24; Kettl, *Leadership at the Fed*; Conti-Brown, *Power and Independence*, 40–68; Chappell Jr., McGregor, and Vermilyea, *Committee Decisions on Monetary Policy*.

9. Paul Volcker, Ben Bernanke, and Janet Yellen fall into this more inclusive category. See, respectively, Andrew Bailey and Cheryl Schonhardt-Bailey, "Does Deliberation Matter in FOMC Monetary Policymaking? The Volcker Revolution of 1979," *Political Analysis* 16, no. 4 (2008): 404–27; Anne M. Khademian, "The Paracademic and the Fed: The Leadership of Chairman Benjamin Bernanke," *Public Administration Review* 70, no. 1 (2010): 142–50.

10. Maisel (1973, 110) estimates the residual decision-making authority is spread among the board governors (20 percent) and reserve bank presidents (10 percent).

11. Conti-Brown, *Power and Independence*, 70–74, 84–91.

12. Board of Governors of the Federal Reserve System, "Policy Tools," https://www.federalreserve.gov/monetarypolicy/policytools.htm.

13. Federal Reserve Bank of Philadelphia, "A Day in the Life of the FOMC," https://www.philadelphiafed.org/education/teachers/resources/day-in-life-of-fomc.

14. The FOMC experimented with monetary aggregate targets under Paul Volcker's "practical monetarism" program, but some see this as a rhetorical effort to avoid blame for steep rate hikes. Greider, *Secrets of the Temple*, 538–40; Peter A. Johnson, *The Government of Money: Monetarism in Germany and the United States* (Ithaca: Cornell University Press, 1998), 177–82.

15. Federal Reserve Bank of Philadelphia, "A Day in the Life of the FOMC."

16. Meltzer, *A History*, vol. 1, 742; Binder and Spindel, *Myth of Independence*, 178–79.

17. Meltzer, *A History*, vol. 2, 672.

18. Milton Friedman, "The Role of Monetary Policy," *American Economic Review* 58, no. 1 (1968): 1–17.

19. J. B. DeLong, "The Triumph of Monetarism?" *Journal of Economic Perspectives* 14, no. 1 (2000): 83–94.

20. Aaron Steelman, "The Federal Reserve's 'Dual Mandate': The Evolution of an Idea," *Economic Brief* no. 11–12 (Dec. 2011), Federal Reserve Bank of Richmond, https://www.richmondfed.org/publications/research/economic_brief/2011/eb_11-12.

21. Bailey and Schonhardt-Bailey, "Does Deliberation Matter in FOMC Monetary Policymaking?"

22. Meltzer, *A History*, vol. 2, 475; Romer and Romer, "A Rehabilitation of Monetary Policy."

23. Jacobs and King, *Fed Power*, 73–75, 98–111.

24. Michael D. Bordo and Arunima Sinha, "A Lesson from the Great Depression that the Fed Might Have Learned: A Comparison of the 1932 Open Market Purchases with Quantitative Easing," NBER Working Paper 22581 (Cambridge, MA: National Bureau of Economic Research, 2016).

25. See Eichengreen, *Hall of Mirrors*; Eric Helleiner, *The Status Quo Crisis: Global Financial Governance after the 2008 Meltdown* (New York: Oxford University Press, 2014).

26. Benjamin Strong to Walter Stewart, August 3, 1928. Quoted in Chandler, *Benjamin Strong*, 460.

27. Blyth, *Great Transformations*, 167–72.

28. See, for example, Greta Krippner, "The Making of US Monetary Policy: Central Bank Transparency and the Neoliberal Dilemma," *Theory and Society* 36, no. 6 (2007): 477–513; Binder and Spindel, *Myth of Independence*, 185–87, 215–17.

29. Orren and Stephen Skowronek, *The Search for American Political Development*, 123.

30. DeLong, "The Triumph of Monetarism?"; Daniel S. Jones, *Masters of the Universe: Hayek, Friedman, and the Birth of Neoliberal Politics* (Princeton: Princeton University Press, 2012).

31. Ira Katznelson and Martin Shefter, eds. *Shaped by War and Trade: International Influences on American Political Development* (Princeton: Princeton University Press, 2002).

32. Trubowitz, *Politics and Strategy*.

33. See, respectively, Oatley, *A Political Economy of American Hegemony*; Schwartz, *Subprime Nation*; Kreps, *Taxing Wars*.

34. Kindleberger, *The World in Depression*; Ikenberry, *After Victory*; Legro, *Rethinking the World*; Mastanduno, "System Maker and Privilege Taker"; Kirshner, *American Power*.

35. Skowronek, *Politics Presidents Make*, 33–52, 442.

36. Ibid.

37. Ibid., 32.

38. Curt Nichols, "Reagan Reorders the Political Regime: A Historical-institutional Approach to Analysis of Change," *Presidential Studies Quarterly* 45, no. 4 (2015): 703–26.

39. Jacob S. Hacker and Paul Pierson, "Winner-Take-All Politics: Public Policy, Political Organization, and the Precipitous Rise of Top Incomes in the United States," *Politics & Society* 38, no. 2 (2010): 152–204.

40. Adolph, "The Missing Politics of Central Banks."

41. Federal Reserve Board of Governors, *Federal Reserve Bulletin*, May 1947, 518–19, https://fraser.stlouisfed.org/title/62/item/21149.

42. "Credit and Liquidity Programs and the Balance Sheet," Board of Governors of the Federal Reserve System, https://www.federalreserve.gov/monetarypolicy/bst_recenttrends.htm.

43. Bailey and Schonhardt-Bailey, "Does Deliberation Matter in FOMC Monetary Policymaking?"

44. William Greider, *Secrets of the Temple*, 711–14, notes that Volcker "persuaded only Governor Wayne Angell. The other three governors appointed by Ronald Reagan declared, rather bluntly, that they would vote down the chairman if he tried it."

45. Chappell Jr., McGregor, and Vermilyea, *Committee Decisions on Monetary Policy*, 128–32.

46. Polsky, "Partisan Regimes," 12.

47. Bill Dudley, "The Fed Shouldn't Enable Donald Trump," *Bloomberg*, Aug. 27, 2019, https://www.bloomberg.com/opinion/articles/2019-08-27/the-fed-shouldn-t-enable-donald-trump.

48. John Revill and Brenna Neghaiwi, "Fed Chair Powell Repeats Vow to Act 'as Appropriate,'" *Reuters*, Sept. 6, 2019, https://www.reuters.com/article/us-usa-fed-powell/fed-chair-powell-repeats-vow-to-act-as-appropriate-idUSKCN1VR26B.

Bibliography

Abdelal, Rawi. *Capital Rules: The Construction of Global Finance.* Cambridge: Harvard University Press, 2007.
Acosta, Juan, and Beatrice Cherrier. "The Transformation of Economic Analysis at the Federal Reserve during the 1960s." Center for the History of Political Economy at Duke University Working Paper Series 4. Durham, NC: Duke University, 2019.
Adolph, Christopher. *Bankers, Bureaucrats, and Central Bank Politics: The Myth of Neutrality.* New York: Cambridge University Press, 2015.
———. "The Missing Politics of Central Banks." *PS: Political Science & Politics* 51, no. 4 (2018): 737–42.
Ahamed, Liaquat. *Lords of Finance: The Bankers Who Broke the World.* New York: Random House, 2009.
Aldrich, Nelson. "Banking Reform in the United States." *Proceedings of the Academy of Political Science* 4, no. 1 (1913): 31–91.
Alesina, Alberto, and Lawrence H. Summers. "Central Bank Independence and Macroeconomic Performance: Some Comparative Evidence." *Journal of Money, Credit and Banking* 25, no. 2 (1993): 151–62.
Andrews, David. "Kennedy's Gold Pledge and the Return of Central Bank Collaboration: The Origins of the Kennedy System, 1959–1962." In *Orderly Change: International Monetary Relations since Bretton Woods,* edited by David Andrews, 100–19. Ithaca: Cornell University Press, 2008.
Axilrod, Stephen. *Inside the Fed.* Cambridge: MIT Press, 2011.
Backhouse, Roger, and Beatrice Cherrier. "The Ordinary Business of Macroeconometric Modeling: Working on the Fed-MIT-Penn Model, 1964–74." *History of Political Economy* 51, no. 3 (2019): 425–47.
Bailey, Andrew, and Cheryl Schonhardt-Bailey. "Does Deliberation Matter in FOMC Monetary Policymaking? The Volcker Revolution of 1979." *Political Analysis* 16, no. 4 (2008): 404–27.

Bearce, David. *Monetary Divergence: Domestic Policy Autonomy in the Post–Bretton Woods Era*. Ann Arbor: University of Michigan Press, 2009.

———, and Mark Hallerberg. "Democracy and de facto Exchange Rate Regimes." *Economics & Politics* 23, no. 2 (2011): 172–94.

Bensel, Richard. *Sectionalism and American Political Development, 1880–1980*. Madison: University of Wisconsin Press, 1984.

———. *Yankee Leviathan: The Origins of Central State Authority in America, 1859–1877*. New York: Cambridge University Press, 1990.

———. *The Political Economy of American Industrialization, 1877–1900*. New York: Cambridge University Press, 2000.

Berk, Gerald, and Dennis Galvan. "How People Experience and Change Institutions: A Field Guide to Creative Syncretism." *Theory and Society* 38, no. 6 (2009): 543–80.

Binder, Sarah, and Mark Spindel. *The Myth of Independence: How Congress Governs the Federal Reserve*. Princeton: Princeton University Press, 2017.

———. "Monetary Politics: Origins of the Federal Reserve." *Studies in American Political Development* 27, no. 1 (2013): 1–13.

Blinder, Alan S., and John Morgan. "Are Two Heads Better than One? Monetary Policy by Committee." *Journal of Money, Credit and Banking* 37, no. 5 (2005): 789–811.

Bloomfield, Arthur. *Monetary Policy under the Gold Standard: 1880–1914*. New York: Federal Reserve Bank of New York, 1959.

Blum, John. *From the Morgenthau Diaries: Years of Crisis, 1928–1938*. Boston: Houghton Mifflin, 1959.

Blyth, Mark. *Great Transformations: Economic Ideas and Institutional Change in the Twentieth Century*. New York: Cambridge University Press, 2002.

———. "Structures Do not Come with an Instruction Sheet: Interests, Ideas, and Progress in Political Science." *Perspectives on Politics* 1, no. 4 (2003): 695–706.

Bodenhorn, Howard. *A History of Banking in Antebellum America: Financial Markets and Economic Development in an Era of Nation-Building*. New York: Cambridge University Press, 2000.

Bopp, Karl. "Confessions of a Central Banker." In *Essays in Monetary Policy in Honor of Elmer Wood*, edited by Pinkney C. Walker, 3–17. Columbia: University of Missouri Press, 1965.

Bordo, Michael D. "Could the United States Have Had a Better Central Bank? An Historical Counterfactual Speculation." *Journal of Macroeconomics* 34, no. 3 (2012): 597–607.

———, and David Wheelock. "The Promise and Performance of the Federal Reserve as Lender of Last Resort 1914–1933." In *A Return to Jekyll Island: The Origins, History, and Future of the Federal Reserve*, edited by Michael

D. Bordo and William Roberds, 59–97. New York: Cambridge University Press, 2013.

Bordo, Michael D., and Barry Eichengreen. "Bretton Woods and the Great Inflation." In *The Great Inflation: The Rebirth of Modern Central Banking*, edited by Michael D. Bordo and Athanasios Orphanides, 449–89. Chicago: University of Chicago Press, 2013.

Bordo, Michael D., and Arunima Sinha. "A Lesson from the Great Depression that the Fed Might Have Learned: A Comparison of the 1932 Open Market Purchases with Quantitative Easing." NBER Working Paper 22581. Cambridge, MA: National Bureau of Economic Research, 2016.

Brandeis, Louis. *Other People's Money and How the Bankers Use It*. New York: Frederick A. Stokes Company, 1914.

Brands, Hal. *What Good Is Grand Strategy? Power and Purpose in American Statecraft from Harry S. Truman to George W. Bush*. Ithaca: Cornell University Press, 2014.

Bremner, Robert P. *Chairman of the Fed: William McChesney Martin Jr., and the Creation of the Modern American Financial System*. New Haven: Yale University Press, 2004.

Broz, J. L. *The International Origins of the Federal Reserve System*. Ithaca: Cornell University Press, 1997.

Bruner, Robert F., and Sean Carr. *The Panic of 1907: Lessons Learned from the Market's Perfect Storm*. Hoboken: John Wiley and Sons, 2008.

Burgess, W. R. "What the Federal Reserve System Is Doing to Promote Business Stability." *Proceedings of the Academy of Political Science in the City of New York* 12, no. 3 (1927): 139–47.

———. *The Reserve Banks and the Money Market*. 2nd ed. New York: Harper and Brothers, 1936.

Capoccia, Giovanni, and Daniel Kelemen. "The Study of Critical Junctures: Theory, Narrative, and Counterfactuals in Historical Institutionalism." *World Politics* 59, no. 3 (2007): 341–69.

Chandler, Lester V. *Benjamin Strong, Central Banker*. Washington: The Brookings Institution, 1958.

———. *American Monetary Policy, 1928–1941*. New York: Harper and Row, 1971.

Chappell Jr., Henry, Rob R. McGregor, and Todd A. Vermilyea. *Committee Decisions on Monetary Policy: Evidence from Historical Records of the Federal Open Market Committee*. Cambridge: MIT Press, 2004.

Charles S. Hamlin Papers, Library of Congress, Washington, DC.

Chwieroth, Jeffrey. "International Liquidity Provision: the IMF and the World Bank in the Treasury and Marshall Systems, 1942–1957." In *Orderly Change: International Monetary Relations since Bretton Woods*, edited by David Andrews, 52–77. Ithaca: Cornell University Press, 2008.

Clarke, Stephen. *Central Bank Cooperation: 1924-31*. New York: Federal Reserve Bank of New York, 1967.
Clifford, Albert. *The Independence of the Federal Reserve System*. Philadelphia: University of Pennsylvania Press, 1965.
Cohen, Benjamin. *Organizing the World's Money: The Political Economy of International Monetary Relations*. New York: Basic Books, 1977.
———. "The Triad and the Unholy Trinity: Lessons for the Pacific Region." In *Pacific Economic Relations in the 1990s: Conflict or Cooperation*, edited by Richard Higgott, Richard Leaver, and John Ravenhill, 133-58. Boulder: Lynne Rienner, 1993.
———. "The Macrofoundations of Monetary Power." In *International Monetary Power*, edited by David M. Andrews, 31-50. Ithaca: Cornell University Press, 2006.
Collins, Robert. "The Economic Crisis of 1968 and the Waning of the 'American Century.'" *The American Historical Review* 101, no. 2 (1996): 396-422.
Conti-Brown, Peter. *The Power and Independence of the Federal Reserve*. Princeton: Princeton University Press, 2016.
Coombs, Charles A. *The Arena of International Finance*. New York: John Wiley and Sons, 1976.
Cooper, Milton. *Pivotal Decades*. New York: W. W. Norton, 1990.
Cukierman, Alex, Steven B. Webb, and Bilin Neyapti. "Measuring the Independence of Central Banks and Its Effect on Policy Outcomes." *The World Bank Economic Review* 6, no. 3 (1992): 353-98.
D'Arista, Jane. *Federal Reserve Structure and the Development of Monetary Policy: 1915-1935*. Staff Report of the Subcommittee on Domestic Finance, Committee on Banking and Currency. 92nd Cong., 1st Sess., 1971. Committee Print 68-574.
De Long, J. B. "The Triumph of Monetarism?" *Journal of Economic Perspectives* 14, no. 1 (2000): 83-94.
Diamond, Douglas W., and Philip H. Dybvig. "Bank Runs, Deposit Insurance, and Liquidity." *The Journal of Political Economy* 91, no. 3 (1983): 401-19.
Eccles, Marriner S. *Beckoning Frontiers*. New York: Alfred A. Knopf, 1951.
Eichengreen, Barry. *Golden Fetters: The Gold Standard and the Great Depression, 1919-1939*. New York: Oxford University Press, 1992.
———. *Globalizing Capital: A History of the International Monetary System*. Princeton: Princeton University Press, 1996.
———. *Exorbitant Privilege: The Rise and Fall of the Dollar and the Future of the International Monetary System*. New York: Oxford University Press, 2011.
———. *Hall of Mirrors: The Great Depression, the Great Recession, and the Uses-and-Misuses-of-History*. New York: Oxford University Press, 2014.
———, and Marc Flandreau. "The Federal Reserve, the Bank of England, and the Rise of the Dollar as an International Currency, 1914-1939." *Open Economies Review* 23, no. 1 (2012): 57-87.

Eichengreen, Barry, and Peter Temin. "The Gold Standard and the Great Depression." *Contemporary European History* 9, no. 2 (2000): 183–207.
Epstein, Gerald, and Thomas Ferguson. "Monetary Policy, Loan Liquidation, and Industrial Conflict: The Federal Reserve and the Open Market Operations of 1932." *The Journal of Economic History* 44, no. 4 (1984): 957–83.
Feis, Herbert. *The Diplomacy of the Dollar: First Era, 1919–1932*. Baltimore: John Hopkins University Press, 1950.
Fisher, Irving. "The Mechanics of Bimetallism." *The Economic Journal* 4, no. 15 (1894): 527–37.
———. "A Compensated Dollar." *The Quarterly Journal of Economics* 27, no. 2 (1913): 213–35.
Fleming, J. M. "Domestic Financial Policies under Fixed and under Floating Exchange Rates." *IMF Staff Papers* 9, no. 3 (1962): 369–80.
Forder, James. "'Independence' and the Founding of the Federal Reserve." *Scottish Journal of Political Economy* 50, no. 3 (2003): 297–310.
FRASER Digital Library, Federal Reserve Bank of St. Louis, St. Louis.
Friedberg, Aaron. "Why Didn't the United States Become a Garrison State?" *International Security* 16, no. 4 (1992): 109–42.
Frieden, Jeffry. "Sectoral Conflict and Foreign Economic Policy, 1914–1940." *International Organization* 42, no. 1 (1988): 59–90.
———. "Invested Interests: The Politics of National Economic Policies in a World of Global Finance." *International Organization* 45, no. 4 (1991): 425–51.
———. "Economic Integration and the Politics of Monetary Policy in the United States." In *Internationalization and Domestic Politics*, edited by Robert Keohane and Helen Milner, 108–36. New York: Cambridge University Press, 1996.
———. *Global Capitalism: Its Fall and Rise in the Twentieth Century*. New York: W. W. Norton, 2006.
Friedman, Milton. "The Case for Flexible Exchange Rates." In *Essays in Positive Economics*, 157–03. Chicago: University of Chicago Press, 1953.
———. *A Program for Monetary Stability*. New York: Fordham University Press, 1960.
———. "The Role of Monetary Policy." *American Economic Review* 58, no. 1 (1968): 1–17.
———, and Anna J. Schwartz. *A Monetary History of the United States, 1867–1960*. Princeton: Princeton University Press, 1963.
Friedman, Milton, and Robert V. Roosa. *The Balance of Payments: Free versus Fixed Exchange Rates*. Washington: American Enterprise Institute for Public Policy Research, 1967.
Gavin, Francis J. *Gold, Dollars, and Power: The Politics of International Monetary Relations, 1958–1971*. Chapel Hill: University of North Carolina Press, 2004.
Gholz, Eugene, and Daryl G. Press. "The Effects of Wars on Neutral Countries: Why It Doesn't Pay to Preserve the Peace." *Security Studies* 10, no. 4 (2001): 1–57.

Glass, Carter. *An Adventure in Constructive Finance*. Garden City: Doubleday, Page, 1927.

Goldenweiser, Emanuel. *American Monetary Policy*. New York: McGraw-Hill, 1951.

Goodhart, Charles. *The Evolution of Central Banks*. Cambridge: MIT Press Books, 1988.

Gourevitch, Peter A. *Politics in Hard Times: Comparative Responses to International Economic Crises*. Ithaca: Cornell University Press, 1986.

Gorton, Gary. "Clearinghouses and the Origin of Central Banking in the United States." *The Journal of Economic History* 45, no. 2 (1985): 277–83.

Greider, William. *Secrets of the Temple: How the Federal Reserve Runs the Country*. New York: Simon and Schuster, 1989.

Griffin, G. *The Creature from Jekyll Island: A Second Look at the Federal Reserve*. Westlake Village, CA: American Media, 1998.

Hacker, Jacob S., and Paul Pierson. "Winner-take-all Politics: Public Policy, Political Organization, and the Precipitous Rise of Top Incomes in the United States." *Politics & Society* 38, no. 2 (2010): 152–204.

Hall, Rodney Bruce. *Central Banking as Global Governance: Constructing Financial Credibility*. New York: Cambridge University Press, 2008.

Hamilton, Alexander. "Report on a National Bank, December 13, 1790." In *Writings*, edited by Joanne B. Freeman, 613–46. New York: Library of America, 2001.

Harding, W.P.G. *The Formative Period of the Federal Reserve System: During the World Crisis*. London: Constable, 1925.

Helleiner, Eric. *States and the Reemergence of Global Finance: From Bretton Woods to the 1990s*. Ithaca: Cornell University Press, 1996.

———. *The Status Quo Crisis: Global Financial Governance after the 2008 Meltdown*. New York: Oxford University Press, 2014.

Hetzel, Robert. *The Monetary Policy of the Federal Reserve: A History*. New York: Cambridge University Press, 2008.

———, and Ralph Leach. "The Treasury-Fed Accord: A New Narrative Account," *FRB Richmond Economic Quarterly* 87, no. 1 (2001): 33–56.

———. "After the Accord: Reminiscences on the Birth of the Modern Fed." *FRB Richmond Economic Quarterly* 87, no. 1 (2001): 57–64.

Hoffmann, Susan. *Politics and Banking: Ideas, Public Policy, and the Creation of Financial Institutions*. Baltimore: John Hopkins University Press, 2001.

Hoover, Herbert. *The Memoirs of Herbert Hoover: The Great Depression 1929-1941*. New York: MacMillan, 1952.

Huntington, Samuel P. *American Politics: The Promise of Disharmony*. Cambridge: Harvard University Press, 1981.

Hyman, Sidney. *Marriner S. Eccles, Private Entrepreneur and Public Servant*. Palo Alto: Graduate School of Business, Stanford University, 1976.

Ikenberry, G. J. *After Victory: Institutions, Strategic Restraint, and the Rebuilding of Order after Major Wars*. Princeton: Princeton University Press, 2000.

Jabko, Nicolas, and Adam Sheingate. "Practices of Dynamic Order." *Perspectives on Politics* 16, no. 2 (2018): 312–27.
Jacobs, Lawrence R., and Desmond King. *Fed Power: How Finance Wins*. New York: Oxford University Press, 2016.
James, Harold. *International Monetary Cooperation since Bretton Woods*. New York: Oxford University Press, 1996.
James, Scott C. *Presidents, Parties, and the State: A Party System Perspective on Democratic Regulatory Choice, 1884–1936*. New York: Cambridge University Press, 2000.
Jeong, Gyung-Ho, Gary Miller, and Andrew Sobel. "Political Compromise and Bureaucratic Structure: The Political Origins of the Federal Reserve System." *Journal of Law, Economics, and Organization* 25, no. 2 (2009): 472–98.
John F. Kennedy Oral History Collection, John F. Kennedy Presidential Library, Boston.
Johnson, Peter A. *The Government of Money: Monetarism in Germany and the United States*. Ithaca: Cornell University Press, 1998.
Johnson, Robert. *The Peace Progressives and American Foreign Relations*. Cambridge: Harvard University Press, 1995.
Jones, Daniel S. *Masters of the Universe: Hayek, Friedman, and the Birth of Neoliberal Politics*. Princeton: Princeton University Press, 2012.
Katznelson, Ira, and Martin Shefter, eds. *Shaped by War and Trade: International Influences on American Political Development*. Princeton: Princeton University Press, 2002.
Kellogg, Edward. *Labor and Other Capital: The Rights of Each Secured and the Wrongs of Both Eradicated*. New York: Published by the Author, 1849.
Kettl, Donald. *Leadership at the Fed*. New Haven: Yale University Press, 1986.
Keynes, John M. *The Economic Consequences of the Peace*. New York: Harcourt, Brace and Howe, 1920.
———. *The Economic Consequences of Mr. Churchill*. London: L. and V. Woolf, 1925.
Khademian, Anne M. "The Pracademic and the Fed: The Leadership of Chairman Benjamin Bernanke." *Public Administration Review* 70, no. 1 (2010): 142–50.
Kindleberger, Charles. *The World in Depression, 1929–1939*. Berkeley: University of California Press, 1973.
Kirshner, Jonathan. *Appeasing Bankers: Financial Caution on the Road to War*. Princeton: Princeton University Press, 2007.
———. *American Power after the Financial Crisis*. Ithaca: Cornell University Press, 2014.
Kreps, Sarah. *Taxing Wars: The American Way of War Finance and the Decline of Democracy*. New York: Oxford University Press, 2018.
Krippner, Greta. "The Making of US Monetary Policy: Central Bank Transparency and the Neoliberal Dilemma." *Theory and Society* 36, no. 6 (2007): 477–513.

Legro, Jeffrey W. *Rethinking the World: Great Power Strategies and International Order*. Ithaca: Cornell University Press, 2005.

Lewis, David. *The Politics of Presidential Appointments: Political Control and Bureaucratic Performance*. Princeton: Princeton University Press, 2008.

Lieberman, Robert C. "Ideas, Institutions, and Political Order: Explaining Political Change." *American Political Science Review* 96, no. 4 (2002): 697–712.

Link, Arthur S. *The New Freedom*. Princeton: Princeton University Press, 1956.

Lowenstein, Roger. *America's Bank: The Epic Struggle to Create the Federal Reserve*. New York: Penguin, 2015.

Lowi, Theodore J. *The End of Liberalism: The Second Republic of the United States*. New York: W. W. Norton, 1979.

Mahoney, James, and Kathleen Thelen. "A Theory of Gradual Institutional Change." In *Explaining Institutional Change: Ambiguity, Agency, and Power*, edited by James Mahoney and Kathleen Thelen, 1–37. New York: Cambridge University Press, 2009.

Maisel, Sherman J. *Managing the Dollar*. New York: W. W. Norton, 1973.

Martin, William M. "Introduction." In *Men, Money and Policy: Essays in Honor of Karl R. Bopp*, edited by David Eastburn, 35–39. Philadelphia: Federal Reserve Bank of Philadelphia, 1970.

Mastanduno, Michael. "System Maker and Privilege Taker: U.S. Power and the International Political Economy." *World Politics* 61, no. 1 (2009): 121–54.

McAdoo, William G. *Crowded Years: The Reminiscences of William G. McAdoo*. New York: Houghton Mifflin, 1931.

McCulley, Richard T. *Banks and Politics during the Progressive Era*. New York: Garland, 1992.

McKinnon, Ronald. *The Unloved Dollar Standard: from Bretton Woods to the Rise of China*. New York: Oxford University Press, 2013.

Meltzer, Allan H. *A History of the Federal Reserve, Volume 1*. Chicago: University of Chicago Press, 2003.

———. *A History of the Federal Reserve, Volume 2*. Chicago: University of Chicago Press, 2009.

Moe, Terry M. "Political Institutions: The Neglected Side of the Story." *Journal of Law, Economics, & Organization* 6 (1990): 213–53.

Moen, Jon R., and Ellis W. Tallman. "New York and the Politics of Central Banks, 1781 to the Federal Reserve Act." Working Paper 2003-42. Atlanta: Federal Reserve Bank of Atlanta, 2003.

Morone, James A. *The Democratic Wish: Popular Participation and the Limits of American Government*. New York: Basic Books, 1990.

Mundell, Robert A. "Capital Mobility and Stabilization Policy under Fixed and Flexible Exchange Rates." *Canadian Journal of Economic and Political Science* 29, no. 4 (1963): 475–85.

Nelson, Mark. *Jumping the Abyss: Marriner S. Eccles and the New Deal, 1933–1940*. Salt Lake City: University of Utah Press, 2017.

Nichols, Curt. "Reagan Reorders the Political Regime: A Historical-Institutional Approach to Analysis of Change." *Presidential Studies Quarterly* 45, no. 4 (2015): 703–26.

Nixon, Richard. *Six Crises*. New York: Doubleday, 1962.

Oatley, Thomas. *A Political Economy of American Hegemony*. New York: Cambridge University Press, 2015.

Odell, John S. *US International Monetary Policy: Markets, Power, and Ideas as Sources of Change*. Princeton: Princeton University Press, 1982.

Orren, Karen, and Stephen Skowronek. *The Search for American Political Development*. New York: Cambridge University Press, 2004.

Papers of Allan Sproul, Federal Reserve Bank of New York, New York.

Papers of Benjamin Strong, Jr., Federal Reserve Bank of New York, New York.

Papers of Lyndon B. Johnson, LBJ Presidential Library, Austin.

Parsons, Craig. "Ideas and Power: Four Intersections and How to Show Them." *Journal of European Public Policy* 23, no. 3 (2016): 446–63.

Paul, Ron. *End the Fed*. New York: Grand Central Publishing, 2009.

Pauly, Louis. "Woodrow Wilson's Problem in Reverse: The Continuing Challenge of Making American Democracy Safe for the World." In *Political Science as Public Philosophy: Essays in Honor of Theodore J. Lowi*, edited by Benjamin Ginsberg and Gwendolyn Mink, 113–32. New York: W. W. Norton, 2010.

Pollack, Sheldon D. *War, Revenue, and State Building: Financing the Development of the American State*. Ithaca: Cornell University Press, 2009.

Polsky, Andrew J. "Partisan Regimes in American Politics." *Polity* 44, no. 1 (2011): 1–30.

———. *Elusive Victories: The American Presidency at War*. New York: Oxford University Press, 2012.

Primm, James N. *A Foregone Conclusion: The Founding of the Federal Reserve Bank of St. Louis*. St. Louis: Federal Reserve Bank of St. Louis, 1989.

Rauchway, Eric. *The Money Makers: How Roosevelt and Keynes Ended the Depression, Defeated Fascism, and Secured a Prosperous Peace*. New York: Basic Books, 2015.

Records of the Federal Reserve System, Record Group 82, National Archives and Records Administration, College Park.

Ritter, Gretchen. *Goldbugs and Greenbacks: The Antimonopoly Tradition and the Politics of Finance in America, 1865–1896*. New York: Cambridge University Press, 1999.

Ritter, Lawrence S. "Allan Sproul, 1896–1978. 'A Tower of Strength.'" In *Selected Papers of Allan Sproul*, edited by Lawrence S. Ritter, 1–21. New York: Federal Reserve Bank of New York, 1980.

Romer, Christina D., and David H. Romer. "The Most Dangerous Idea in Federal Reserve History: Monetary Policy Doesn't Matter." *American Economic Review* 103, no. 3 (2013): 55–60.

———. "A Rehabilitation of Monetary Policy in the 1950's." *American Economic Review* 92, no. 2 (2002): 121–27.

Roosa, Robert. "Reconciling Internal and External Financial Policies." *Journal of Finance* 17, no. 1 (1962): 1–16.

———. *Monetary Reform for the World Economy*. New York: Harper and Row, 1965.

———. "Capital Movements and Balance-of-Payments Adjustment." In *Men Money & Policy: Essays in Honor of Karl R. Bopp*, edited by David P. Eastburn, 171–94. Philadelphia: Federal Reserve Bank of Philadelphia, 1970.

Roosevelt, Franklin D. "Annual Message to Congress." January 11, 1944. In *The Public Papers and Addresses of Franklin D. Roosevelt*, edited by Samuel I. Rosenman, 40–42. New York: Harper and Bros., 1950.

Ruggie, John G. "International Regimes, Transactions, and Change: Embedded Liberalism in the Postwar Economic Order." *International Organization* 36, no. 2 (1982): 379–415.

Salant, Walter S. "Competitiveness and the US Balance of Payments." In *The US Balance of Payments in 1968*. Washington, DC: The Brookings Institution, 1963.

Saldin, Robert P. *War, the American State, and Politics since 1898*. New York: Cambridge University Press, 2010.

Sanders, Elizabeth. *Roots of Reform: Farmers, Workers, and the American State, 1877–1917*. Chicago: University of Chicago Press, 1999.

Schickler, Eric. *Disjointed Pluralism: Institutional Innovation and the Development of the US Congress*. Princeton: Princeton University Press, 2001.

Schwartz, Herman M. *Subprime Nation: American Power, Global Capital, and the Housing Bubble*. Ithaca: Cornell University Press, 2009.

Shull, Bernard. *The Fourth Branch: The Federal Reserve's Unlikely Rise to Power and Influence*. Westport: Praeger, 2005.

Sibert, Anne. "Central Banking by Committee." *International Finance* 9, no. 2 (2006): 145–68.

Silber, William. *When Washington Shut Down Wall Street: The Great Financial Crisis of 1914 and the Origins of America's Monetary Supremacy*. Princeton: Princeton University Press, 2007.

Skowronek, Stephen. *Building a New American State: The Expansion of National Administrative Capacities, 1877–1920*. New York: Cambridge University Press, 1982.

———. *The Politics Presidents Make: Presidential Leadership from John Adams to Bill Clinton*. 2nd ed. Cambridge: Harvard Belknap, 1997.

Snyder, Carl. *Capitalism the Creator: The Economic Foundations of Modern Industrial Society*. New York: Macmillan, 1940.

Sparrow, Bartholomew H. *From the Outside In: World War II and the American State*. Princeton: Princeton University Press, 1996.

Sproul, Allan. "Reflections of a Central Banker." *The Journal of Finance* 11, no. 1 (1956): 1–14.

———. "The 'Accord'—A Landmark in the First Fifty Years of the Federal Reserve System." *Monthly Review: Federal Reserve Bank of New York* 58, no. 11 (1964): 227–36.

———. "Policy Norms in Central Banking." In *Men, Money, and Policy: Essays in Honor of Karl R. Popp*, edited by David P. Eastburn, 67–78. Philadelphia: Federal Reserve Bank of Philadelphia, 1970.

Stein, Herbert. *The Fiscal Revolution in America: Policy in Pursuit of Reality*. 2nd ed. Washington, DC: American Enterprise Institute Press, 1996.

Steinmo, Sven H. "American Exceptionalism Reconsidered: Culture or Institutions." In *The Dynamics of American Politics: Approaches and Interpretations*, edited by Lawrence C. Dowd and Calvin Jillison, 106–31. New York: Routledge, 1994.

Stockwell, Eleanor, ed. *Working at the Board: 1930s-1970s*. Washington, DC: Board of Governors of the Federal Reserve System, 1989.

Streeck, Wolfgang, and Kathleen Thelen. "Introduction: Institutional Change in Advanced Political Economies." In *Beyond Continuity: Institutional Change in Advanced Political Economies*, edited by Wolfgang Streeck and Kathleen Thelen, 1–39. New York: Oxford University Press, 2005.

Sylla, Richard. "Federal Policy, Banking Market Structure, and Capital Mobilization in the United States, 1863–1913." *The Journal of Economic History* 29, no. 4 (1969.): 657–86.

———. "Financial Foundations: Public Credit, the National Bank, and Securities Markets." In *Founding Choices: American Economic Policy in the 1790s*, edited by Douglas Irwin and Richard Sylla, 59–88. Chicago: University of Chicago Press, 2011.

Taliaferro, Jeffrey W. "State Building for Future Wars: Neoclassical Realism and the Resource-Extractive State." *Security Studies* 15, no. 3 (2006): 464–95.

Timberlake, Richard H. "Mr. Shaw and his Critics: Monetary Policy in the Golden Era Reviewed." *The Quarterly Journal of Economics* 77, no. 1 (1963): 40–54.

———. "The Central Banking Role of Clearinghouse Associations." *Journal of Money, Credit and Banking* 16, no. 1 (1984): 1–15.

———. *Monetary Policy in the United States: An Intellectual and Institutional History*. Chicago: University of Chicago Press, 1993.

———. *Constitutional Money: A Review of the Supreme Court's Monetary Decisions*. New York: Cambridge University Press, 2013.

Todd, Walker F. *The Federal Reserve Board and the Rise of the Corporate State, 1931–1934*. Great Barrington, MA: American Institute for Economic Research, 1995.

Toniolo, Gianni. *Central Bank Cooperation at the Bank for International Settlements, 1930–1973*. New York: Cambridge University Press, 2005.
Tooze, Adam. *The Deluge: The Great War, America, and the Remaking of the Global Order, 1916–1931*. New York: Penguin, 2014.
Triffin, Robert. *Europe and the Money Muddle: From Bilateralism to Near-Convertibility, 1947–1956*. New Haven: Yale University Press, 1957.
———. *Gold and the Dollar Crisis: The Future of Convertibility*. New Haven: Yale University Press, 1960.
Trubowitz, Peter. *Defining the National Interest: Conflict and Change in American Foreign Policy*. Chicago: University of Chicago Press, 1998.
———. *Politics and Strategy: Partisan Ambition and American Statecraft*. Princeton: Princeton University Press, 2011.
Tsebelis, George. "Decision Making in Political Systems: Veto Players in Presidentialism, Parliamentarism, Multicameralism and Multipartyism." *British Journal of Political Science* 25, no. 3 (1995): 289–325.
Tulis, Jeffrey K., and Nicole Mellow. *Legacies of Losing in American Politics*. Chicago: University of Chicago Press, 2018.
Walter, Stefanie. *Financial Crises and the Politics of Macroeconomic Adjustments*. New York: Cambridge University Press, 2013.
Warburg, Paul M. *Federal Reserve System, Its Origin and Growth*. Vol. 1. New York: Macmillan, 1930.
Warburg, Paul M. "The Owen-Glass Bill as Submitted to the Democratic Caucus: Some Criticisms and Suggestions." *The North American Review* 198, no. 695 (1913): 527–55.
———. "Defects and Needs of Our Banking System." *Proceedings of the Academy of Political Science in the City of New York* 4, no. 4 (1914): 7–22.
———. "A United Reserve Bank of the United States." *Proceedings of the Academy of Political Science in the City of New York* 1, no. 2 (1911): 302–42.
Ware, Alan. *The Democratic Party Heads North, 1877–1962*. New York: Cambridge University Press, 2006.
Weir, Margaret M. "When Does Politics Create Policy? The Organizational Politics of Change." In *Rethinking Political Institutions: The Art of the State*, edited by Ian Shapiro, Stephen Skowronek, and Daniel Galvin, 171–86. New York: New York University Press, 2006.
West, Robert C. *Banking Reform and the Federal Reserve, 1863–1923*. Ithaca: Cornell University Press, 1977.
Whittington, Keith E. *Political Foundations of Judicial Supremacy: The Presidency, the Supreme Court, and Constitutional Leadership in US History*. Princeton: Princeton University Press, 2009.
Wicker, Elmus. *Federal Reserve Monetary Policy, 1917–1933*. New York: Random House, 1966.

———. *The Great Debate on Banking Reform: Nelson Aldrich and the Origins of the Fed*. Columbus: Ohio State University Press, 2005.

Widmaier, Wesley. *Economic Ideas in Political Time*. New York: Cambridge University Press, 2016.

William McChesney Martin Jr. Papers, Missouri History Museum, St. Louis.

Williams, John H. *Post-War Monetary Plans: And Other Essays*. London: Oxford, Basil, Blackwell, 1949.

———. "The Postwar Monetary Plans," *The American Economic Review* 34, no. 1 (1944): 372–84.

———. "International Monetary Plans: After Bretton Woods," *Foreign Affairs* 23, no. 1 (1944): 38–56.

Wood, John H. *A History of Central Banking in Great Britain and the United States*. New York: Cambridge University Press, 2005.

———. *Central Banking in a Democracy: The Federal Reserve and Its Alternatives*. New York: Routledge, 2014.

Wheelock, David C. "National Monetary Policy by Regional Design: The Evolving Role of the Federal Reserve Banks in Federal Reserve System Policy." In *Regional Aspects of Monetary Policy in Europe*, edited by Jurgen von Hagen and Christopher J. Waller, 241–74. New York: Kluwer, 2000.

———, and Mark A. Carlson. "Navigating Constraints: The Evolution of Federal Reserve Monetary Policy, 1935–1959." In *The Federal Reserve's Role in the Global Economy: A Historical Perspective*, edited by Michael D. Bordo and Mark A. Wynne, 50–83. New York: Cambridge University Press, 2016.

White, Eugene N. *The Regulation and Reform of the American Banking System, 1900–1929*. Princeton: Princeton University Press, 1983.

Zakaria, Fareed. *From Wealth to Power: The Unusual Origins of America's World Role*. Princeton: Princeton University Press, 1999.

Zelizer, Julian E. *The Fierce Urgency of Now: Lyndon Johnson, Congress, and the Battle for the Great Society*. New York: Penguin, 2015.

Index

agenda-setting: and the Board of Governors, 5, 25, 47, 92, 112, 137, 140–141, 144, 151; and Martin, 118, 137; and the New York Fed, 15, 118; in politics, 30, 34, 36, 50, 58–59, 91–92, 126, 129, 157, 160
Agricultural Adjustment Act of 1933, 87
agricultural crisis, 80
Aldrich, Nelson, 29–30, 34–35, 43
Aldrich Plan, 29–31, 35–37, 41–42, 51
autonomy. *See* central bank independence
attorney general, 40, 45–47, 52, 57

balance-of-payments, 71, 101–102, 121–122, 128–130, 134, 143; as a policy signal, 123–124, 128, 133, 137, 142–143
Bank for International Settlements, 89, 122, 130, 137
Banking Act of 1933, 91–93
Banking Act of 1935, 81, 89, 94, 107, 148
Bank of England: collaboration with New York, 61–62, 66–67, 72, 83, 88; and Hamiltonian ideology, 9; and the London Gold Pool, 126
Bank of the United States, 12–13, 32, 41–42, 52

bank runs, 33, 86
Bernanke, Ben, 37, 200n9
bill of exchange, 33, 49–50, 56, 70
bill rate, 49, 72, 77, 92
Binder, Sarah, 6–7, 106
"bluebook," 138, 151
Board of Governors of the Federal Reserve System, 1–4; appointment procedures, 12, 17–18, 39–40; domestic orientation of, 13; and Fed policy regime, 20–21, 69–75, 141–146, 150–151; populist view of, 11, 148; progressive view of, 11, 37, 45, 92, 107, 147; reform of, 17–18, 60–61, 81, 94, 111, 123–124, 129, 132–141
Bopp, Karl, 1–2, 139
Brandeis, Louis, 35, 37
Bretton Woods system: activation of, 119–121; and central banks, 124–126, 129, 159; collapse of, 131–132; and Democratic policies, 112, 122, 128, 130–131, 141–142; and embedded liberalism, 22–23, 101–103; Triffin's critique of, 121
Bryan, William J., 10–11, 31, 37–38, 40, 43
Burgess, W. Randolph, 64–67, 78, 89, 102, 108
Burns, Arthur, 1, 160; and Fed

217

reform, 112, 136–141, 143–146, 150; and Nixon, 135–136, 140

Carter, Jimmy, 160
central bank: functions, 31–33, 35, 40–43, 55; ideological images of, 4, 9, 11–13, 24–25, 153
central bank independence: academic literature on, 17–18; Burns's views on, 136, 140; Eccles's views on, 82, 92, 107–108; and the Federal Reserve Act, 12, 46, 81, 94; Glass's views on, 57, 94, 121, 148; and Hamilton, 25; Heller's views on, 126–127; Martin's views on, 118–119, 125, 141–143; and political time, 17–19, 60–61, 70, 72, 79–82, 99, 123–124, 132–134, 159–160; populist attacks on, 60–61, 93, 95–96, 117; Strong's views on, 47–48; and the Treasury-Fed Accord, 6, 106–107; Warburg's views on, 33–34, 44–48
Chandler, Lester, 24, 89
chair of the Board of Governors: agenda-setting role, 137, 140–141, 144, 150–151; New Deal reconstitution of, 81, 94; origin as a partisan office, 11. *See also individual occupants of*
comptroller of the currency, 39, 45, 60, 70, 92, 127
Conti-Brown, Peter, 52, 107, 151
Council of Economic Advisors, 123, 126, 136
currency: and the Aldrich Plan, 35; American variants of, 31–33, 88; and the Federal Reserve Act, 41–44, 48, 50, 79, 85, 91, 94, 148; and Hamiltonian ideology, 12, 158; hoarding of, 97; and international power, 25; and international reform, 101–103, 120–121, 124–126, 129, 131–132; and populist ideology, 9–11, 24–25, 36–37, 87; stability and monetary policy, 13–16, 19–20, 22, 49, 58, 62, 64, 67, 99, 112, 115. *See also* dollarization
Currie, Lauchlin, 92

Daane, J. Dewey, 127
decentralization: Glass's support of, 36–37, 39, 52, 68, 90, 92, 94; and Jeffersonian ideology, 12, 153; Martin's support of, 113, 115; of reserve banks, 6, 12, 39, 43, 51, 54; Warburg's criticism of, 43, 46–47
deflation, 22, 31, 53, 57, 58, 60, 61, 84, 100; Fed avoidance of, 78, 85, 113, 119; and the gold standard, 20, 101, 103
De Gaulle, Charles, 131
Democratic Party: factions, 10, 36; and Fed reform, 36–40, 93–96, 107, 126–127, 132–134; ascendance, 36, 82, 112, 122; platform, 36; declines, 56–58, 79, 82, 118, 129, 132
Dillon, C. Douglas, 123, 124, 127, 130
discount rate: conflict over, 47–48, 57, 60, 67–69, 73, 77–80, 84, 92, 133, 134–135; legal ambiguity, 5, 47, 68, 95
"discount window," 73, 85, 91
Douglas, Paul, 106
dual mandate, 108, 152

Eccles, Marriner, 82, 86, 140; and Fed reform, 95–96; and Glass, 92–94; legacy of, 107–108, 151, 159; and Morgenthau, 97–98, 100; and New Deal, 90; populist vision of, 22, 82, 92, 148; and Roosevelt, 90–91; and the Treasury-Fed Accord, 105–106; and Truman, 104–105

Index

economic forecasts, 16, 138–139, 141, 150
economic growth, 3, 12, 26, 122–123, 126, 130, 136
Eichengreen, Barry, 13
Eisenhower, Dwight, 118–123, 127, 142

embedded liberalism, 101, 103, 118–119
Employment Act of 1946, 104, 108, 152
Eurodollar markets, 142
"even keel," 118–119, 128
Exchange Stabilization Fund, 88–89, 96–97

farmers, 31, 32, 58, 59, 60, 66, 70, 75

Federal Advisory Council, 72
Federal Deposit Insurance Corporation, 24, 88–89, 134
Federal Reserve Act of 1913, 3, 29, 42–43, 45, 87, 146; ambiguity of, 5, 41, 51–53; amendment of, 49, 55–56, 60–61, 85, 147–148; board diversity requirement, 3, 12, 23, 127, 149; embedded ideologies, 4, 11–13; legal opinions on, 45–47, 57; partisan construction of, 30, 36–40; Strong's criticism of, 13, 50; Warburg's criticism of, 43, 46, 48
Federal Reserve Bank of Chicago (Chicago Fed), 62–63, 65, 67, 68, 75, 78, 85, 126
Federal Reserve Bank of Minneapolis (Minneapolis Fed), 68–70, 127
Federal Reserve Bank of New York (New York Fed): and agenda-setting, 21, 80, 85, 97, 127; conflict with the board, 55, 57, 60, 68–75; conflict with the treasury, 98, 105; criticism of Bretton Woods, 101–103; and the depression, 93; diplomacy of, 75, 87–88, 122–123, 126; gold reserve of, 61, 86; ideational authority of, 26, 112, 127, 141, 150; 65–67, 75–77, 83, 128, 133, 135; and open market operations, 2, 53, 63, 64, 95, 151–152; wartime empowerment, 19, 100, 113. *See also* Burgess, W. Randolph; Harrison, George L.; Roosa, Robert; Sproul, Allan; Strong, Benjamin; Young, Allyn
Federal Reserve Bank of San Francisco (San Francisco Fed), 68, 76–78
Federal Reserve Bank of St. Louis (St. Louis Fed), 45, 60, 96, 114, 116
Federal Reserve Banks, 1, 5: autonomy of, 24, 46, 70–75, 80, 90, 96, 107–108, 153; conflicts among, 67–68, 75–78; fiscal agency of, 40, 55; inequalities among, 6, 21, 117; and Morgenthau, 97; power of, 19, 79, 85; reform of, 4, 12–14, 39, 41–50, 52, 92–95, 143–144, 146–148, 150; and state-building, 87–89. *See also names of individual banks*
Federal Reserve System *see* Board of Governors of the Federal Reserve System; Federal Reserve Banks; Federal Open Market Committee
Federal Reserve Board. *See* Board of Governors of the Federal Reserve System
Federal Open Market Committee: conflict over structure, 64, 69, 71–72, 77–78, 113–117; legalization of, 80, 92; origin of, 63; policies of, 65, 67, 76, 83–85, 89, 97–99, 119, 124–129, 133–136; reform of, 74–75, 94–96, 100, 106–108, 111–112, 118, 137–153

fiscal policy, 24, 90, 105–106, 112, 125, 131, 142
Fisher, Irving, 11, 53, 143
FOMC. *See* Federal Open Market Committee
Fowler, Henry, 130
fragmentation: of American government, 19, 25, 31, 52, 155; of the Federal Reserve, 8, 15, 18–20, 30, 74, 80, 108, 113, 147, 158
France, 67, 78, 83, 99, 131
Frieden, Jeffry, 13
Friedman, Milton, 2, 8; advocacy of dollar flexibility, 121, 142; critique by Hamiltonians, 24; and the Federal Reserve's struggle for power, 6, 54, 89–90; populism of, 11, 23–25; praise of the New York Fed, 73; influence on modern Fed, 26, 79, 152–154, 158

Glass, Carter: and the Federal Reserve Act, 37–39, 51–52, 55, 82, 85, 90–95; and Jeffersonian ideology, 13, 36; and Strong, 57, 68–69; and Warburg, 46, 50
gold standard: and central banks, 15, 108, 142; collapse of, 23, 54, 83, 140–141; and Hamiltonian ideology, 3, 13, 54, 142; international constraints of, 13–14, 57; in interwar era, 21–22, 24, 58, 61, 62, 66, 69, 71, 80; and Jeffersonian ideology, 10, 12, 146; Keynes's critique of, 101–103; legalization, 31, 38, 88; and populist ideology, 11; and progressive ideology, 12. *See also* Bretton Woods system
government debt: European, 54, 59, 62, 83, 90, 100; and Fed policy, 24, 57, 106, 113, 125, 128, 158–159; monetization of, 105, 142; and the Treasury-Fed Accord, 106; and war, 19, 57–58, 100, 104, 155
"greenbook," 138
Greenspan, Alan, 160
gridlock, 20, 61, 75

Hacker, Jacob, 157
Hamilton, Alexander. *See* Hamiltonian ideology
Hamiltonian ideology: central bank vision, 9, 11–12, 25, 41–42, 52, 158; decline of, 142, 148; influence on Aldrich Plan, 30–31, 35; and Martin, 149; in the modern Fed, 26, 153–154, 161; and the New York Fed, 3–4, 54, 70, 103, 146; and the Republican Party, 10; and Sproul, 113–114; and Strong, 13, 21, 48–50, 79; wartime empowerment, 18–19, 156
Hamlin, Charles, 40, 45, 64–65, 68–69, 73–74
Harding, Warren G., 58
Harding, W. P. G., 40, 45, 61

Harrison, George L., 72–78, 80, 94, 98
Heller, Walter, 122, 124, 126–127, 129, 131, 133
historical institutionalism, 26–27
Hoover, Herbert, 55, 70–71, 75, 80, 82–86, 105, 159, 178n8
House, Colonel, 36, 40, 45

ideas: and currency stability, 11, 15; and economic policy, 6, 54, 61, 69, 124, 127, 152; and Fed culture, 5, 27; and political time, 16–17, 90; and reform, 20–22, 29, 116–117, 130, 147; and technocracy, 26, 146

ideology, 5, 9, 161. *See also* Hamiltonian ideology; Jeffersonian

Index   221

ideology; populist ideology; progressive ideology
Independent Treasury System, 40, 55
inflation: and the Bretton Woods system, 23, 112, 120; and central bank independence, 7; and currency stability, 14, 20, 31, 61–62, 66–67, 78, 142–143, 150; and the dual mandate, 108, 152; Fed as an "engine of," 22, 104–105, 108, 148, 159–160; and the Federal Reserve Act, 43; and Fed policy, 63, 96–97, 113, 128, 133–138, 140; and Fed reform 1, 82, 157; Fisher's view of, 53; Hamilton's view of, 12; Martin's view of, 119; and war, 19, 57, 60, 100, 115, 130–131
interest rates, 1, 21, 23, 60–61, 67, 73, 78, 92, 94, 105, 107, 123–125, 127–129, 134–136, 142, 153, 159–161
isolationism, 75, 99–100, 119

Jacobs, Lawrence, 6–7
Jeffersonian ideology: central bank vision, 8–9, 12–13, 36, 41; and the Democratic Party, 10, 30; and Fed reform, 21–22, 25, 112–113, 115, 146–149; and Glass, 36; and the gold standard, 11, 14; in the modern Fed, 153; and political time, 17–19, 156; view of Fed history, 4, 29, 27, 29, 51, 54
Jekyll Island, 3, 29–30, 38, 43, 51
Johnson, Lyndon B., 112, 129–134, 142, 149

Katznelson, Ira, 154
Kellogg, Edward, 31, 153, 168n38
Kennedy, John F., 122–128, 133, 137, 140, 149
Keynesianism, 90, 113, 121–124, 129–132, 135, 137, 157

Keynes, John M.: and embedded liberalism, 22, 101–104; and the Versailles treaty, 56; and sterling restoration, 67; and fiscal policy, 90; and monetary policy, 113, 121
Kindleberger, Charles, 24
King, Desmond, 6–7

Lindbergh, Charles, 35
Link, Arthur, 37
London Gold Pool, 126, 131–132

Maisel, Sherman, 111, 131, 133–134, 137–139, 151
Martin, William M., Jr.: and the Bretton Woods system, 121–123, 126, 132; childhood of, 114; and Fed policy, 128–129, 134–135; and Fed reform, 2–4, 6–7, 22, 27, 108, 111–113, 115–117, 137–141, 143, 145–146, 148–152, 159; and U.S. presidents, 119–120, 125–127, 130–131, 133, 136; view of Fed independence, 118, 160
McAdoo, William, 37, 39–41, 44–47, 49, 55, 60
McDougal, James, 62, 68
Mellon, Andrew, 59–60, 63, 66, 69, 83
Mellow, Nicole, 27
Miller, Adolph, 40, 78, 127, 149; criticism of Strong, 67, 69, 71, 76; and Fed policy, 78, 83; and Fed reform, 22, 53, 63–64, 70, 72–74, 80, 94, 143, 147
monetary policy, 1–2, 94, 113, 133; and central bank independence, 7, 97–98, 105, 125; and economic ideas, 8, 126, 136, 142; international dimensions of, 3, 14–15, 102, 112, 133, 135; and Martin, 118; in the

monetary policy *(continued)*
  modern Fed, 23, 26, 138–140, 146, 149–153, 161
monetization, 10, 19, 105, 106, 129, 142
"money trust," 35–36
monetarism, 11, 53–54. *See also* Friedman, Milton; Schwartz, Anna
Morgenthau, Henry, 97–98, 100

national banking system, 31
National Monetary Commission, 34–35
New Deal, 22, 80, 82, 86, 89–92, 95, 98, 103–104, 108, 118, 129, 147–148, 157–160
New York Times, 61, 129
Nichols, Curt, 157
Nixon, Richard, 122, 132, 135–136, 140–141, 149–150
Norman, Montagu, 61–67, 72, 73, 83, 88, 140

Owen, Robert, 31
Open Market Investment Committee. *See* Federal Open Market Committee
Open Market Policy Conference. *See* Federal Open Market Committee
"operation twist," 125–126

partisan regime: and Aldrich, 30; and Fed power, 161; and Hoover, 82; and Kennedy, 122; and political time, 16–18, 20, 99, 141, 156; and Reagan, 157; and Roosevelt, 86
peace, return to: and economic problems, 56, 58–59, 103–104; and Fed reform, 60–61, 112, 115; and political time, 4, 9, 16–19, 26, 100, 147, 156
Pierson, Paul, 157

policy regime, 3, 5, 7, 15, 74, 108, 146
political development, 5, 144–150, 154–155
political time: and agency, 5, 16, 156; and Fed reform, 21, 30, 51–52, 54, 80, 82, 90, 108–109, 111, 118, 141, 159; and Skowronek, 4; and state-building, 9, 17–18; waning of, 26, 154, 157, 160–161
populist ideology: central bank vision, 9, 11–12, 21; and the Democratic Party, 10, 36, 40, 51; in the Federal Reserve Act, 37–38, 41, 147; and Fed reform, 21–22, 37, 44, 61, 87, 90, 93, 95, 104–105, 113, 117, 148–149; and Friedman, 121; and Kellogg, 31, 153, 168n38; in the modern Fed, 23, 26, 153; and political time, 17–18, 30, 60, 79, 81–82, 86, 99, 123; view of Fed history, 4, 25, 27, 54, 107. *See also* Bryan, William J.; Eccles, Marriner; McAdoo, William
power: and currency stability, 20, 62, 143; of the Fed, 8, 23–26, 75, 79, 99, 145, 156–161; Federal Reserve Act restraints of, 11, 29, 39, 41–43, 53, 57; Fed struggle for, 2–6, 21–23, 37, 45–51, 55, 60–61, 63–65, 68–75, 79–80, 82, 90–99, 104–106, 108–109, 111–115, 117, 120–121, 124, 134, 137, 140–141, 144, 146–149; and ideology, 4, 12, 17–19, 21, 27, 34, 36, 38, 41, 54, 107, 142, 153–154; in the modern Fed, 7, 81, 150–152; of political parties, 10–11, 18, 20, 36, 52, 85–86, 100, 129; purchasing, 76, 78, 87, 104; of the U.S., 31, 56; of Wall Street, 32, 35, 58
President of the United States: agency of, 4–5, 16, 20, 155–156; and Fed

Index

reform, 17–18, 39, 56, 92, 95, 111, 127, 141, 149, 160–161; and war, 19, 100. *See also names of individual presidents*

progressive ideology: and the Aldrich Plan, 35; central bank vision, 9, 11–12, 147; and the Democratic Party, 36, 38, 51, 56, 91; in the Federal Reserve Act, 37, 41; and Fed reform, 21–22, 82–83, 148; in the modern Fed, 23, 26, 153; and political time, 18; and the Republican Party, 10–11, 30, 34; view of Fed history, 4, 27, 29, 51, 54, 69, 75, 78, 81, 106–107, 111; and Warburg, 33, 45, 48

Quadriad, 123
quantitative easing, 152, 158

Reagan, Ronald, 157, 160
Reichsbank, 9, 33, 35, 44, 67, 83
Republican Party: factions of, 10, 34; and Fed reform, 60–61, 75, 79; and gold standard legalization, 31; ascendance, 58–59, 118–119, 160; declines, 51, 75, 80, 85–86, 160
Reserve Bank Organization Committee, 39, 47, 52
reserve requirements, 42, 92, 94–98, 107, 119, 151
Roosa, Robert, 123–126, 130, 142
Roosevelt, Franklin D.: death of, 103; and Democratic ascendance, 85–86, 129; and dollar devaluation, 87–88; and Fed reform, 81–82, 90–91, 95, 97–98, 104, 107–108, 148; and World War II, 99
Roosevelt, Theodore, 10, 35–36

Schwartz, Anna, 2, 6, 8, 11, 23–26, 54, 69, 73, 79, 89

secular time, 9, 20, 118
Shefter, Martin, 154
Skowronek, Stephen, 4, 16, 26, 156–157
Snyder, Carl, 78, 163n7
Spindel, Mark, 6–7, 106
Sproul, Allan, 24, 102, 105, 112–118
St. Louis Star, 69
Strong, Benjamin: and Congress, 60, 66, 71; death of, 69, 72; and Glass, 57; and Fed reform, 44–45, 47–51, 53, 55–56, 63–64, 73, 79, 147, 152, 158–160; on the Federal Reserve Act, 43, 68; "great idea" of, 21, 58, 65, 75, 78; and Hamiltonian ideology, 13, 52, 54, 161; international collaboration of, 22, 61–62, 67, 70, 126; and Martin, 114; on protectionism, 59, 80
Supreme Court of the United States, 88, 107

Taft, William H., 10, 34–35, 57
technocracy, 1, 3, 21, 26, 109, 137, 140, 144, 146, 149–150
trade acceptance. *See* bill of exchange
Treasury-Fed Accord of 1951, 6, 22, 81–82, 106–108, 111, 113, 118, 133, 143, 148
Trubowitz, Peter, 154–155
Truman, Harry S., 101, 103–105, 148

Vanderlip, Frank, 38
Volcker, Paul, 160

Wall Street Journal, 68–70
war: in Afghanistan, 161; and agency, 16, 156; the Civil War, 10, 31; debt legacy of, 58–59, 62, 83; and dollarization, 25; empowers the New York Fed, 19, 56, 100, 108, 113; and inflation, 22, 57, 60, 67,

war *(continued)*
  105; and international regimes, 20, 23, 54, 93, 142; in Korea, 106, 118–119; and political time, 4, 9, 17, 26; and state-building, 5, 18, 24, 154–155; in Vietnam, 1, 112, 129–133, 159; World War I, 15, 23, 50, 52, 55, 79, 147; World War II, 82, 99, 103–104, 115, 148

Warburg, Paul: and the Aldrich Plan, 35; board appointment, 40, 56; central bank idea of, 31–34; on the Federal Reserve Act, 5, 29, 43, 147; and Fed reform, 27, 46–47, 50–52, 55; and McAdoo, 45; and Strong, 44, 48–49; and Wilson, 36–37

Widmaier, Wesley, 16
Williams, John H., 96, 102, 103, 120
Williams, John S., 60
Wilson, Woodrow: board appointments of, 39–40, 56; and Democratic ascendance, 10–11, 51; and the Federal Reserve Act, 36–38, 41, 55; loss of domestic support, 56–58, 147; and McAdoo, 44–46; reelection of, 51–52; and Roosevelt, 91; and World War I, 54

Young, Allyn, 70, 114
Young Plan, 75
Young, Roy, 69–70, 72–73, 74–76, 85

www.ingramcontent.com/pod-product-compliance
Lightning Source LLC
Chambersburg PA
CBHW030135240426
43672CB00005B/141